THE WORLD'S MOST BEAUTIFUL

ORCHIDS

THE WORLD'S MOST BEAUTIFUL

ORCHIDS

GREG ALLIKAS & NED NASH

THUNDER BAY
P·R·E·S·S

San Diego, California

Thunder Bay Press
An imprint of the Advantage Publishers Group
5880 Oberlin Drive, San Diego, CA 92121-4794
www.thunderbaybooks.com

Produced by PRC Publishing
The Chrysalis Building
Bramley Road, London W10 6SP, United Kingdom

An imprint of **Chrysalis** Books Group plc

ISBN-13: 978-1-59223-509-4
ISBN-10: 1-59223-509-3

Printed and bound in China

1 2 3 4 5 09 08 07 06 05

Acknowledgements

This book would not have been possible without high-quality subject matter.
There are many talented orchid growers and fine commercial establishments who exhibit at the shows and monthly AOS judgings at which much of the
awards photography was done. You cannot take great photos of poor orchids. We would like to thank all of our friends and growers whose awarded orchids have
been subjects for the portraits in this book.

Many fine people helped indirectly with this book, but a few made more direct contributions. We thank the following profusely: Anita Aldrich, Lee Cooke,
Pam Giust, Leo Holguin, Irene Holguin, Ernest Hetherington, Merritt Huntington, Bill Peters, and Will Rhodehamel. A special thanks to Kathy Figiel for her
tireless work proofreading and editing the manuscripts.

While some authors live alone and work in a vacuum, I don't. Without the help and support of my family, this book simply could not have been written. If the
homefires hadn't been kept burning while I traveled and worked endless hours, if my children hadn't had a great mother, this book could not have been
written. So, thanks to my wife, Debra, especially, and my kids, Aaron and Lilian, for putting up with me while I lived enough to be able to write.
Ned Nash

Greg Allikas is the proprietor of the popular Orchid Photo Page on the Web at www.orchidworks.com. Greg and his wife Kathy maintain a mixed collection of
over 1,200 orchids comprised of Cattleyas, Laelias, Vandaceous, Dendrobiums, and Oncidium allies, as well as many unusual species orchids.

Picture credits: All pictures and captions by Greg Allikas.

CONTENTS

INTRODUCTION

Although the aim of this book is to present a collection of the world's most beautiful orchids, beauty is truly in the eye of the beholder.

There are orchids in this book that many will consider as being more "interesting" than truly beautiful. Some might find them curious, or even grotesque. However, all of them are definitely exceptional. You may also notice that this book contains a preponderance of cattleyas, but any collection of "the most beautiful" simply must contain a high proportion of what is, for so many, the archetypal orchid. Orchids are the starlets of the plant world and, like human starlets, often photograph differently than they appear "in the flesh." For this reason, so many fine orchids could not be included for lack of an image that did them justice.

This well-grown Cattleya skinneri *has flowers of only average quality and shows that floral presentation can easily overshadow modest flowers.*

What, exactly, makes a beautiful orchid beautiful? Why do some orchids remain in cultivation for decades, while others seem to vanish after only a few years? What attracts people to certain flowers and not to others? What characteristics do "beautiful orchids" share? The answer to these questions depends on who is providing that answer. Certainly, commercial growers throughout the world are continually searching for the "next" phalaenopsis (by far the most commonly sold orchid on the world market) or *Vuylstekeara* Cambria or *Oncidium* Sharry Baby. Most of the orchids we see today on the mass market are the large growers' answer to these questions. They are fast-growing plants, easily produced by tissue-culture (or seed, if results are sufficiently uniform), simply transported to a final selling point, with long-lasting and decorative blooms. Is it any wonder why we see so many phalaenopsis, which grow and flower in less than half the time of many other types? One answer, then, to our question is that a beautiful orchid is one that is not just beautiful and eye-catching in a picture, at one unique moment in time, but one that performs and grows well under a variety of circumstances.

Small pot, big display! Orchid growers with cool conditions can grow colorful miniature orchids such as Masdevallia strobelii.

When orchid plants reach large "specimen size," they show their true potential, such as Coelogyne cristata 'Woodlands'.

Of course, orchid judges have an entirely different set of criteria. Most international judging systems—for example, the American Orchid Society's—do an admirable job of performing the task for which they are designed: the evaluation of superior examples of advances in any given line of breeding, recognition of superior or different or new examples of orchid species, and the giving of awards to exemplary culture. The equivalent in the UK is the RHS (Royal Horticultural Society) the UK's leading gardening charity dedicated to advancing horticulture. Plants that are judged to be of particular merit receive awards, indicated by AOS or RHS, after the plant name. The American Orchid Society (AOS) has many types of awards. The common awards are HCC (Highly Commended Certificate), AM (Award of Merit), JC (Judges' Commendation) and FCC (First Class Certificate). But since so few of us are commercial growers or orchid judges, why do we allow ourselves to be bound by their criteria? The answer to this question is bound up in the psyche of the particular orchid grower. Collectors are collectors, after all, no matter what they are

Oncidium *Sharry Baby may well be one of the most significant commercial orchid success stories of recent years. Shown here is a sport from 'Sweet Fragrance'. It shows a lighter color pattern than the original.*

collecting. Whether it is fish or snakes or roses, there comes a time when the urge to simply "collect" morphs into the urge to have something better, or different, than the next guy. This is when some hobbyists begin to be seduced by the lure of orchid judging.

They want to know what is new and different and superior, according to those who should know. They want to learn how to use these criteria not only to find and obtain superior orchids by learning about breeding trends, but they yearn for the validation given by an award system. And there is nothing wrong with this. It is one of the most important parts of the hobby to many. However, it is not the be-all and end-all that some would have it. Just because an orchid grows quickly and flowers young, is it suitable for your collection? If, on some isolated occasion, an orchid flowers well enough to gain the attention of orchid judges, does this necessarily mean that it will do the same under differing circumstances for a different grower? And if it does, will it do it year in and year out, without any special tricks or coincidences, and without any propensity for disease or susceptibility to mistakes?

Top: Certified orchid judges from organizations such as the Royal Horticultural Society and American Orchid Society must go through years of training to be able to recognize the best qualities of orchids. Ken Roberts examines the details of a Masdevallia while Ursula Ploch researches previous awards.

Above: Teams of judges consider nominated plants carefully and compare them against previous awards given to similar orchids. Bonnie Riley and the late Jean Merkel consider the merits of a Paphiopedilum hybrid.

After all, what good is an awarded orchid that rarely—or never—blooms? Or if it does, it is substantially affected, adversely

Cattleya lueddemanniana *has a reputation for producing flowers of varying quality from year to year.*

so, by culture, so much so that it may be almost unrecognizable as the same orchid in the award photo?

An added difficulty to the selection of truly "good" orchids, those that perform reliably and well, is the changing nature of the orchid market today. Formerly, orchid hobbyists could visit any one of a number of commercial growers in their area and see plants produced and grown on site. The staff was ready and willing to discuss the plants under their care. They had intimate knowledge of their particular varieties and knew what went into their proper culture. Many nurseries stocked a wide variety of species and hybrids so that they could better serve their local area, and this led to widely knowledgeable staff members who could answer customer questions based on personal experience. Also, many nurseries were vertically integrated, producing what they sold, from seed to bottle to tray to pots. The staff knew the plants from their inception. Over the past fifteen years, nurseries have become increasingly stratified in their production. That is, some produce seedlings in flask, sell to those who grow young plants, who then provide to the growers of slightly larger sizes, who in turn send plants off to the final retailer. Unfortunately, this often leads to the plants being sold by people who haven't a clue about the plants so briefly in their care. Today, by far the majority of orchid plants

Florália, in Niteroi, Brazil, is a popular destination for plant seekers. During the holiday season, they offer poinsettias and mums alongside flowering native orchids.

sold are by the mass market, where the staffs simply have no idea what goes into the successful culture of the orchid plants they are charged with selling. Even at orchid shows or smaller orchid nurseries—once the bastions of high quality knowledge for local conditions—the vendors often don't have sufficient experience to give their customers good quality information about the plants they are selling because they haven't grown them. However, there are still real orchid growers out there, orchid growers who know their product and, in many cases, orchids in general.

FINDING THE RIGHT ORCHID

This is certainly an important criteria for a "good orchid": the label of a reputable, trustworthy, and experienced orchid nursery. A good orchid nursery cultivates its clients the same way it cultivates its orchids, slowly and over a period of time. Given a climate of mutual respect, such relationships are the heart of the orchid hobby. How do you find a good orchid nursery? Orchid magazines are one good source, as are online Web site listings of vendors. Local orchid shows are another good place to start.

However, buyer beware. Just because a vendor has a nursery name and plants in front of him or her does not qualify that person as an expert. Take a minute to chat with the vendors. Are they interested in you, in your needs and growing conditions? Can they answer your questions in a sensible and unambiguous manner? Did they grow the plants they are selling, or have they only recently brought them in from another source? (This, in and of itself, does not disqualify a nursery from being "good," as many very good nurseries also buy products from other reputable sources.)

Displays of healthy, flowering orchids, such as those found at R.F. Orchids in Homestead, Florida, are a consumer's assurance of buying a quality product.

Basically, don't get carried away in the moment. Take some time to visit with the vendors.

What makes a good orchid is also dependent on the particular area in which it is to be grown. Here is another aspect that demands good-quality information from a knowledgeable source. A good orchid for Connecticut may not be any good at all in Kansas, vandas just don't do well in California (in general), and odontoglossums (odonts) are given a death warrant in Florida and the Gulf States. Plants appropriate for the greenhouse or patio are simply going to be too massive for a windowsill or for growing under lights.

Conversely, the miniature plants so beloved of growers who cultivate them inside their home often get "lost" in greenhouses or outdoors. Joining your local orchid society is one of your best sources for information on locally successful types. The experienced staff of local nurseries will also be of help. A local orchid nursery can serve as an invaluable repository of years of experience with what works and what doesn't. The staff also have a vested interest in cultivating you as a potential customer, so it is to the nursery's advantage to help you succeed in growing orchids and offer some of its valuable experience.

What are the physical characteristics you should look for in a good orchid? Some you will be able to observe on your own, and some will require the longer-term observations of your trusted nursery professional. First and foremost, look at the plant. If the plant looks weak or sickly, or has no roots, just forget it. A strong and healthy plant is the first indicator of a good orchid. Remember, what good is an awarded plant that never flowers? And if the

A nurseryman's attention to detail usually means healthy easy-growing orchids for the orchid customer. Here a display plant is being staked at The Little Greenhouse in Baltimore, Maryland.

Even warmth-loving vandas can be grown in a greenhouse in chilly Vermont.

professional grower is unable to succeed, well, why might you? (If you must try, though, you do have the advantage over the commercial grower in that you can take the individual care of your plants that he cannot. In other words, you may be able to have a plant succeed under your more specific care that does not perform well under the generalized care available in most nurseries.) Next, look at the general growth habit. Is the plant generally compact for its type? Does it branch freely, as opposed to "marching" straight across the pot? How about the distance between bulbs? If the plant is listed as "flowering size" or if it's a division, does it show a good history of flowering from every bulb? Are the leaves clean, giving evidence of freedom from disease and a tolerance of cultural mistakes? (All of these characteristics will be discussed at greater length later in the book, as will strategies for accomplishing the optimum performance from your plants.) Given

the choice between the strongest plant in a batch and the one in bud or flower, always take the strongest plant. An orchid has to first grow well to have any chance at all of flowering well. Yes, immediate gratification seems to be the operative mode for orchid buyers today, but it doesn't have to be that way. Orchid plants are long-term investments. Time spent in thoughtful selection today will pay off in the months and years to come with healthy, reliable, and robust plants that will give higher quality blooms on a regular basis, rather than just once before dying.

The flowering habit of a particular plant or hybrid group is more difficult to assess on the spot and will usually require prior knowledge on your part or the assistance of the knowledgeable grower. Some species or hybrids are simply more free-flowering than others. For example, *Brassavola nodosa* and *Cattleya aurantiaca* are both famous for their free-blooming habits as well

Top: Healthy orchids should have leaves that are medium-green and blemish-free, such as these phalaenopsis seedlings.

Above: Inspect potential orchid purchases for pests. Not only are pests bad for the orchid, they can spread to the rest of your collection.

as their floriferous progeny best exemplified by *Brassocattleya*

Maikai (*B. nodosa* x *C. bowringiana*) and the legion of spring-

flowering orange cluster types sired by *C. aurantiaca*. It is often

easier to know the species that flower profusely, with a broad

Top: A bounty of orchids at the peak of flowering can easily cloud one's judgment. A specialty orchid grower such as Carib Plants Inc. can make buying decisions easier by offering products not found elsewhere.

Above: Stay away from orchids that show color break in the flowers such as this Cattleya *hybrid seen at an orchid show. The mottled breaking of pigment in the flowers indicates that it probably has an incurable virus.*

range of examples from *Lycaste aromatica* to *Paphiopedilum*

callosum, *Neofinetia falcata* to *Dendrochilum magnum*. Flowers

should be of consistent quality from year to year and long-lasting.

Inflorescences should be strong and self-supporting, insofar as is

Above: Brassavola nodosa *is a perennial favorite species among both novices and longtime orchid growers. It presents a sweet nighttime fragrance.*

Right: Laeliocattleya *Puppy Love 'True Beauty' HCC/AOS shows the erect stem of flowers typical of* L. anceps *hybrids.*

possible, with the flowers emerging above the foliage. For example, *Laelia anceps* and its hybrids tend to have a wonderful flowering habit, with flowers held well above the plant on strong stems. *Lc.* Puppy Love is perhaps the archetypal *L. anceps* hybrid. A strong inflorescence will provide good flower carriage, optimizing the display qualities of the plant. Crowded or nodding flowers are usually not as attractive as those individually displayed on a well-spaced inflorescence. For windowsill growing, don't overlook *C. walkeriana* and its hybrids, such as *Lc.* Love Knot, for their compact stature, relatively large and long-lasting blooms, and attractive perfume. Modern hybrids from the Oncidium alliance are becoming almost universally available. Wilsonaras, colmanaras, alicearas, miltonidiums, and many others reward successful culture with abundant sprays of long-lasting and colorful blooms. However,

some hybrids have the unfortunate habit of having their flowers poorly arranged in a bunch at the end of a proportionately overlong inflorescence. Many of the hybrids from *Neofinetia falcata* are proving to be fine examples of "good orchids," as is the species itself. Perhaps no other orchid of its size has a sweeter and more attractive fragrance. Compact stature and a growing color palette show in such hybrids as the blue or pink *Neostylis* Lou Sneary (x *Rhy. coelestis*), shades of cerise in *Ascofinetia* Cherry Blossom (x *Asco. ampullaceum*), and the blue, white, or pink *Darwinara* Charm (x *Vascostylis* Tham Yuen Hae). An overlooked group of species and hybrids are the so-called soft-leaf types, related to *Zygopetalum* and *Lycaste*. Species and hybrids from *Bollea*, *Cochleanthes*, *Pescatorea*, and others not only have some of the most pleasing of all orchid foliage but also some of the most exotically colored and patterned blooms. No one who sees *Pesc. lehmanni* in all its purple-striped glory or *Coch. amazonica*, with its enormous round white lip with grape purple stripes, can doubt that these are "good orchids." A word of caution, though, that while some of the complex hybrids involving these species with zygopetalums may look good in pictures, many are quite difficult to grow and flower reliably.

An important feature of many orchids, often overlooked, is fragrance. It never ceases to amaze me how many people think, "most orchids aren't fragrant." Well, many are, and they are worth

searching out. Who could forget the perfume of *Zygopetalum mackayi* or *Cattleya walkeriana* or *C. labiata*? Some orchids may not smell good but are unforgettable nevertheless. From the musky scent of *Ansellia africana* to the carrion scent of *Bulbophyllum phalaenopsis* or *Cirrhopetalum graveolens*, orchid fragrance exists to attract pollinators, not people. Nevertheless, fragrant orchids do attract people.

So far, we have not even discussed flower quality. Without the above characteristics, an orchid plant may not even flower, so the floral aspects would be meaningless. When I think of what makes a good orchid, I think of what would look attractive on my coffee table or on my mantle or end table. In other words, what would make the best possible display subject in my home? Honestly, an orchid plant with good growth habit, that performs easily and well and flowers reliably and freely, will make the best display plant, regardless of the appearance of the individual

Above: Lycaste aromatica *from Mexico and Central America has flowers scented of cinnamon.*

Left: A fine-flowered form of Laelia anceps.

blooms. In other words, consider the entire aspect of the orchid plant in evaluating its beauty.

Nevertheless, most orchids are grown for the flowers. And it is the flowers that this book will focus on. We will show plant habit where possible and where appropriate, and orchid flowers that catch our attention. First must come color; flowers that are pleasing, definite, and with good texture are the characteristics that first catch the eye. What makes any given color or color combination attractive is so personal that it is impossible to discuss. Some like the pastel shades, others must have strong reds and oranges and yellows. I happen to like white. Substance is another feature that often, but not always, gives a hint about floral longetivity. For example, stanhopeas have very heavy substance and only last a day or two, while some dendrobiums in the *Nigrohirsute* group have relatively thin substance but last for weeks and weeks. When discussing orchids as display subjects, a round flower shape just doesn't matter. It is the overall aspect of the plant and its flowers that does.

It is important to note that there are entire classes of orchids that are grown for their overall display characteristics, which may or may not include their flowers. Oriental cymbidiums, prized for centuries by their Chinese or Japanese custodians, are as much loved for their graceful foliage as for their often-idiosyncratic blooms and heavenly fragrance. Don't overlook the jewel orchids—terrestrial plants of the forest floor that dazzle with patterned and veined foliage, which sparkles in subdued light.

Above: The small stature of Cattleya walkeriana *has sired a whole generation of large-flowered mini-catts suitable for the windowsill grower.*

Above right: The delicate vanilla-scented flowers of Neofinetia falcata *in profile, showing the distinctive spur-like nectary.*

Below: Zygopetalum *Rhein Clown is a colorful modern hybrid.*

Many grow their first orchids without even knowing it by stumbling across plants of *Anoectochilus* or *Ludisia* in their local garden centers and walking away with what is a simply stunning foliage plant, never mind that it is an orchid! Another group—artificial to be sure in its assembly—is comprised of orchids whose individual flowers are insignificant or even bizarre, but whose inflorescence as a whole creates a lovely and striking display.

In the end, what makes a good orchid is one that you enjoy. It is not what a commercial grower has to sell you, nor is it what an AOS judge evaluates as worthy of an award. It is not what your neighbor has (necessarily) or what you see in this book or any one

Above: The fetid stench of Cirrhopetalum graveolens *attracts the species' pollinator, flies.*

Top right: Once encountered, the sweet fragrance of Cattleya labiata *is never forgotten.*

of a number of popular orchid periodicals, though it might be. A "beautiful orchid" is one that performs reliably for you and satisfies your personal sense of beauty. The answer is that simple.

Nor is the above discussion intended only for the connoisseur, the dedicated hobbyist, or the aesthete. No, the same characteristics that make a good orchid, make it good for anyone, gardener or not. Indeed, the nonhobbyist has an advantage in the marketplace, because they can simply go on beauty alone. That plant in your garden center or plant shop that attracts your eye, if it meets most of the criteria set out previously, can be a delightful and long-lasting addition to your home decor at a fraction of the cost of keeping cut-flower arrangements. If it grows well enough to flower again for you, it is a bonus. If not, you've gotten your cost-benefit from it and can discard it, like you could any one of a number of other flowering potted plants.

Top right: Dendrobium formosum *is a member of the* Nigrohirsute *section of* Dendrobium *because the plant parts have fine black hairs.*

Top: Orchids are best enjoyed when they grace our living space with their beauty.

Above: Stanhopea tigrina *from Mexico has large spotted flowers that emerge downward from the base of the plant.*

WHAT IS AN ORCHID?

Members of the orchid family share a host of floral and vegetative features that give them a distinctive aspect. So distinctive are the

Top: Ludisia discolor, *one of the jewel orchids, is grown mainly for its attractive foliage.*

Top: Arpophyllum giganteum *has flowers arranged on cylindrical racemes that from a distance look more like an aquatic plant than an orchid.*

Above: The fernlike foliage of Isochilus linearis *is attractive even when not in flower.*

Above: The bright fuchsia, campanulate (bell-shaped) flowers of Isochilus linearis *are beautiful in detail when viewed closely.*

foliar characteristics, in fact, that even moderately experienced orchidists have little trouble saying about some new plant or other "Well, it sure looks like an orchid." Many of the most popularly cultivated orchids are epiphytes ("upon a tree") that grow up in the forest canopy in nature as an adaptation to insufficient light and nutrients on the woodland floor. Many other types of commonly seen houseplants have similar habits. A visitor to a tropical or subtropical forest would see such familiar plants as begonias,

Field trips offer opportunities to see how orchids grow in their native habitats. This Elleanthus species was rescued from a roadside clearing in the Colombia cloud forest.

bromeliads, gesneriads (African violets and their relatives), ferns, cacti, peperomias, and tradescantias (wandering Jews) growing right alongside more unusual plants, such as orchids.

It has to be clearly stated that not all orchid plants look alike. However, there is a shared set of features that enable most to quickly spot orchids in situ or at the garden center. Perhaps the most characteristic and universal among orchids are the fleshy, velamen-covered roots. The velamen is a water-absorbent tissue able to catch the first nutrient-rich moisture available as well as capture trace amounts of moisture in the sometimes-marginal habitats where orchids are often found. Interestingly, velamen is also present in most terrestrial orchids. This is an important "hint" to successful orchid culture, as even orchids that grow on the ground in nature often do not really grow in the ground. That is, their roots ramble about in the humusy forest duff, where air circulation is good and moisture is even, though often light. Therefore it is easy to project a cultivated orchid plant's need for an open potting medium that allows not only some moisture retention but air circulation as well. When media is kept constantly sodden and soggy, the roots essentially drown from lack of gas exchange. Whether epiphytic or "terrestrial," an orchid's velamen-coated roots are key to its amazing capacity to survive—indeed, thrive—in what are in many cases marginal habitats. An epiphytic orchid's roots can serve many functions and take a variety of forms. They may be rounded and rambling about, even unattached to the substrate.

They may be flattened and racing around the bark of the host tree, holding the plant tight to the surface and seeking out whatever ephemeral moisture and nutrients that may be available. They may be fat and succulent, serving as water and nutrient storage. In some cases, they may even have chlorophyll and be photosynthetic, allowing the plant to do without leaves entirely. For example, *Polyradicon gracilis* does very well with no leaves, albeit in some of the most humid and uncomfortable of all environments. Finally, some orchids—*Ansellia*, *Cyrtopodium*, *Grammatophyllum*, and some others—have what are known as "bird's-nest roots," which project upward in a wiry mass and serve to catch debris, which both nourishes the plants and serves as a water catchment system. Orchid roots have evolved in some species, such as *Phalaenopsis schilleriana* and *Phal. stuartiana*, adventitious buds that form into plantlets, thereby asexually propagating the plant over a favorable area. In concert with the almost always present foliar water-storage schemes, such as thickened stems (pseudobulbs), fleshy leaves, and thick, water-resistant cuticles, orchid roots help to make up what are among the most hardy and adaptable of all flowering plants.

What about terrestrial orchids? The species' progenitors of some of the best-known and most widely grown (where conditions permit) of all orchids, cymbidiums, live in the rich forest duff that accumulates on the forest floor. Their thick, fleshy roots serve a multitude of functions for the plant, from anchorage to storage of water and nutrients. Sobralias, with their reed-like stems and

Epidendrum nocturnum *shows typical epiphytic growth.*

alternating leaves, inhabit wide ranging habitats throughout South and Central America. We have seen *Sob. gloriosa* in the Colombian cloud forest, *Sob. fragrans* growing on a tree in Belize, and *Sob. liliastrum* growing six feet tall in the full sun of open fields

The spongy layer that covers orchid roots is known as velamen.

in the Gran Sabana. These are some of the most attractive of all orchids for their foliage alone. The large, generally short-lived *Cattleya*-like blooms are borne in succession from the apex of the canes. *Sobralia* roots are truly among the most amazing of all terrestrial orchids, if only for their succulence, profusion, and sheer mass. Again, storage functions are chief among their attributes. Indeed, with this type of orchid, transplanting from the wild into cultivation can be especially difficult owing to the extremely important role played by the roots, which are easily damaged and lost in transit or transplanting. Many terrestrials, though, do not have well-developed foliar water storage schemes and so rely almost entirely on their fleshy roots for sustenance during hard climatic times. Prime examples of these are the various slipper orchids (*Paphiopedilum*, *Phragmipedium*, *Cypripedium*) as well as many temperature zone terrestrials. While slippers are not, many terrestrials are seasonally deciduous, doubling up on adaptive schemes with their sustaining root masses, which carry them over the dry, cold, or otherwise unfavorable seasons. Unfortunately, the deciduous terrestrials also live in a very close relationship with the

soil fauna of their environment and so are very difficult to cultivate even by the most dedicated.

A brief discussion of the two growth habits of orchids— sympodial (primitive) and monopodial (derived)—will suffice here. Many orchids have the sympodial habit of growing along a horizontal rhizome from the base of which new growths emerge. The best analogies are ginger, irises, or bamboo. Flowering stems may grow from the apex of the newest growth or from the axils of the leaves. The growths may be succulent, with pronounced thickening to form pseudobulbs for storage—cattleyas are an excellent example of this—or may have soft leaves arranged more or less in a fan as in paphiopedilums. Monopodial orchids, on the other hand, grow basically straight up along a stem, with one main terminal apex. Branching may occur anywhere along the stem, but there is almost always a dominant stem. Flowering stems emerge from the axils of the continuously developing leaves along the

Sterilized bark from Douglas fir trees is a popular potting media that retains moisture yet allows air circulation.

stem. Think, here, of a palm tree: straight up. Vandas and phalaenopsis are commonly seen monopodial orchids.

But this book is about beautiful orchid flowers. What makes orchid flowers, orchid flowers? What sets them apart from other, "common" blooms? First and foremost is the often-present highly modified petal, known as the labellum, or lip. Orchids, being monocots, have flowers arranged in whorls of three. Three sepals, or the outer whorl, encase the inner whorl of three petals. One of the three petals, often the lowest, is modified into pollinator-attracting labellum, or lip. Orchid lips have evolved a startling array of bizarre, arcane, and colorful ways to attract and trap various animals—birds, bees, moths, bats, gnats, and others—into pollinating their flowers. The lip is generally lowermost of the three petals. This is because orchids are usually resupinate; that is, the flower ovary (the stem of the flower) twists 180 degrees during development to present the lip, which develops at the top of the bloom, at the bottom. Those orchids that present the lip

Sobralia liliastrum *growing in full sun in front of a Venezuelan farmhouse in the Gran Sabana.*

uppermost twist through an entire 360 degrees. The lip encloses to some greater or lesser extent the most marvelous of the orchid's adaptive features, the column, which unites the male stamens and the female stigmatic surface into one. The evolutionary advantage to this is startling. Orchids have fine, dust-like seeds that are extraordinarily profuse—to say millions in a seedpod is no exaggeration—and are scattered by wind in the hope of one or a few finding just the right spot to germinate and grow. For these many seeds to be fertilized necessitates a mechanism that guarantees the precise placement of enough individual pollen grains to fertilize each ovule. This is accomplished by orchid pollen grains being bound together in a few large masses called pollinia.

The structure of the orchid bloom is adapted to allow precise placement of a high number of pollen grains where the pollen tubes may reach waiting ovules for fertilization. Additionally, the pollinaria are structured to prevent, insofar as is possible, self-fertilization, which is undesirable. The method by which this is accomplished is generally one of movement of the stipe—twisting, bending, and turning—after removal from the column, from a position where self-fertilization is improbable to one where cross-pollination is possible. Another ingenious structure that helps to prevent self-pollination is the rostellum, a barrier between the pollinia and stigmatic surface. In some self-pollinating orchids, the premature drying and loss of the rostellum allows self-pollination before the flower opens. Of course, self-fertilization occurs in orchids, sometimes intentionally, but is normally as undesirable in orchids as it is in any other organism.

In their process of relatively rapid speciation and habitat radiation, orchids have evolved into one of the largest of all plant families with more than 25,000 naturally occurring species discovered to date. Because orchids inhabit such a wide range of habitats, many of them very localized, there are surely many, many orchids still to be uncovered, some of which, owing to habitat loss, will never be known. In this process, the variety of plant forms and habits has evolved to fill just about every imaginable niche and to give every competitive advantage. Some of the largest orchids are truly massive, such as the tropical *Grammatophyllum speciosum* and *Gram. papuanum*, which can reach several yards in height and weigh over a ton when mature. Other examples of mass are the various vining members of the genus *Vanilla*,

Above: Paphiopedilum delenatii *is a beautiful terrestrial species from Vietnam.*

Below left: The typical growth habit of a sympodial orchid.

whose overall weight would be difficult to calculate, as the vines can reach many yards in length (one nursery-grown plant was over 400 feet long before it flowered for the first time when light was increased). Some of the New World sobralias recently discovered can be over twenty feet tall! Of course, many orchids are large, such as *Cattleya guttata*, which can reach over six feet tall, but even more are miniscule, such as the tiny "champs," *Platystele jungermanoides* and *Bulbophyllum odoardii*, both at less

Above: Monopodial orchids grow upward instead of along a rhizome.

Right: Encyclia radiata *(syn.* Prosthechea radiata, *syn.* Anacheilium radiatum*) is a good example of a nonresupinate flower.*

than a quarter inch. As with the giants, where there are large plants and there are LARGE plants, there are the nearly invisible, and the merely small, of which there are many. One of the best-known of the merely small is *Pleurothallis grobyi*, representative of an entire group of miniature orchids that inspire nearly fanatic devotion among windowsill growers, as so many plants can be crammed into such a compact space. Perhaps strangest of the many habitats that orchids occupy is underground. The subterranean *Rhizanthella*, of Australia, is never seen above ground, with its flowers only appearing when temporarily uncovered at the surface by rooting animals. Another type of "subterranean" orchid is the saprophytic type, which lives off rotting vegetation in the soil substrate, not unlike fungi, with only flower spikes emerging to show that there are orchid plants present in the environment.

Nor are orchids exclusively tropical or subtropical with a cosmopolitan range from northern Sweden and Alaska to Tierra del Fuego and Macquarie Island, from sea level to over 12,000 feet in the Andes. Indeed, according to Robert Dressler, orchids occupy habitats that are "near the limits of vegetation." Their ecology has a profound influence on their cultivation. In many cases, orchids have evolved great stress tolerance, an almost "weedy" habit. Orchids are often among the first to colonize disturbed or marginal habitats such as road cuts, slopes damaged by landslides, or new volcanic islands. I have seen zygopetalums in roadside ditches in Brazil, with their leaves sawed off by road maintenance, flower stems emerging proudly from developing growths. In Colombia, we

Top: Beautiful gold veining leads the pollinator to the column, which contains both male and female sex organs.

Above: An orchid seedpod (capsule) can contain a hundred thousand fine seeds that rely on the wind to carry them to a place where proper conditions exist for germination.

Top right: Orchid pollen is fused into waxy masses known as pollinia. The stipe can be seen at the top of the pollen mass in this photo.

were puzzled by what were clearly orchid seedlings popping up in the clay soil of a recent road cut, only to discern that they were *Phragmipedium* seedlings from seed rained down from a mother plant above the cut. I often discuss "coyote orchids" in conservation talks, referring to the amazing ability many orchids have to adapt to changing conditions, whether the result of human intervention or natural catastrophe. Not unlike coyotes, which have easily adapted to, and spread with, man's changing environment, many orchids are denizens of the changing environment, growing in an area before other plants can emerge. However, there are also "panda orchids," orchids that have evolved such a high degree of interdependence with their environment that any change—rainfall, shade or sun, pollinator—leads to their rapid decline and possible extinction. Happily, these plants seem to be the exception, but they do serve as the warning for habitat preservation, much as pandas do in the animal kingdom.

Also, many orchids have a very stress-tolerant metabolism known as CAM. This photosynthetic pathway produces one metabolic product during the day when light is abundant but moisture may be limited and finishes the job during dark hours, when the stomata can be open for gas and moisture exchange without overly taxing the plants' moisture reserves. The CAM mechanism is particularly favorable for epiphytic orchids, where moisture may be quite limited during the day hours but humidity

Artificially, we can create orchid hybrids or species by placing the pollinium onto the stigmatic surface.

rises as the temperature drops at night, allowing the dew to collect and recharge the moisture-absorbing velamen of the roots.

Another aspect of orchid ecology that influences not only their distribution within a given habitat but also their cultivation is their intimate relationship with mycorrhizal fungi. As previously noted, orchid seed is very fine and dustlike. It contains essentially no endosperm, the starchy, nutritive material that gives most angiosperm seedlings the energy to germinate and grow until their own photosynthetic pathways can kick in. In nature, orchid seed must be invaded by the mycorrhizae, whose metabolic by-products serve as nutrition and enable the orchid seedling to germinate and grow. Such explicit conditions only exist in a limited number of places—just the right tree, the favorable soil, a crack in a rock—and so, from the many opportunities, only a vanishingly small number of seedlings ever germinate from any seedpod. This can lead, in nature, to a particular tree being an "orchid tree" or to a species being locally abundant, where the conditions are right and the mother plant provides seed. In cultivation, the nutrients are

provided—much like a hospital culture—in a sterile environment,
usually in an agar-based medium. Here, countless orchid seeds
have the chance to germinate and grow, for convenient and cost-
effective distribution into cultivation.

Orchids' complex adaptation into the epiphytic habit has many
ramifications both for the student of the plants and the grower.
Why, exactly, did orchids—or any plant—begin to take to trees?
It helps to think about a tropical or subtropical forest as a whole.
Most of the biomass of such a forest is tied up in the existing
vegetation. When a tree or other organism falls, it is very quickly
transformed and recycled by other forest organisms, leaving very
little to go back into the soil. The multilayered canopy filters
photosynthetic rays extremely efficiently, allowing little or none to
reach the lowest, floor level. The common image of a natural forest

Top left: This vine of Vanilla planifolia *climbs thirty feet up the tree.*

Top right: Cattleya guttata *can reach six feet tall.*

Above: Macroclinium wullschlaegelianum *has a name that is bigger than the plant itself.*

Above: Spathoglottis plicata *is reported to have been one of the first plants to colonize the devastated islands surrounding Krakatau after the huge 1883 volcanic explosion.*

Left: Arundina graminifolia *has achieved weed status in parts of Hawaii.*

being a solid, impenetrable layer from top to bottom is based on Tarzan movies as well as views from along, say, a river course, where light can reach all the way to the surface. In fact, the floor of a forest is more often open and nearly sterile, park-like in its appearance. How, then, can an herbaceous plant get a start? By moving up in the world, up into the canopy itself, where it can intercept both light and nutrients before they are filtered out by larger plants. Orchids live in the trees, stratified according to their type and preference, from the topmost perches at the fringes of the forest where light is intense and moisture less dependable, to further down in the canopy where light is of lower intensity but moisture and nutrients are more constant. The plant habit of any

given orchid will reflect its position in the forest. Thicker, more succulent leaves with a waxy protective cuticle team with swollen, water-retentive pseudobulbs on plants exposed to brighter light and drier conditions. Softer, broader leaves and less conspicuous water-storage organs are the norm on plants in shadier, moister environments. Such clues give the experienced orchid grower a real advantage for the successful culture of an unknown plant.

THE HISTORY OF ORCHID CULTURE

The early history of orchids can be traced back nearly to the beginning of modern learning. We cannot know what was thought of them prior to the invention of writing, of course, but they are mentioned almost from the very beginning of this crucial development. The earliest known mention of orchids must go to the Chinese, where *Bletilla hyacinthina* was first mentioned in a twenty-eighth century BCE herbal. Confucius noted them as "lan,"

We were amazed to see volunteer Phragmepedium *seedlings on a rocky road cut in Colombia.*

The seed that produced these Encyclia tampensis *seedlings found just the right conditions for germination.*

(or orchid) and called them the "king of fragrance" as early as 500 BCE. This King of Fragrance was almost certainly *Cymbidium ensifolium*, still revered in Eastern culture for its delicate foliage and heavenly perfume. Countless cultivars are still grown today, where aberrant foliar or floral characters set apart the most venerated and valuable. Here in the West, interestingly, *Cym. ensifolium* is prized as much for its contribution to heat-tolerant hybrids as for its intrinsic appeal. Asiatic interest in orchids has, therefore, the longest continuous history, and continues unabated today.

Surely, the Japanese inherited their love of orchids from the Chinese. Two Japanese native orchids, especially, deserve

mention as historical pieces with modern relevance. Orchids have played an important part in traditional Japanese culture, where they were appreciated for their serenity and beauty, as well as their symbolic representation of royalty and elegance. Various cultivars of *Dendrobium moniliforme* have been important in Japanese royal collections for hundreds of years and today are exhibited occasionally where they attract considerable attention from the public not only for their multitude of foliar and floral differences but also as symbols of wealth and privilege. The Samurai were passionately fond of *Neofinetia falcata*, the "wind orchid," which they collected not only for the diminutive fan-shaped foliage,

A Cattleya mossiae *in full bloom growing epiphytically in the Venezuelan jungle.*

but for the sweetly scented, birdlike blooms of purest white. Indeed, stories abound of Samurai even carrying their plants of *Neof. falcata* with them into battle, both to protect the plants and to enjoy a moment of serenity with the plants in between skirmishes.

Today, distinctive cultivars of this orchid, as with *Den. moniliforme*, are very highly prized and sought-after, not only by discriminating Japanese growers, but by Western aficionados as well. The finest cultivars of either of these orchids can fetch prices—on the rare occasion when divisions may be available—well into the thousands, and occasionally tens of thousands, of dollars.

The Western history of orchids is more complete and relevant to this particular book. As with Asian history, orchids probably first entered Western knowledge as herbal remedies. Theophrastus, the "Father of Botany" and pupil of Plato and Aristotle, first wrote of orchids in his *Enquiry into Plants* around 300 BCE. He coined the name orchis in reference to the testicle-like appearance of the orchid's bulbs. Later, Dioscorides wrote about orchids in his *Materia Medica* of ca. 70 CE. All of this ties into the so-called Doctrine of Signatures, prevalent in early Western medicine. The basic tenet of the doctrine was that if a naturally occurring object or organism resembled a part of the human anatomy, it must somehow affect that organ or body part if ingested. Therefore, the testicle-like tubers of orchis were thought to influence male virility.

The contemporary history of orchids is a complex and interwoven story, beginning at the start of the modern scientific revolution in the early eighteenth century, and is exemplary of the progress of our Western culture, shot through with the same drama and same humanity. Indeed, the history of the people, the innovation, the collectors and collections, the science, and the business of orchid growing is a microcosm that cannot be discussed in isolation, one aspect from another. Only the high points, the critical junctures can be presented here.

With increasing exploration and the wealth that inevitably followed, leisure was available for the sort of scientific and intellectual pursuits that the advance of knowledge requires. The hunger of science for new materials of potentially great economic value, coupled with the aristocracy's need for novelty, sent collectors fanning out across both the New and Old Worlds in search of newer and more distinct plants and animals. The capital made available by the opening of new sources of raw materials drove the race for further discovery. As the recently discovered New World began to give up its secrets to explorers looking for more than just the quick, golden discoveries, new plants and animals began to flood back to Europe. Simply, these new plants and animals needed names, and to be named, they had to be more closely investigated using the developing scientific method. It must be remembered that much of this predates Linnaeus and his binomial system, so plants were named, more or less randomly,

Schomburgkia tibicinis (*syn.* Myrmecophila tibicinis) *prefers bright or full sun exposure in its Central American habitats.*

according to their attributes, in a descriptive way. Indeed, the family name *Orchidaceae* was not applied until early in the nineteenth century. One of the most important aspects of the process—and a part that led to the eventual binomial Linnaean system—was the storage and cataloging of items so that, once categorized, they could be referenced and compared with other, newer organisms. Thus it was that the first tropical orchid entered cultivation in England in 1731 as a "dried" herbarium specimen. The observant recipient, noting what he perceived to be some life still in the plant, potted it up. It grew and flowered. Here, as in much of scientific discovery, happy chance played a great part. If the plant hadn't

Above: Cymbidium ensifolium *'Iron Bone' is a beautiful cultivar of the species that has a citrusy fragrance.*

Below: Bletilla hyacinthina *was mentioned in ancient Chinese herbals.*

Above: Dendrobium *Ise is a primary hybrid of Den. moniliforme x Den. stricklandianum. The hybrid exhibits many of the desirable qualities of the* Den. moniliforme *parent but is of easier culture.*

originated where it had (the Bahamas), if it hadn't been dormant, and if the grower was not exceptionally lucky, the plant would have simply gone onto its herbarium sheet. The descriptive, non-Linnaean name given this new species was *Helleborine virginianum flore rotundo luteo*. As it was, what was later named *Bletia verrucunda* was the vanguard of many tens of thousands of plants to follow.

The potential economic value of the discoveries was so great that the explorers often equivocated as to the exact location of their finds, even if they knew it, which too often they did not (this was long before precise location could easily be determined.) It must be remembered, too, that every plant and animal evidencing even the slightest potential interest was being sent back to Europe. So, if the plant sent back was not the supposed object of interest, the location of its collection might not have even been noted.

Above: Species of bletia are found throughout the tropical Americas and Caribbean. Bletia verrucunda (syn. Bletia purpurea) *was one of the first tropical orchids cultivated in Europe.*

Right: Cattleya labiata *is a beautiful species in its own right.*

The most famous example of this concerns one of the premier orchids of all time, *Cattleya labiata*. The first plants of this species to arrive in England in the early nineteenth century were sent, so it is said, as packing material around some other plants of supposedly higher interest and value that originated in the Organ Mountains around Rio de Janeiro, Brazil. Mr. William Cattley of Barnet, England, received the package from the collector, Mr. William Swainson, and finding more interest in the packing material than the packed plants, attempted the cultivation of these strange plants. Later that same year, in November 1818, a plant flowered, and it was stunning, simply unlike any flower Swainson had seen to date. John Lindley, another pivotal name in this golden age of

orchids, named the new orchid after its cultivator, noted patron of horticulture, and seminal orchid hobbyist as *Cattleya labiata autumnalis* (autumn-flowering, large-lipped cattleya). Sadly, the exact location of the plants' collection had not been recorded, and the few plants were much treasured for a period of nearly twenty years while others eagerly sought out more plants in their native land.

Eventually, in 1836, a Dr. Gardner refound the species and recorded its habitat in his journal. In a pattern that has been repeated time and again in the ensuing decades, commercial collectors flocked to the locale, decimating the habitat to provide plants for demanding clientele.

One of the most important of early orchid collectors, arguably the most important for his starting the "fad" of aristocratic orchid collections, is William Spencer Cavendish, sixth Duke of Devonshire, popularly known as the "Bachelor Duke." At a horticultural exhibition in London in 1833, at the Royal Horticultural Society, C. Loddiges & Sons (one of first nurseries to regularly grow and stock orchids for sale) exhibited a plant of the "butterfly orchid," *Oncidium (Psychopsis) papilio*. At this time, most epiphytic orchids were known as "Epidendrums" or "air plants." Cavendish was so impressed with this novel new plant that he purchased it, thus beginning one of the great amateur orchid collections at his estate of Chatsworth. Of course, when it became known that Cavendish was collecting orchids, it became the "thing to do" among the wealthy and landed rich. Among other early hobbyists are such names as Hugh Cuming, Skinner and Bowring, Harrison and Moss, Cattley, Rucker, and Day, all of whom are immortalized in orchid history by species named after them such as *Cattleya* and *Lycaste skinneri* (among others), *C. bowringiana*, *C. harrisoniana* and *Bifrenaria harrisoniae*, the genus *Cattleya*, *Anguloa ruckeri*, and *Coelogyne dayana*.

As new locales were explored, new plants were sent back, grown, and flowered. Such a simple exposition does not give real credit to the difficulties of the time. Anyone who has imported orchids from another country, even from an established nursery, knows the headaches and heartaches with which such an undertaking is fraught, even today with our modern methods of communication and transportation. Imagine, if you will, a day when orchids collected from the wild would be taken to a port by donkey or horseback, to be loaded onto a sailing ship or, in later days, a steamship to travel for many days back to a European port, where they would be distributed by auction. Imagine the loss rate. Besides the marginal cultural methods employed in the early years of the nineteenth century, just the attrition rate of those orchids that actually made it to England or France or Belgium was fantastic. This leaves aside the many more that never made it to a port, for whatever reason, or those lost in transit when the ship sank or was delayed by a storm or breakdown. Mechanical breakdown was the least of the problems faced by collectors trying to get orchids back to the European market. The literature is rife with stories of collectors who perished in the line of duty. Nevertheless, we can only admire these stout men—for women orchid collectors were few and far between in the prim Victorian climate—who faced unknown geography, new insects and diseases, and often hostile natives on their way to finding the new and desirable plants they sought. Orchid collectors, too, were honored by specific names: Warszewicz and the genus *Warszewiczella*, Roezl and *Miltoniopsis roezlii*, Linden and *Oncidium lindenii*, Wallis and *Pescatorea wallisii*, Lobb and *Bulbophyllum lobbii*, Low and *Paph. lowii*—the list could go on and on. And as noted with *C. labiata*, the collectors were not shy in the amounts of plants they stripped—for this is the only appropriate word—from the habitat. This was not only to meet demand and hedge against losses in transit, but if an area were completely depleted of a given species, it would be impossible for competitors to gather any and to thereby affect the market. Indeed, the orchids weren't the only targets, as often the trees in which they grew would be removed as well, not just to make the collection easier but to ruin the habitat for any survivors. Huge numbers of plants, therefore, were sent off to European markets, as often as not measured in crates or tons. Records tell of shipments of 10,000 *Odontoglossum crispum* or thirty boxes of the same species, which resulted in their being "extinguished in this spot."

As new plants flowered, they were given to the leading botanists of the day to be recorded by painting or drawing, officially described, and named. As more and more plants came into Europe, systemic botany began to truly come into its own. Each family or genus certainly had its experts, and the preeminent expert of orchids was John Lindley, often called the Father of Modern Orchidology. While he worked in other groups as well, his contributions to the study and classification of the orchids known at the time are beyond compare. Indeed, he is credited with the coining of the family name, *Orchidaceae* (from the earlier *Orchideae of de Jussieu*) in his *The Genera and Species of Orchidaceous Plants*. Another of his significant works is *Folia Orchidaceae*, which set out to be a monographic treatment of all orchid genera, and, was, unfortunately, never completed. If his contributions to orchid classification were the extent of his accomplishments, it would be enough to guarantee him a place in the pantheon of orchid greats. However, perhaps more significant was his suggestion to Joseph Paxton (later Sir Joseph) about how to successfully cultivate orchids.

As new lands were explored, information about them traveled at differing rates, leading to many popular misconceptions about their climate, populations, animals, and plants. The early nineteenth century was not that far removed from the era of maps that had vast areas of terra incognita, and were labeled with "Here Be Monsters." As a result, equatorial zones were still considered to be uniformly hot, damp, and shady. Hence, the "stove" house was conceived, where the owner did his best—or his estate gardener did—to emulate the sticky tropics. Very little light and less air were admitted, and the "stove" portion of the equation was a coal fire kept constantly burning to add a furious heat. Epiphytic, often higher-elevation orchids were plunged into peat beds where, more often than not, they expired very quickly, sometimes flowering before dying, sometimes not. Of course, it was not to the advantage of the commercial collectors to let too much be known about the habitats where they obtained any particular plant, both because others might find it and because a dead plant is a plant that needs replacing, from them. Growers rather early on discovered that epiphytic orchids appreciated having their roots exposed, and their perches were emulated by placing the imported plants onto sticks or limbs with some mossy material to bind them in. This worked, after a fashion. However, when Lindley suggested to Paxton the admission of outside air to create a more buoyant and fresh atmosphere, even one that was cooler for the higher-elevation plants, a revolution was born. Paxton succeeded with previously intractable plants beyond the wildest dreams of even the most optimistic. From being the "graveyard of tropical orchids," England went on to lead the Western world in the cultivation and exhibition of new and fine varieties. Indeed, it held this position until the world wars and their privations intervened. Paxton first published his methods in the influential *Gardener's Chronicle* in 1859, opening the floodgates to modern orchid culture. After decades of failure and seeing plants—many of which involved the "investment" of many hundreds or thousands of dollars—summarily expire after only a short time, one can only imagine the excitement of seeing, for the first time, a plant prosper and flower, not just for a few months but, really, as long as the grower cared to keep it going.

Cattleya skinneri was named after George Ure Skinner, its discoverer. The pictured clone, 'Casa Luna', has received an Award of Merit from the American Orchid Society.

Orchid collecting as a hobby and as a business was undergoing an evolution, as well. In its earliest days, the orchid hobby was strictly the pursuit of the landed rich, who financed collection expeditions with their own money, hoping to populate their greenhouses with something new with which to impress their wealthy peers. The same estate gardeners who grew their cut flowers and vegetables and tended their considerable estates cared for their plants. Today, we know little of this formerly honorable and sought-after profession. Boys were apprenticed out at an early age to learn from expert gardeners, and as they learned, they often moved up within the estate or were lucky or good enough to be hired by another estate's patron. These men were the first to learn successful orchid culture and to teach a select fortunate few their secrets—and in many cases, secrets they were, because the success of a particular Duke's or Earl's estate-grown orchids was a great source of pride and status. Inevitably, more orchid growers were trained than could be supported by the available estates and some few, joined by opportunistic peers, struck out on their own to form the first orchid nurseries.

These earliest orchid nurseries were not simply those we know today but are evolved from seed merchants into more general

Top: The colors of Bifrenaria harrisoniae *from Brazil range from white to dusty rose. All forms have intricate lip details. It was named in 1825 in honor of Mrs. Arnold Harrison, owner of a fine orchid collection.*

Above: Cattleya harrisoniana *was introduced as a variety of C. loddigesii by Richard Harrison of Liverpool in 1836. Named in honor of his relative, Mrs. Arnold Harrison, it is now recognized as a distinct species.*

tropical nurseries where a gentleman could obtain the latest *Anthurium*, as well as something a little different in the orchid family. The same collectors who went out around the world for orchids were on the lookout for other desirable exotics, and so the partnership was logical. One of the earliest successful orchid purveyors was C. Loddiges & Sons, a nursery in Hackney, founded in 1812 and active until the dissemination of their collection in 1852. Remember, it was they who displayed the plant that first caught the fancy of the Bachelor Duke.

One of the most famous and influential of all orchid nurseries started life as a seed nursery around 1802 as James Vietch and Sons. It was at this establishment that an event occurred that would change the course of orchid history. At the suggestion of a physician, Dr. John Harris, who had worked out what went where to successfully pollinate an orchid flower, Vietch's foreman, John Dominy, made a series of hybrid orchids that culminated with the first flowering, in 1856, of an artificial orchid hybrid, later to be named *Calanthe* Dominii. Other hybrids soon followed, and a rage was born. It is impossible to underestimate the impact of this event. In the middle of the nineteenth century, genetic affinities had not yet been worked out; no one even knew about genetics. Nor had successful seed culture been perfected, though occasional success with sowing of the seed around the base of the mother plant was sometimes seen.

Imagine, then, the acclaim that would follow not only making a hybrid but also persuading the seed to grow into plants and tending them until they flowered and proved their qualities unique from either parent. After decades of dominating the orchid trade with world-ranging collectors and show-stopping auctions of their finds, the Vietch firm morphed into Black & Flory—with its sale after the retirement of Sir Harry Vietch—which was a very influential player in the period between the two World Wars.

Of course, other English firms were important during this developmental phase. Stuart Low & Co. was originally founded by Hugh Low in 1820 and made their mark in post–World War I orchids. The House of Sander came along in 1860 and rivaled, at its peak, the Vietch firm. And while it was certainly topflight in its provision of new species and hybrids, being ultimately responsible for some of today's best orchids through their development of early

Top: Miltoniopsis roezlii *is a beautiful species from Panama, Colombia, and Ecuador. It has been used to make many Miltonia hybrids known as "pansy ochids." It is named after Benedict Roezl.*

Above: The popular species Paphiopedilum lowii *was introduced by Hugh Low from a discovery made on Sarawak around 1846.*

breeding lines, its work on *Sander's List of Orchid Hybrids* is where its name will live forever. Personally tended by the Sander family until being turned over to the Royal Horticultural Society in 1961,

Sander's List is one of the aspects of orchidology that is very nearly unique in the world of horticulture. No other family of plants has such a complete and relatively transparent record of all hybrids made since the dawn of time. This was not an easy accomplishment in the latter years of the nineteenth century, when records were incomplete and often conflicting. But Sander's did impose order, and today we can trace the full lineage of almost any orchid registered from 1856 with *Cal.* Dominii to today with the most complex hybrid phalaenopsis or paphiopedilum. For example, *Blc.* Bryce Canyon, a cattleya-type hybrid registered by the late firm of Armacost & Royston, could trace its parentage back nine generations to the species, all of whose hybrids were made by the nursery. Pretty impressive. There are, of course, some breaks in the record where parentage was not recorded by the originator, the originator is or was unknown, or there was an unavoidable mix-up in the raising of the seed. This is not too difficult to understand when one considers that the formation of a seedpod was not always a sure thing, so records weren't always kept; germination around the mother plant was slow, and a particularly good mother plant might have multiple sowings around its base, leading to inevitable confusion; where a seedling originated might not be known or remembered (if it takes so long to flower an orchid, this is understandable); and, finally, the maker of the hybrid might not want anyone else to know what he had done, leading to, well, equivocation. Thankfully, these early "blips" in the system did not affect its long-term viability, and today, orchid students can have endless discussions about what species' influence is where and how much.

The beginning of what could be seen as truly modern orchid-culture techniques started with Charlesworth & Co., founded in the waning years of the nineteenth century. Charlesworth specialized in *Odontoglossum crispum*, collected at higher elevations in Colombia. It made a business of knowing and obtaining the very best and finest varieties of this highly variable and extraordinarily beautiful species. The "premier" series of *Odm. crispum* was their hallmark, and a good premier *crispum* remains to this day one of the most beautiful of all orchids. Charlesworth's was highly influential in both the line-breeding (breeding together select varieties of the same species to get better examples) of *Odm. crispum* and in the breeding of its hybrids. It was able to enter into truly commercial production of unheard-of quantities with its collaboration with a Dr. Ramsbottom, who helped to perfect the "symbiotic" method of orchid culture. As discussed earlier, orchid seed germinates in close association with a symbiotic fungus that provides nutrition to the developing seedling.

To this time, seed sown around a mother plant germinated with some limited success, probably because of the presence of the mycorrhizal fungus in the wild-collected plant. Charlesworth's and Ramsbottom's success was based in the application of recently gained knowledge of the presence and function of the invading fungus. The appropriate and necessary strain of fungus was isolated and used to inoculate the sterilized seedling media, where

AOS judge John Naugle still maintains an old-style glass greenhouse near the west coast of Florida. Once the only kind of greenhouse, they are becoming scarce today.

it was quickly discovered that, when properly done, orchid seed germinated freely and in quantities much greater than ever expected. From the occasional one or a dozen orchid seedlings closely held and seldom released, Charlesworth had found the mother lode of orchid hybridization, leading to the sensational "odonts" of today.

Marking the final transition to the modern orchid world was the collection of Sir George Holford at Westonbirt, tended by his grower, H. G. Alexander. Arguments could be made that Alexander was the greatest hybridizer of all time. Based on the track record of his many hybrids—including, but not limited to, *Cymbidium*

alexanderi 'Westonbirt', *Laeliocattleya lustre* 'Westonbirt', and *Paphiopedilum hellas* 'Westonbirt'—and their countless progeny, his observational skills and uncanny intuition mark him as a once-in-a-lifetime personality. However, one of Alexander's unsung roles in the history of orchid growing might be his role in the early training of a gentleman who was to transform the American, and the world's, concept of commercial orchid growing through his association with Armacost & Royston, B. O. Bracey. In Bracey, we have the culmination and final stage of the evolution of the orchid grower from estate gardener, to nurseryman growing wild-collected plants, to the truly commercial nurseryman specializing in the

Odontioda Picotee *is a modern hybrid heavily influenced by* Odontoglossum crispum.

Modern orchid growing began in 1922 when Dr. Louis Knudson of Cornell University, building on the same research of Bernard and Burgeff used by Charlesworth and Ramsbottom in their symbiotic approach to orchid seedling culture, devised the asymbiotic method (described above). When Knudson went west to California, to Armacost & Royston of Sawtelle, and taught B. O. Bracey his methods, a revolution began. Armacost, building on the fabulous Doheny collection purchased some years previously and the association of Bracey with Alexander, immediately began growing tens of thousands of hybrid cattleyas for its own cut-flower use and that of other growing nurseries in the United States. With Bracey's keen observational powers, his access to the best of English breeding, and the ability to grow thousands of a hybrid from which to select the very best for further breeding, Armacost became the powerhouse of a new orchid industry in the United States. American orchid culture started in the middle of the nineteenth century, when gentlemen sought to emulate everything English, including their hobbies. Commercial growing was somewhat slower coming, with firms like Butterworth's in Massachusetts. Sander's made an effort to start an American branch, but the financial and managerial strain caused by long distances and steamship travel intervened, and the site was sold to Lager & Hurrell, another of the early and very influential U.S. nurseries.

Armacost's production of orchid seedlings fueled a rapidly growing and very profitable market in cut orchid blooms, especially

hybridization and cultivation of hybrid orchid plants. Sadly, this same era was to see the passing of the English orchid scene as an influential part of the world orchid stage. Two world wars forced many nurseries into a position where they could not economically operate, and the United States, repository of their best and brightest, took the lead. This leadership was not only based on good English hybrids but also on a more favorable climate and a larger market necessary to drive commercial exploitation of orchid hybrids.

cattleyas. Because the flowers were so profitable, orchid plants were not widely available to the public in those years between the wars. This was the time of the Great Depression, when expendable income for hobbies simply wasn't available. Demand for orchid cut flowers built over the years, and nurseries such as George E. Baldwin, Thomas Young, and the Rod McLellan Co. capitalized on the highly profitable and exclusive market. Production buildup and demand peaked during World War II, when, for the first time in many years, the working class had, thanks to the war-driven economy, available excess income for frivolities like orchid plants.

Demand for orchid cut-flowers, largely cattleyas but later cymbidiums, has waned over the years, and orchid production has shifted to the more hobby-oriented novelty types and orchids suitable as flowering potted plants. Hobby-oriented orchid nurseries began to be seen after World War II, as excess cut-flower stock was sold as potted plants and orchids became more widely available to the masses. A big step in this process was the formation of the American Orchid Society in 1921. Originally formed by wealthy Easterners and the orchid nurseries that supplied them to fight the onset of a proposed orchid quarantine, the AOS morphed after World War II into an organization intimately concerned with the popularization of the orchid hobby. Thanks to its prescient editor and executive director, Gordon Dillon, the AOS has played and continues to play a significant role in introducing the hobby to the public.

The last cultural breakthrough that enabled far more to enjoy successful orchid culture came about in the early 1950s. A lumber mill owner, John Ivory, began to look for other uses for what were essentially mill waste products. In concert with O. A. Matkin of California's Soil and Plant Laboratory, he became convinced that the bark stripped from the logs in the milling process could be used in orchid culture. This came at a critical juncture in the nursery business. Osmunda, the roots of a fern, which had long been used for growing orchid plants, was becoming increasingly scarce, of decreasing quality, and of rapidly escalating cost. Nor was it the easiest for amateurs to pot with and grow in. Matkin and O. W. Davidson of Rutgers University conducted initial, highly favorable tests that showed the potential of the product. With increased processing and suitable fertilizers, fir bark became the potting medium of choice for the next forty years, with its ease of use enabling the rapid growth of the hobby orchid industry.

This hobby industry was served by an increasingly sophisticated coterie of speciality nurseries, some of them founded on the collections of the wealthy (Fred A. Stewart Inc., Jones & Scully, Kensington Orchids), some morphing from previously successful cut-flower nurseries (Armacost & Royston, Rod McLellan Co., Carter & Holmes), while some were begun simply as a way to support an out-of-control hobby. Many succeeded wildly during the decades of the 1960s through the 1990s. Over the past fifteen years or so, we have, sadly, seen many of these formerly great nurseries go by the wayside as a changing market

The American Orchid Society visitor center features a large display greenhouse and lush tropical gardens landscaped with orchids.

and the associated economic pressures drove them under. Offshore growers, looking to continue their rapid growth based on less expensive land, heat, or labor, are invading the United States with product, first looking to U.S. nurseries to finish (bring into flower) and now establishing facilities here in the United States where practical.

As a result, domestic orchid nurseries are beset on all sides by competition from homegrown garden centers and the ominous Big Boxes (Home Depot, Lowe's, etc.), where good-quality plants are readily available year-round at very reasonable prices. Is there the knowledge base to instruct newbies in successful orchid culture? No, but that is not the intent. The intent is provide a high-value,

relatively low-cost flowering potted plant that can be discarded after flowering, if the consumer desires.

ORCHID CONSERVATION

The conservation of wild orchids is a topic that engenders strong feelings. There can be no doubt that wild-collected orchids are no longer a viable option for most people in the developed world. The areas from which commercially valuable orchids are collected are some of the most endangered, most biologically diverse, most remote, and most easily disturbed habitats in the world. Few remain. In such areas of high biodiversity, the web of life that maintains the fragile balance here on earth is very easily disrupted.

The loss of a single facet of the ecological system can spell the end of a species, never again to be seen. For example, an unintentional pesticide spraying kills the pollinators of a particular orchid, or a rapacious collector takes the last few mature plants of a species from its only habitat, or, perhaps, a section of forest is burned for agriculture. There are those who would argue for "rescue"—salvaging and maintaining populations in captivity—as a viable alternative. Quite simply, this is a naïve notion. First, the only real reason to "salvage" is against a time of possible reintroduction to the wild. This, to date, has never successfully occurred. Also, if the plants are "rescued" from a doomed forest, as in the case of *Epidendrum ilense*, there would be nowhere to reintroduce the plants. No one ever seems to want to rescue the "ugly ducklings," either—only the pretty or commercially important. Real rescue would involve all aspects of a particular ecosystem.

This is not to say that wild-collection of plants is always and necessarily bad. Some new plants have to enter the trade to provide propagation stock. Such plants should only be collected in a limited and sustainable way. The last one should never be taken. There is debate, however, whether the propagation is something that ethically should be done in the range state (i.e., where the species originates) to allow the benefits of the native species to accrue to the land of origin, whether the more sophisticated technology of the developed countries guarantees better, quicker, and more efficient production and distribution. While many are familiar with the effects of CITES (Convention on International Trade

in Endangered Species of Wild Flora and Fauna), far fewer know about CBD (Convention on Biological Diversity, the Rio Convention). CITES is a trade-oriented treaty that seeks to track and manage trade in wild species whose survival may be or is affected by international trade. It is the main boogeyman of orchid hobbyists who believe that unrestricted trade in their beloved plants is the only way to go. CBD, on the other hand, seeks to maintain biodiversity and to ensure that countries are able to profit from the biodiversity originating within their borders. In other words, if a special plant was found in Panama that cured cancer, Panamanians—especially the indigenous people on whose ancestral land the plant was found—should benefit equally with those from the developed world who exploit the resource. How this will affect the orchid trade remains to be seen. However, it is already clear that orchid production from the range states is to be encouraged.

Whatever the source of the propagation, nursery-raised species are the ethical way to go. Do remember, though, that your local orchid nursery charges a higher price for their plants for a reason: they take the losses that can occur from long-distance transport or seasonal change across hemispheres. When you buy from a foreign nursery, be aware that any losses will be yours. However, you will be supporting a business that returns something to the country of origin. This is a very important aspect for some. The species that you do grow should be tended carefully and propagated by division for local distribution. This is one of the most

Above: The striking species, Laelia milleri, *is severely threatened in its Brazilian habitat due to iron ore mining as well as overcollection.*

Right: The 2005 United Nations release of endangered orchid postage stamps created in conjunction with CITES feature twelve endangered orchid species.

effective ways of conservation, simply making rarer plants more available by propagation. There are several very effective means by which the individual orchid grower can promote conservation:

- Grow your plants well. Fewer killed, less trade in potentially endangered plants needed.

- Patronize nurseries that demonstrate good conservation practices, i.e., effective propagation of existing species and procuring new species from ethical sources. Don't patronize businesses you know practice ethically shady methods.

- Don't be greedy. You don't have to have the first of a new species collected from the wild. Nursery-raised plants will be along very soon and will grow much better and will probably have superior flowers.

- Support your local and national orchid societies. They are the main source of knowledge on how to better grow your plants as well as gathering points for advocacy.

Artificially cultured orchid species not only reduce pressure on native populations but offer flowers that are generally of better quality than jungle plants. Additionally, seed-grown seedlings are usually more vigorous than wild plants.

In a time of rapidly diminishing wild areas, of escalating population and pressure on what wild lands remain, it is necessary for thinking people to do all they can to reduce their adverse effect on our world. Above all, be aware of your actions and their potential effects. Who cares? You should.

BRASSAVOLA NODOSA
AND ITS HYBRIDS

It may seem odd to begin a book dedicated to orchid beauty with a species that is perhaps better characterized as charming or graceful, or damned by the faint praise of "interesting."

However, *Brassavola nodosa* has beauty that is more than skin-deep. Not only do charming and graceful serve as very apt descriptors but lovely may also be added when its spicy, clovelike fragrance is included. If parental prowess is considered, few species have such a dependable legacy of truly delightful progeny.

B. nodosa was one of the first New World orchids to appear in European literature, and is also one of the most widespread, occurring from Mexico south through northern South America. As with any widespread species, variations occur, some more horticulturally desirable than others. Today, the most popular form originates from Panama, and is recognizable by its flatter leaves and upright stems of generally larger blooms (and may be known as *B. grandiflora or B. venosa*). A wide geographic range can account for another of *B. nodosa*'s favorable traits, its ease of culture. The species and its hybrids both have a prolific habit that makes large plants relatively easy to attain, though even modestly sized specimens flower freely, often more than once a year. The successful grower is rewarded with fine displays of the pale green,

fragrant blooms. Because of their compact size, *B. nodosa* and its hybrids are outstanding for the windowsill or under grower lights, and the gardener who enjoys frost-free winters can often succeed with these plants on the patio or in the sunroom, where the plants will appreciate very bright light. Often, *B. nodosa*'s primary hybrids with larger species result in modestly sized plants that can be accommodated in limited growing areas. *Brassocattleya* Nodata (*B. nodosa x Cattleya guttata*) is a prime example of a very fine primary (species x species) hybrid utilizing *B. nodosa*, showing the many fine traits of both parents.

Above: Bc. Nodata bears colorful flowers on compact plants.

Right: The graceful flowers of Brassavola nodosa *belie the value of the species for creating extraordinary hybrids. Its ease of growth makes it a perfect "first orchid."*

BRASSOLAELIA RICHARD MUELLER

Bl. *Richard Mueller* may well be the most popular B. nodosa *hybrid. The cross has been remade numerous times and is usually easy to find.*

B. nodosa is not the only member of the genus that hybridizers have utilized. Indeed, many fascinating results have come from the use of *B. cucullata*, *B. perrinii*, and *B. subulifolia* (syn. *cordata*). However, with rare exceptions, these have mainly been of interest (or available) to aficionados and serve primarily to demonstrate why *B. nodosa* is the superior parent for its particular "type." A notable exception is *Brassolaeliocattleya* Everything Nice, a hybrid of *Blc.* Mem. that Helen Brown crossed with *B. perrinii*, which is notable for its upright inflorescences of pippin green blooms offset by a full rose lip and is a highly sought-after novelty.

Of the many hybrids involving *B. nodosa*, some stand out as exceptional, both for their own intrinsic beauty and as significant parents. Few have been as popular as *Brassolaelia* Richard Mueller (*B. nodosa* x *Laelia milleri*). By way of comparison, *Bl.* Martha Miller (*L. angereri* x *B. subulifolia*) is attractive but lacks the panache of *Bl.* Richard Mueller. *Bl.* Martha Miller also lacks the distinguished and growing number of successful progenies that *Bl.* Richard Mueller is currently producing. Like the goose that lays the golden egg, beautiful orchids that consistently produce quality progenies are highly valued and tend to remain in cultivation. *Bl.* Richard Mueller demonstrates both some of *B. nodosa*'s strong and weak points as a parent. Few would argue that *L. milleri* is among the most brilliant reds in the cattleya alliance. It has a history of producing good, red progeny. However, crossed with *B. nodosa*, which tends to lend softer, more pastel colors, yellows and oranges are the result. Happily, the flowers are relatively flat, lending a full star shape. The key is that, while the color does not

B. subulifolia *is closely related to* B. nodosa *and produces many smaller, night-fragrant flowers.*

This attractive hybrid, Bl. *Martha Miller, demonstrates the potential of using* B. subulifolia *to produce more floriferous* Bl. *Richard Mueller-type hybrids.*

manifest itself fully in this generation, it is "available" genetically to its progeny.

BRASSOLAELIOCATTLEYA COPPER QUEEN

A theme that will recur throughout this book in discussions of hybrids is consistency, coupled with the hybridist's knowledge of the "right" combinations to obtain the desired results. Such knowledge comes only as a result of experimentation, observation, and time. The average generational time frame in orchids can range from as little as five or six years (in phalaenopsis) to decades in cattleyas or cymbidiums, the generational time being that span necessary to bloom the original hybrid, select superior cultivars, and begin their testing in further breeding. *Brassolaelia* Richard Mueller, particularly the superior tetraploid form used in Hawaii, is a fairly well known quantity, breeding-wise, having been registered in 1965. It has been remade with better parents since; another mark of the successful hybrid is the popular demand that drives businesses to want more of a given product.

Brassolaeliocattleya Copper Queen (*Bl.* Richard Mueller x Toshi Aoki) demonstrates the great attraction of this sort of breeding. Brilliant color, coupled with the characteristic boldly dotted red lip on large blooms, appears on relatively compact, free-branching plants. The breeding behaviors of both parents are well known, and the combination of the two gave the sort of populations that orchid nurseries love to stock because of the highly satisfactory overall quality of the results. *B. nodosa* and its hybrids are very popular in hot summer areas, especially in South Florida, where 'Crownfox' JC/AOS was awarded, owing to their tolerance of warmer nights and higher humidity. Indeed, such conditions drive *B. nodosa* hybrids to extreme performance, creating large plants that flower freely throughout the year.

Blc. *Copper Queen 'Crownfox' JC/AOS uses Bl. Richard Mueller to take B. nodosa breeding one generation further toward creating attractive, easy-growing orchids.*

BRASSOLAELIOCATTLEYA GOLDEN TANG

Brassolaeliocattleya Waikiki Gold is one of the most popular cattleyas of recent years owing to its ease of care and delightful blooms, which are highly perfumed. While the color is not strong, because of its *C. forbesii* background, the shades of chartreuse and soft yellow have found favor with many growers. Breeders, too, have succumbed to the appeal of *Blc*. Waikiki Gold and have used it in a variety of combinations, some successful, some less so. It is only natural that it is bred to another similarly popular parent whose parental attributes are widely known, *Brassolaelia* Richard Mueller. The resulting *Blc*. Golden Tang has been an instant sensation among orchid hobbyists, as much for its colorful blooms as its heady fragrance and superb ease of growth.

Above: The somewhat variable but always valuable breeder, Blc. *Waikiki Gold.*

Left: Blc. *Golden Tang 'Alberta' AM/AOS combines* Bl. *Richard Mueller with another valuable breeder,* Blc. *Waikiki Gold.*

Today, mass-market-oriented nursery strategies mitigate against many cattleyas as potted plants, as results are often too slow or too variable to give cost-effective product. However, with such parents as *B. nodosa* and *Bl.* Richard Mueller, particularly when the tetraploid versions are used, populations have the uniformity and rapidity of growth to give the amount of uniform flowering results needed. Comparisons with F1 hybrid corn or other highly structured breeding can fairly be drawn. For this reason, and coupled with the quick growth seen in tropical areas such as South Florida, Hawaii, and Thailand, some cattleyas are very appropriate candidates for periodic remaking of known seed for the mass market. Where this is impractical or impossible, often owing to the breeder lacking the precise parents needed to remake the cross—such advantages are closely held by the originators whenever possible—cloning is a viable alternative, as the clones will be as quick to grow and flower as the seed population is. The only danger when cloning is overdone is that when too many are produced from too little initial tissue, it results in unfortunate mutations.

BRASSOLAELIOCATTLEYA
APACHE SUNRISE

The upside of the mass-market-oriented production of orchid seedlings is the rapid dissemination of desirable hybrids. Growers can expect to see a spectrum of results that are widely available in time frames unheard of even a few years ago. Proven breeding lines, as with *Brassolaeliocattleya* Apache Sunrise, which combines *Brassavola nodosa* with the relatively new *Blc*. Apache Gold—itself a result of the proven breeding of *Blc*. Papa Sam and *Blc*. Toshi Aoki—give reliable results at a low price to an exceptionally broad market. Additionally, judging systems will also see an influx of new cultivars exhibited by nurseries and individuals over a short, by orchid standards at least, period, allowing even wider popular knowledge of new products.

In the past, by the time a given hybrid had begun to show up on judging tables, it was far too late to search out seedlings in the hope of getting your own award, or, indeed, even a "good one." This is largely because any seedlings that might remain on suppliers' shelves would be the runts, or the slower or poorer growers, which are always tickets to disappointment. Traditional wisdom for the informed orchid purchaser dictates that the best method for good seedling selection is to go on the word of a trusted orchid purveyor and/or based on a knowledge of the parents involved in a hybrid. In many cases, this has not changed. But with faster-growing lines of breeding, as with *B. nodosa* and its secondary hybrids, it is increasingly common to be able to purchase good, unbloomed seedlings based on a flowering sample or picture of a first bloom. Better meristemming technology is also allowing more rapid distribution of highly select new clones into the market. Formerly, it was not uncommon for a period of nearly ten years to go by before something "new" might be available as a clone. This interval has been substantially reduced in many cases to a more acceptable span of only a few years.

Above right: Blc. Apache Sunrise, created by hobbyist Marianne Matthews, is evidence that many fine hybrids originate in the hobby sector of the orchid world.

Right: Blc. Apache Sunrise 'Redland Surprise' HCC/AOS.

Far right: Beautiful lip details are one of the attractions of B. nodosa breeding, as shown by Blc. Apache Sunrise 'Carola' AM/AOS.

BRASSOLAELIOCATTLEYA
MORNING SONG

Brassavola nodosa types are not confined to bright yellow and orange shades. A Hawaiian remake of the unlikely hybrid of *Brassolaelia* Morning Glory (*B. nodosa* x *L. purpurata*), using tetraploid forms of the species, gave a very fine and uniform population that has been widely distributed. The vigorous plants produce strong nflorescences of well-spaced blooms in shades of white, offset by a good-sized, boldly veined lip. In many cases, such hybrids can seem to be dead ends, that is, so beautiful and distinct that it would be difficult to imagine a mate that would give an improvement. Thankfully, a gifted hybridizer's insight, coupled with knowledge of proven breeding lines, can result in unexpected advancements in the type. In *Brassolaeliocattleya* Morning Song knowledge and insight are happily married.

Cattleya Horace is arguably the most important hybrid parent today, thanks to its proven ability in multiple breeding lines, ranging from lavenders through to the most brilliant and fiery shades. A fortunate surprise of recent years was the semi-alba (white with colored lip) *Laeliocattleya* Melody Fair that resulted from the Japanese hybrid of *C.* Horace crossed with *Lc.* Stephen Oliver Fouraker. The expectation would be shapely soft lavenders with darker lips. But in this case, and thanks to the unique capabilities of *C.* Horace, a percentage of true semi-albas clones resulted. When one of these was crossed with *Bl.* Morning Glory, *Blc.* Morning Song resulted, giving the many good traits of traditional semi-albas without huge plants and poor uniformity of flower quality. What growers obtained were charming white flowers with large solid magenta lips on relatively compact and easy-to-grow plants.

Opposite: The large flowers of Bl. *Morning Song 'Rosita' HCC/AOS present a striking contrast.*

Left: Beautiful veining in the lip of Bl. *Morning Glory comes from the* Laelia purpurata *parent.*

BRASSOCATTLEYA MAIACA

While breeders need their share of insight and courage, they also need a proportion of good sense and a willingness to use proven lines in the production of uniform, and hence marketable, seedlings. *B. nodosa* and its hybrids are a time-tested method to this end. One of the most widely distributed of all *B. nodosa* hybrids is *Brassocattleya* Maikai, bred from the floriferous multiflora lavender species, *Cattleya bowringiana*. Its many good qualities of highly prolific growth (producing multiple leads, resulting in multiple flower heads), perky lavender blooms, and favorable Christmas blooming season give it a wide-ranging appeal that growers have been quick to capitalize on by continuous propagation by division and cloning.

Bc. Maikai, for a variety of reasons, has not been an especially good parent. Its few registered offspring have not appreciably affected the market, nor are they well known. However, when *Bc*. Maikai was mated to the prolific and proven species, *C. aurantiaca*, the resulting *Bc*. Maiaca gives proof that there may yet be worth in its future utilization. *C. aurantiaca* is well known to produce colorful and floriferous hybrids, and with *Bc*. Maikai, its promise has once again been fulfilled. The added feature of a main blooming season of winter into spring, when consumer demand is at its highest, coupled with a propensity to truly bloom multiple times a year, makes this a sought-after hybrid. Again, the Gulf State region of the United States is prime territory for this type, as the warmer climate enables growers to devote more space to their plants, which translates into specimens literally covered in colorful blooms. Light, warmth, and humidity are the keys to top productivity with hybrids such as *Bc*. Maiaca and *Bc*. Maikai, though their background also enables them to be successful cymbidium companions in frost-free climates as on the west coast of the United States.

Right: Bc. Maiaca combines the orange tones of C. aurantiaca *with* Bc. Maikai *to produce a fall-blooming multiflora.*

Below: Bc. *Maikai has long been a popular, easy-to-grow* B. nodosa *hybrid.*

CATTLEYA AURANTIACA
AND ITS HYBRIDS

There is something cheery, something charming, about *Cattleya aurantiaca* that attracts the eye of the experienced orchid grower as well as the novice.

Perhaps it is the striking color, or perhaps it is the clusters of blooms so freely borne on the upright pseudobulbs. The mid-winter season is another draw, seemingly giving a bit of sunshine during otherwise gray months. Widespread from Mexico into Guatemala, El Salvador, and Honduras, *C. aurantiaca* shares the characteristic of other widespread species in having a variety of color forms and floral sizes. While this is the smallest flowered of the genus, it more than makes up for this lack in its number of blooms and production of multiple new leads. Additionally, it is one of the easiest cattleyas for new growers to master, tolerant of a wide array of conditions from greenhouse to sunroom to patio and garden where frost does not threaten.

In the early days of taxonomy, *Cattleya* was separated from *Epidendrum*—the catchall generic name given to "air plants," i.e., epiphytes—by their "large" flower size. Because of the smallish size of *C. aurantiaca* flowers, the species has occasionally been reclassified as an *Encyclia*. This is not entirely satisfactory, and, for the time being, *Cattleya* is the preferred genus, though modern systematic methods may change this situation any day now. As with other well-known species in generic flux, though, growers will probably always know this as *C. aurantiaca*.

Above: The color of C. aurantiaca varies from orange to yellow, but flowers bear the typical starry, cupped shape and open lip.

Left: C. aurantiaca bears heads of waxy flowers in the late winter, early spring.

Right: A selection of multiflora hybrids made using C. aurantiaca. From left to right: Lc. Red Gold, C. Roman Rainbow, and Blc. Laurie Tsuda.

CATTLEYA GUATEMALENSIS

Speciation, the natural process by which new species separate one from another, can take several forms. Two distinct forms of an existing species can be geographically separated and, over time, evolve into separate populations with distinct pollinators. With *Cattleya* Guatemalensis (*skinneri* x *aurantiaca*), we may be witness to another speciation event, one the result of a naturally occurring primary hybrid stabilizing into a specieslike form. Both *C. auran-tiaca* and *C. skinneri* can occur in the same area, *C. skinneri* occurring from Guatemala to Panama. Indeed, *C. skinneri* is the national flower of Costa Rica. Where the ranges of these two species meet, hybrid swarms are often seen. Of course, man-made *C.* Guatemalensis is also in cultivation.

C. Guatemalensis is a variable hybrid that comes in a range of colors from white to sunset pink.

Another aspect of the hybrid nature of this very beautiful, naturally occurring hybrid is introgression, where the hybrids themselves freely breed among themselves and with either species parent. This results in a continuum of flower types ranging from one parent to the other. For example, a slightly small, more brightly colored *C. skinneri* would almost certainly have *C. aurantiaca* genes in its background. This process also results in many of the more unusually colored *C. aurantiaca* that find their way into the trade, particularly the white clones, which must be part of the hybrid continuum. Breeders in the range states have proven this by the reproduction of this type of hybrid, as well as by the selfing of unusually colored *C. aurantiaca*, which, rather than breeding true as would be expected, give a range of color types as would be expected from the selfing of a hybrid.

None of this diminishes the appeal of *C.* Guatemalensis. Indeed, the availability of a range of floral sizes, shapes, and colors adds to the appeal of this floriferous plant. Entire collections may be devoted to *C.* Guatemalensis in Central America, based on just this diversity. Colors from red, through salmon and orange, to pink and white, with flower shapes from starry to full, assure this plant a continuing place in orchid lovers' hearts.

Cattleya skinneri, *the national flower of Costa Rica, is a wonderful species in its own right.*

LAELIOCATTLEYA RED GOLD

Orange is one of the most highly sought-after colors in cattleyas. This, coupled with the species' highly tolerant nature and range of bright colors, has led to *C. aurantiaca* being a popular and widely used parent. *C. aurantiaca* figures not only as a direct parent in an entire range of fine hybrids, but its progenies have gone on to sire other valuable horticultural types. The early breeders were, by necessity, constrained to the use of species and primary (species x species) hybrids in their hybridizing programs. Today, some breeders are revisiting older hybrids and species with the thought of re-creating lines of breeding using superior species clones in primary and near-primary crosses. However, the argument can be made that the early breeders, given essentially first choice from the wild-collected clones, had better material with which to work. Where genetic manipulation in the creation of artificial tetraploids is not a factor, this may well be true. Thus, it is easy to see the attraction in the utilization of older clones, as in the production of *Laeliocattleya* Red Gold, a cross registered in 1964 by Alberts & Merkel, made with *C. aurantiaca* and the very old *Lc. charlesworthii* (*C. dowiana* x *L. cinnabarina*)—registered in 1900!

The mark of a truly successful cross is both in its longetivity and its usefulness for further breeding. Both of these characteristics are present in *Lc.* Red Gold, a truly beautiful and worthwhile "heritage" orchid as well as a parent that has made a lasting impression on cattleya breeding. This is the more remarkable as the *C. dowiana* grandparent is known to cause crippling in progeny for several generations if great care is not used in their use in breeding.

Lc. *Red Gold* blooms reliably for Christmas and brightens the season with its cheery colors.

LAELIOCATTLEYA GOLD DIGGER

Crippling (a curling and deformation of the petal edges) has not proven to be present in the widely known and popularly grown *Laeliocattleya* Gold Digger, a cross of *Lc.* Red Gold and *Cattleya* Warpaint, itself a hybrid of *C. aurantiaca* crossed with *C.* Tango. The two doses of *C. aurantiaca*, combined with other brilliant species, influence led to one of the most floriferous of all cattleya hybrids. Prior to Hurricane Andrew's devastation in concert with the Benlate disaster, which led to the loss of many of Florida's oldest and best cattleya specimens, it was not a question of what was going to win the "Best Specimen of Show," at the prestigious Miami Show, but rather which *Lc.* Gold Digger, grown by whom. Florida's favorable climate allows growers the space to produce enormous plants, often exceeding three feet across, of the widely distributed cultivars 'Orchidglade's Mandarin' and 'Orchid Jungle' HCC/AOS.

Lc. Trick or Treat (*L.* Icarus x Chit Chat) is another, very similar, *C. aurantiaca*–based hybrid that has not only enjoyed wide acclaim and cultivation but has also gone on to sire further hybrids as a parent (unlike *Lc.* Gold Digger). In some cases, it takes a breeder

A sign of any good orchid hybrid is how long its popularity lasts. The pictured hybrid, Lc. Gold Digger 'Orchidglade's Mandarin', is still a popular hybrid and valuable display plant at early spring shows.

to "champion" the use of a particular parent as much as it does a willing marketplace. Such is the case with *Lc*. Trick or Treat. The Hawaiians, in particular, have been very active with this grex (group of progeny from a specific cross), not only as a parent to impart rapid growth and early flowering, but also in sibling and selfing crosses, to produce more *Lc*. Trick or Treats. These crosses have generally used a chance tetraploid plant of *Lc*. Trick or Treat 'Orange Princess' HCC/AOS and have been uniformly good.

Right: Lc. Gold Digger 'Orchid Jungle' HCC/AOS is a good display plant because of the many brightly colored flowers it produces.

Below: Lc. Trick or Treat has created a whole family of orange hybrids.

SOPHROLAELIOCATTLEYA BRASS TOWN

Another avenue of *Cattleya aurantiaca* breeding shown productive over the years is its use with larger-flowered parents in hopes of imparting not only its brilliance of color, but also its floriferous and easy nature. Perhaps the best-known, archetypal, hybrid of this type is *Sophrolaeliocattleya* Jewel Box (Anzac x *C. aurantiaca*). *Slc.* Anzac was one of the early, and very famous, parents to use for "red" cattleyas, although its color was arguably more lavender than "red" and was profoundly affected by both climatic and light factors. For many years, different clones of *Slc.* Jewel Box, notably 'Scherezade' AM/AOS and 'Dark Waters' HCC/AOS, have remained on the market and are especially popular on Valentine's Day, where their bright reddish-orange color is quite appropriate. *Slc.* Jewel Box also exemplifies the compact stature of many *C. aurantiaca* hybrids and can give quite a stunning display of multiple flower heads even in a six-inch pot.

If *Slc.* Jewel Box had a drawback as a cross, it came from the lavender tones imparted by the *Slc.* Anzac parent giving a slightly "muddy" or less-than-brilliant appearance. In the years since the production of *Slc.* Jewel Box, breeders have used similar, but improved, parents to produce flowers with greater brilliance and depth of color. *Slc.* Brass Town 'Lipstick' HCC/AOS is an example

of the depth of color that can be achieved by using a parent only one generation further along than *Slc.* Anzac, its progeny *Slc.* Mae Hawkins resulting from a cross with the well-known Hawaiian breeder, *Slc.* Naomi Kerns. *Slc.* Brass Town exhibits a clarity and depth of color, which, coupled with extraordinary sheen and texture, makes a flower that simply shines. A search for similar hybrids will yield success when it is remembered to look for · parents whose depth and saturation of color matches that of *C. aurantiaca*.

Above: Slc. *Jewel Box 'Scherezade' AM/AOS is a longtime, compact-growing hybrid that offers its red flowers right around Valentine's Day.*

Opposite: Satiny red flowers are the hallmark of Slc. *Brass Town 'Lipstick' HCC/AOS.*

EPICATTLEYA EPIORANGE

As breeding trends have come and gone, *Cattleya aurantiaca* is again strictly being used in novelty-type hybrids, where its many desirable characters can be best appreciated. No one could argue about the value of *C. aurantiaca* in the production of exhibition-type, high-color cattleyas. Nor could its contribution to highly satisfactory specimen plant hybrids be debated. But it is as a parent in plants intended solely as decorative that this species really shines. In frost-free garden settings, or in cool sunrooms, anywhere the space can be devoted to larger orchid plants, one cannot go very wrong with these decorative plants. Certainly one of the most enjoyable and showy of this type is *Epicattleya* Epiorange (*Encyclia alata* x *C. aurantiaca*) first produced nearly forty years ago and since remade for wider distribution. Showy, slightly starry burnt orange blooms are offset by a boldly veined lip and are proudly held on a tall stem with good spacing for maximum display.

Nor can we ignore such off-the-wall hybrids as *Vaughnara* Fairy Tales (*Brassoepidendrum* Phoenix x *C. aurantiaca*). *Bepi.* Phoenix is the result of the colorful *Encyclia phoenecia* crossed with our old friend, *B. nodosa*. The resulting cultivar 'Great Balls Afire' AM/AOS is remarkable for its tall inflorescences of starry blooms that change color as they age, from the newly opened blooms' lemon yellow to a more pronounced orange. The imagination of breeders truly knows no bounds. With useful parents such as *C. aurantiaca* freely available and constantly improving, we can look forward to a continuing heritage of brightly colored potted plant cattleyas. Growers everywhere can count on reliable and exotic displays from the species and its hybrids.

Above: C. aurantiaca *can also be used to make whimsical novelty hybrids such as* Vgnra. *Fairy Tales 'Great Balls Afire' AM/AOS.*

Right: Epc. *Epiorange holds heads of colorful flowers on strong inflorescences.*

LABIATE CATTLEYAS

What can be said about the quintessential "orchid," *Cattleya labiata*, that has not already been said?

If there is a species that most conveys the word "orchid" to the most people, that exists as the "mind's eye" image of what an

orchid actually is, it must be *Cattleya labiata*. Indeed, the color "orchid" comes from the lavender tones of this plant. It was first flowered by Cattley and was subsequently named by Lindley in 1821, *C. labiata vera*, the true "labiate cattleya." The sensation that *C. labiata* created in nineteenth-century England was heightened when its area of collection was lost for nearly twenty years, and the

species became a rare and sought-after novelty. Once the habitat—the Organ Mountains north of Rio de Janeiro—was relocated in 1836, collectors quickly and thoroughly removed all the plants they could find, making the wild plant rare in nature.

C. labiata is the basis for the group of similar cattleyas, the labiate cattleyas, many of which are not distinguishable by amateurs except by the season in which they bloom. This led to *C. labiata* also having the specific epithet, autumnalis, or autumn flowering, to distinguish it from its cousins flowering at different seasons.

In the early days of orchid growing, orchid fanciers had to rely on the importation of wild-collected plants to satisfy their urges.

Above: Alba forms of the labiate Cattleya *species can be difficult to tell apart. One of the useful indicators is blooming season.*

Right: The floriferousness and fragrance of C. labiata *make it a worthwhile species to grow.*

And in these collections were found an astonishing array of differing flower colors. These included light to intense lavender, white, white with a colored lip, and even what is known as "blue" in orchid circles, which is closer to what most people would call lavender. These color variants were highly valued and propagated.

Even today, in its native Brazil, the best and most varied color forms are eagerly sought and line-bred using selected cultivars for a waiting world market. Interestingly, *C. labiata* was among the first orchids to be line-bred to improve the quality of its flowers and its productivity for cut-flower uses. Even given its initial popularity based on its vigor and ease of growth, demand was such that newer and better cultivars were much sought-after and enthusiastically obtained.

In the past, Brazilian hobbyists tended to keep the best varieties to themselves and to guard them carefully, lest they slip out into general cultivation, especially in foreign markets. This helped to retain the value of the highly select cultivars they held so closely. In recent years, the market has opened up considerably, and Brazilian nurseries are in the forefront of the distribution of line-bred populations of the very best and most unusual *C. labiata* forms, such as the semi-alba Cooksoniae, the fine albas, the dark rubras, the "blue" coeruleas, and others.

It was inevitable that a showy and desirable species like *C. labiata* would be an essential ingredient in the production of improved hybrid types of cattleyas. Of course, modern lavender cattleyas are heavily influenced by *C. labiata*, especially the fall flowering types. Our modern yellows, in many cases, trace their origins, at least partially, to *C.* Fabia (*dowiana* x *labiata*), which in its line-bred forms also contributed to modern semi-alba breeding. Today, we are seeing a resurgence of interest in *C. labiata* both as a parent and for its intrinsic value as a species. A strong and vigorous grower, it is without parallel as a display plant in its September season, especially when its heady fragrance is mixed in. When bred with selected forms of other labiate species, new versions of antique primary hybrids result, with improved vigor.

Top: A sampling of a few of the color forms of C. labiata.

Above: This semi-alba form of C. labiata *shows color flares on the petals and sepals. Breeders look for plants with unique qualities such as this.*

CATTLEYA JENMANII

Cattleya jenmanii is a prime example of how a species can be "lost" to cultivation, misidentified in collections, and finally, when refound in nature, become a valuable addition to our arsenal of unifoliate/labiate cattleya species. Noted by Withner as "not particularly distinctive" and easily mistaken for an older hybrid, more select varieties have trickled into cultivation from Venezuelan growers as they propagate their best. *C. jenmanii* is a worthy addition to any collection, as its Christmas blooming season and small stature combine with good flower production to make a really showy plant. Additionally, *C. jenmanii* is known for its lovely, sweet perfume.

As with most, if not all, of its unifoliate cousins, *C. jenmanii* has a host of color varieties, including the rare "blue" coerulea type. *C. jenmanii* Alba 'Fuchs Snow' FCC/AOS created a sensation when first shown and has gone on to set the standard for this extremely rare color form. Being a winter-flowering species, the pseudobulbs will mature during the warmer summer and fall months, seeming then to rest until lengthening nights trigger the flowering response and buds begin to grow into the sheath.

Occasionally, particularly under less-than-favorable growing conditions, the sheath may begin to yellow and senesce before the buds have grown through it. In cases such as these, the grower should carefully peel the decaying sheath away from the buds and be prepared to stake the unsupported stem as it matures for the best results.

Above: The blue or "Coerulea" form of C. jenmanii *is very desirable.*

Right: Like the closely related C. labiata, *the floriferousness of* C. jenmanii *makes up for any deficiencies in the individual flowers.*

CATTLEYA LUEDDEMANNIANA

The darker colored forms of C. lueddemanniana *come from the state of Lara in Venezuela. Generally they produce fewer flowers than the coastal race.*

Of all the many recent "reintroductions" of cattleya species from Latin America, none is more exciting than *Cattleya lueddemanniana*. Closely related to *C. mossiae*, and also originating in Venezuela, it blooms slightly earlier than *C. mossiae*, generally beginning as early as January, extending into late February and early March. There are two types of *C. lueddemanniana*: a larger growing form that has larger, paler rose blooms and a somewhat smaller variety with intense, sparkling rose flowers. Both have *mossiae*-like veining in the throat of the

shapely, trumpet-shaped lips, highlighted by yellow eyes. *C. lueddemanniana* is simply one of the most beautiful and eye-catching of the labiate cattleyas. Even in the paler forms, which often tend to have the largest flowers, the texture is diamond-dust, sparkling, and catching the light in a way that is unique in the large-flowered cattleya species. Like most cattleya species, *C. lueddemanniana* has a variety of color forms, including the famous *C. lueddemanniana* 'Stanley's', an extraordinary semi-alba.

Until the 1990s, most of the clones of this species seen in cultivation were the result of inbreeding older, often less vigorous varieties, with the result that, while the flowers were often quite nice, the plants were difficult to grow well. Since that time, we have seen many new and vigorous populations enter the United States, with the result that given proper care, *C. lueddemanniana* is no more difficult to grow than any other of its close relatives.

C. lueddemanniana's growth habit is distinctive, with pseudobulbs that are more cylindrical and spreading than others. Some forms have the disadvantage of being slightly sprawling in their growth, with a relatively long interval between bulbs on the rhizome, making them more difficult to contain in an appropriately sized pot. As with most cattleya species, they are seasonal in their

rooting and growth, necessitating a watchful grower, lest he or she repot at an unfavorable time. If this happens, the plant will sulk, rootless and dehydrating, until the season is proper, when it will begin to grow roots and plump up. Unfortunately, this does not always happen in time to save the plant. However, if the grower pots as roots begin to show at the base of the most recent growth, the plants are very easy and vigorous. When selecting plants, a wise grower also looks for a cultivar that has shorter internodes and an upright growth habit, hopefully one that demonstrates a good flowering habit by having old flower stems on every bulb.

Whatever extra effort may be necessary—in the growing or in the initial acquisition—becomes academic when the plant flowers. There is no way to adequately describe the beautiful aspect of these very large—occasionally over eight-inch—blooms, sparkling in the sunlight, glittering in shades of brilliant rose and magenta. Happily, breeders are beginning to use *C. lueddemanniana* again in breeding, both with other species and with more complex hybrids, so we will soon be thrilled to the sight of new populations of late winter cattleyas with all the charm of *C. lueddemanniana* and the increased vigor that hybrids often impart.

C. ueddemanniana *'Blue Drago' HCC/AOS is a fine example of the* Coerulea *or "blue" color form of the species.*

CATTLEYA PERCIVALIANA

Another of the Venezuelan labiate cattleyas that has enjoyed a recent upswing in popularity is the compact-growing *Cattleya percivaliana*. Plants have somewhat rounded, squat pseudobulbs that give a cluster of three to five flowers right around Christmas, hence the popular name of Christmas Cattleya. The only drawback to *C. percivaliana* is its slightly musky scent. Nevertheless, the

The most sought after grexes of C. percivaliana, *such as* C. percivaliana *'Nitsuga's Luis Francisco' AM/AOS, feature flat petals and a full, round form.*

sparkling "champagne" lavender color is striking, especially so when offset by the darker lip, which is often outlined in the same lavender seen in the petals and sepals. Darker forms played an important role in our modern purple cattleya hybrids.

Since the early part of the twentieth century, the standard of excellence for this species was the very fine variety, 'Summit' FCC/AOS, introduced as Summitensis by the famous firm of Lager & Hurrell. A mark of its continuing popularity and quality is the fact that, though in cultivation for decades, it gained its coveted FCC/AOS only in the latter part of the century. In recent years, breeding on with 'Summit' as well as new introductions from Venezuela has raised the average considerably, though rarely to the extent of superceding the quality of 'Summit'. Even though slightly less popular than some of its close relatives, C. percivaliana is known for the same variety of color variations, including a very striking white with colored lip type as well as unusual coerulea ("blue") types exemplified by 'Undine'. Some breeding has incorporated C. percivaliana for its small stature and free-branching habit. Perhaps the most interesting of these is C. Cat Canyon.

Top: C. percivaliana *is a small-growing plant that produces three to five flowers around Christmas. Flowers have a distinctive smell that is offensive to some.*

Above: Semi-alba forms such as C. percivaliana *'Carache' are always in demand.*

CATTLEYA SCHRODERAE

The Colombian labiate cattleyas, the best-known of which is *Cattleya trianaei*, are somewhat underrepresented in modern collections, even though they are among the loveliest of all. *Cattleya schroderae* is characterized by trianaei-like shape and similar, though later, winter season, which led to its being considered first a variety of *C. trianaei* and later a natural hybrid. Like *C. trianaei*, *C. schroderae* is dominant for its good, round shape, characterized by petals that are proportionately broad, forming an equilateral triangle with the lip, with the sepals forming an opposing triangle backing the petal-lip combination. Also like *C. trianaei*, *C. schroderae* is recessive for color, allowing stronger yellow pigments to be expressed when used with yellow-based parents. This ability led to *C. schroderae* being an important parent for our modern yellow cattleyas.

Unfortunately, *C. schroderae* is not easy to grow. Until plants began to come out of Colombia recently—where it is also difficult to obtain, originating far from civilization in almost inaccessible areas—*C. schroderae* was an almost mythical plant. Those who had it treasured it were few and far between, because even having the plant was only part of the battle.

I well remember a very small, struggling division at a nursery with which I was formerly associated. We did all we could to get that plant to grow, but it would not. Some years later, a plant entered cultivation and began to be used for breeding, to remake some of the seminal early hybrids, in the hope of re-creating superior races for further breeding. It caused quite a stir, and the owner was beset by those begging him to part with a division. Perhaps his unwillingness to do so was the reason behind the plant's success in his hands, for he rarely, if ever, divided it. Too many rare and sought-after orchids meet their maker as a result of being divided too small, too often, resulting in a lack of vigor and, eventually, death. Happily, there seem to be a few plants being propagated today, so we can be assured of the ultimate survival of this beautiful and important species.

The soft pink flowers of C. schroderae *are contrasted by an "old gold" lip. Closely related to* C. trianaei.

CATTLEYA WARSCEWICZII

Cattleya warscewiczii, another Colombian native, and often known as *C. gigas*, is the "king" of labiate cattleyas, with flowers often in excess of nine inches. The plants, too, are imposing when mature and can reach in excess of thirty inches in height. Because *C. warscewiczii* blooms in the summer when others of its type are rare, it has long been treasured by both cut-flower growers and breeders. That we have a good selection of this species to enjoy in cultivation again after a long hiatus is due to the increased participation of Latin Americans in the U.S. market. For obscure reasons, *C. warscewiczii* was rarely seen for many years, until seed-raised populations began to be offered in the mid-1990s. Some of these utilized older clones, long in cultivation but unfortunately suspect with virus. An important reintroduction of this time was the alba type, bred from the famous *C. warscewiczii* (*gigas*) Alba 'Firmin Lambeau' FCC/AOS. Introduced by Lager & Hurrell in the early twentieth century, this plant commanded astounding prices, even for today. A propagation sold into Europe at that time garnered such a high price that it was hand delivered via a transatlantic crossing by John Lager himself. Very few seedlings from a selfing of a badly virused mother plant were raised to flowering, two of which subsequently gained a FCC/AOS and an AM/AOS when shown in Southern California. Sadly, neither sibling or selfing crosses of these irreplaceable plants have been successful to date, so they remain rare and highly prized.

As with so many of the labiate cattleyas gaining newfound popularity, *C. warscewiczii* is again being used to remake classic primary crosses, as well as those with modern hybrids, to lock in the desirable summer season. Two hybrids of note are the alba remake of *Laeliocattleya* Callistoglossa, a rare white result from *Laelia purpurata* Alba crossed with the closely held *C. warscewiczii* Alba 'Leo Holguin' FCC/AOS, and *Lc.* Summer Belle, resulting from the cross of the semi-alba *C. warscewiczii* with *Lc.* Princess Margaret, which produced vigorous, "classic" semi-albas for midsummer.

Cattleya warscewiczii may well be the king of labiate cattleyas, featuring heads of large flowers held well on strong inflorescences.

BIFOLIATE CATTLEYAS

Cattleya granulosa: lords of their realm, masters of all they survey, imposing, impressive, and the largest members of the bifoliate cattleyas.

Unlike the labiate, or unifoliate types, two or three leaves top their canelike pseudobulbs, and they can easily exceed six feet when well grown. *Cattleya amethystoglossa*, *C. bicolor*, *C. granulosa*, *C. guttata*, and *C. leopoldii* all originate from Brazil and share the features of heavy-substanced flowers borne in heads of three to thirty or more, their distinctive lips cut by a pronounced isthmus or narrowing. *C. granulosa* has slender pseudobulbs that reach a maximum of twenty-four inches, rendering it the smallest growing of the above-mentioned group. Five to eight medium-sized green blooms whose white lips are marked with lines of rose-red dotting are borne in summer from a green sheath.

As with the similarly colored *C. bicolor*, *C. guttata*, and *C. leopoldii*, the base green coloration can vary from quite light in color to a strong pippin green with various degrees of brown overlay or spotting. Breeders have generally sought out the clearest green examples to use in their hybrids in the search for green flowers. *C. granulosa*, when crossed with the semi-alba *Laeliocattleya* Ethel Merman, produced the seminal green hybrid *Lc.* Ann Follis, progenitor of some of today's best green hybrids.

C. granulosa shares with its other seasonally active relatives a profound dislike of potting at the wrong season. High humidity and warm temperatures will best suit this low-elevation species, making it an outstanding choice for Florida and the Gulf states.

Right: C. granulosa *is named for the grainy or "granulose" appearance of the lip.*

Opposite: Good examples of C. granulosa *have flowers of a clear apple-green color with a contrasting bright magenta lip.*

CATTLEYA LEOPOLDII

At one time considered a variety of *Cattleya guttata*, *C. leopoldii* is now generally recognized to be a good species in its own right. One of the easiest methods of discernment between the two species is their flowering season, *C. leopoldii* flowering earlier in the summer from a green sheath, while *C. guttata* flowers from a dried sheath on fully mature pseudobulbs. *C. leopoldii* is certainly one of the most imposing of all cattleya species, plants reaching a maximum height of more than four feet with flowering heads of twenty to thirty blooms. The tall, cylindrical pseudobulbs are crowned with two, or on the largest and best-grown plants, three leaves. In cultivation, as with others of this type, potting must be done when roots are emerging from the newest lead growth. The best plants I have seen have been grown in shallow clay pans with ample drainage, using one of the heavier rocklike media to help keep the plant upright, as they are very top-heavy, especially in bloom. An advantage to the rock medium is the additional time the plant may remain undisturbed, unlike bark-based media that can break down and necessitate more frequent potting to forestall root loss.

Most commonly seen cultivars of *C. leopoldii* are in varying shades of mahogany with an amethyst veined white lip. The most famous, though still rare, variety resulted from a selfing of *C. leopoldii* (then known as *C. guttata*) Alba 'Bracey's', which gave rise to *C. leopoldii* Alba 'Field's' HCC/AOS, an extraordinary clear

green with a stunning white lip. Further selfing and sibling crosses, at least when 'Field's' was healthy enough to bear flowers or a seedpod, led to later populations, but they remained rather difficult to keep in cultivation, resulting in scarcity to this day. Indeed, rarely available divisions of 'Field's' were offered at several thousand dollars back in the 1970s.

Above: The tall inflorescence of C. leopoldii *can carry more than twenty bubblegum-scented flowers.*

Opposite: The tall heads of jungle-spotted flowers of C. leopoldii *definitely command attention.*

Right: Plants seen labeled as C. guttata *Alba are actually the species pictured here,* C. leopoldii *Alba. Another way to distinguish between these two species is the cut-back side lobes of the* C. leopoldii *lip, which, unlike* C. gutatta, *reveal the column when viewed in profile.*

CATTLEYA ACLANDIAE

Cattleya aclandiae represents, along with the equally diminutive *C. walkeriana*, the other end of the bifoliate spectrum, generally growing to less than eight inches. The rose lip veined with darker rose delightfully offsets the leopard-spotted olive green blooms. This species is one of the most popular among lovers of miniature orchids and has contributed to some of the most famous miniature hybrid cattleyas of all time. Unfortunately, the plants of *C. aclandiae* are not among the easiest to grow, unless certain precautions are taken. The roots are relatively large and thick for the size of the plant and can seem to exceed even those on proportionately larger species. These large roots are adapted to very open and airy conditions, quickly expiring if confined to a soggy medium or damaged by careless potting. The best solution for this species is to grow on a bark raft or mount, or to use a slotted teak basket, either of which solutions will allow the plant to grow uninterrupted for the longest possible duration. A dry rest during the winter months, together with ample humidity, watering, and warmth during growth, will reward the attentive grower with some of the most admired blooms in the genus. While unusual color forms do exist, they are not as common as in other species of this

Opposite: Best grown mounted instead of potted, C. aclandiae 'KG's Pink Tiger' HCC/AOS shows the prolific and rambling roots typical of the species.

Right: The spotting on C. aclandiae *flowers can be open as in this example, cr coalesce to produce nearly solid dark flowers. The latter are the most desirable among collectors.*

Below: The charming flowers of the miniature hybrid, Lc. Jungle Elf, *resulted from the cross of* C. aclandiae *with the rarely used* L. esalqueana.

genus, and the more boldly colored "typical" forms are desirable to most.

C. aclandiae's main contribution is to miniature cattleya breeding. Primary hybrids involving C. aclandiae include C. Quinquecolor (x C. forbesii, another small growing bifoliate species), C. Landate (x C. guttata), C. Small World (x C. luteola), and Laeliocattleya Jungle Elf (x Laelia esalqueana). However, it is Sophrolaeliocattleya Precious Stones, a cross of C. aclandiae with Sl. Psyche (Laelia cinnabarina x Sophronitis coccinea), which has given C. aclandiae the most fame. Besides being one of the finest red miniature cattleyas ever produced, the tetraploid form of Slc. Precious Stones 'True Beauty' AM/AOS is proving to be a red parent beyond compare.

CATTLEYA INTERMEDIA

Cattleya intermedia was one of the earliest cattleyas introduced into England, around 1824, from Brazil. The species favors coastal habitats and is found from Rio de Janiero south to Rio Grande do Sul. The result of this broad distribution is a range of colors, shapes, and sizes typical of such widespread species. The species name *intermedia* was given in reference to their size. They were seen to be intermediate in size between the species already known in the genus, the smaller *C. forbesii* and the larger *C. labiata*. Unlike so many early specific names based on first impressions, *C. intermedia* has proven to be apt. It is a species that is truly intermediate not just in the entire genus but in the bifoliate group, where its twenty-inch pseudobulbs nicely bridge the gap between the smaller and larger bifoliates.

Brazilian nurseries and hobbyists have taken this relatively common member of their country's flora to heart, using the range of colors and types available to not only improve on the type species but also to create new and different forms.

From improved forms of 'Tipo' ("type") to the "blue" coeruleas to the unusually colored 'Aranbeem' AM/AOS, one new type has surpassed them all. This has been named the Orlata type. Significantly larger in flower size and fuller in shape, with an inordinately rounded lip highlighted by a broad dark edge, the Orlata type has taken U.S. growers by storm. This has culminated

A sampling of a few of the color forms of C *intermedia, from left to right; Orlata, Flammea, Tipo, and Amethystina.*

in the highest accolade that can be given to an orchid, the

FCC/AOS, going to *C. intermedia* Orlata 'Crownfox'.

One of the chief diagnostic features that sets *C. intermedia*

plants apart from the closely related *C. harrisoniana* and

C. loddigesii is the habit of blooming from green sheaths in early

summer. Thus, while not as finicky as *C. guttata*, it will appreciate

potting at about the same time.

C. intermedia has been used sparingly, in general, in

hybridizing. Perhaps the most widely grown for many years was

C. Claesiana (*intermedia* x *loddigesii*). This primary hybrid, made

with the alba (white) forms of both species, was a mainstay of

cattleya cut-flowers for quite some time, owing to the waxy pure

white blooms borne in profusion, chiefly in the summer months

but often again throughout the year.

However, it was not the more typical forms of *C. intermedia*

that were to have the greatest impact on cattleya hybridizing. In the

latter years of the nineteenth century, several plants of a new type

of cattleya were found in nature. The petals resembled the lip,

resulting in a very distinctive color combination. Though first

described as *C. aquinii*, these plants were later placed in the

species *C. intermedia*, where they remain today. The epithet Aquinii has come to be widely used for this type of "three-lipped" cattleya. The best of the initial three plants, with the boldest and clearest markings, was further distinguished by the cultivar name 'Vinicolor'. Over the past twenty years, renewed interest in species has led to new populations of *C. intermedia* Aquinii coming from Brazil whose background is confused to say the least. However, we are fortunate to have improved forms of this sought-after species to enjoy. Interestingly, one Brazilian grower crossed the Aquinii type with a coerulea type, interbreeding over several generations to obtain a "blue" splash petal. This was quite an accomplishment of perseverance. It should also be noted that there is some leeway in such horticulturally applied naming, as opposed to the strict botanical conventions, so further descriptive epithets have arisen such as Flammea—indeed, Orlata is another prime example.

Above: Aquinii or Flammea forms of C. intermedia *show an aberration of the petals that mimics the lip. This quality has been instrumental in producing generations of "splash petal" hybrid cattleyas.*

Opposite: Although not truly "blue", coerulea forms of cattleyas are of a pretty violet color or feature this color on the lip, rather than the rose-fuchsia of typical flowers.

SPLASH PETAL CATTLEYAS

Cattleya intermedia Aquinii, the peloric, "three-lipped" cattleya species, has had a profound affect on modern splash petal hybrids.

Today, though, the best and brightest of our splash petal types are created more by "chance" than by the influence of *C. intermedia*. Some species have what is known as "chip flaring," that is, chips of lip color at the tips of the petals. *C. dowiana*, *C. lueddemanniana,* and *C. warneri*, among a few others, all lend this influence when hybridizers properly select their parents.

C. dowiana's influence in this type comes largely from the semi-alba hybrids that result from its progeny, chief among them *Lc*. Wayndora (which produced *Lc*. Mem. Robert Strait when crossed with *C. walkeriana*, and *Brassolaeliocattleya* Segundina Vizcarra with *Blc*. Neal Blaisdell) and *C*. Kittiwake. The influence of bifoliate species such as *C. granulosa* is also seen, which can give curious "reverse" flaring in *Lc*. Ann Follis–based hybrids.

C. loddigesii gives surprise results with *Lc*. Trick or Treat, producing *Lc*. Magic Bell, again with the "reverse" flaring that appears as the flower matures and the background color fades to reveal the flaring underneath.

Modern *C. intermedia* Aquinii breeding has tended more and more toward novelty types, such as *Cattleytonia* Capri (x Jamaica Red). This charming plant has proven to be a popular potted plant and has been a significant parent in the breeding of further brilliant progeny when crossed with other miniature splash petals such as *Lc*. Mari's Song to give *Laeliocatonia* Party Time. These new directions in hybridizing are opening new vistas to orchid growers and windowsill gardeners alike, owing to their compact stature and propensity to freely bloom.

Above right: Lc. *Mem. Robert Strait 'Diana' HCC/AOS has superior form and attractive flaring.*

Right: The influence of Bro. sanguinea *makes* Lctna. *Party Time 'Michael Quest' AM/AOS a compact splash petal type.*

RED, WHITE & BLUE CATTLEYAS

SOPHRONITIS COCCINEA-BASED HYBRIDS

The development of red cattleya hybrids has been a journey that began in the very earliest days with the use of *Sophronitis coccinea*, the dwarf red species from Brazil.

Red cattleya hybridization exemplifies the type of breeding that has been the case when trying to create other unusual colors. Attempts to attain a red color has resulted in a "push me, pull you" effect—in other words, the redder the flower, the smaller it is; the larger the flower, the less intensity and trueness of red color it has. Looking back from today's vantage point, we can analyze the results of misguided ideas. For example, the lavender *Potinara* (*Brassavola* x *Cattleya* x *Laelia* x *Sophronitis*) shows intensity of color but little red. Smaller flowered, red cattleya hybrids, such as *Sophrocattleya* Doris (*C. dowiana* x *Sophronitis coccinea*), *Sc.* Beaufort (*C. luteola* x *Soph. coccinea*) and hybrids from *Sophrolaeliocattleya* Precious Stones are relatively common today, but a true red, large-flowered cattleya is still rare.

Being able to reliably achieve good red color in smaller and very shapely hybrids is both a blessing and a curse. It is a blessing to those many who truly love them and can only afford limited space and a curse to those hybridizers who are continually frustrated in their search for this particular Holy Grail. Thanks to the long-term efforts of such Hawaiian breeders as Masatoshi Miyamoto, we do have large-flowered cattleyas that approach very closely to true red. Continued inbreeding of what amounts to yellow types crossed with lavender types (i.e., the yellow *C. dowiana* crossed with lavender species such as *C. labiata* or *C. mossiae*), coupled with astute selection of those progeny most closely approximating the desired goal and a lot of patience, results in plants with the quality of *Pot.* Cindy Yamamoto 'Crownfox' AM/AOS (Sally Taylor x San Damiano). The basis of this breeding is the particular pigments present in cattleyas. The lavender types overlay the yellows, which, in proper combination (exceedingly rare), produce the intensity of wine red that is sought.

Pot. *Cindy Yamamoto 'Crownfox' AM/AOS shows just how far red* Cattleya *breeding has come. It was the recipient of the 2003 Masatoshi Miyamoto Award for the most outstanding* Cattleya *alliance species or hybrid.*

The influence of L. pumila *can be seen in the richly colored tubular lip of* Slc. Precious Katie 'Naples' HCC/AOS.

Soph. coccinea *is the obvious path to red cattleya hybrids. Because it comes from the cool coastal mountains of southeast Brazil, it requires cool temperatures for successful culture, as do most first generation hybrids.*

Pot. *Newberry Delight 'Carol' AM/AOS was made by using a large red-purple Cattleya hybrid crossed with the ever-popular mini-catt, Sc. Beaufort.*

Red, White & Blue Cattleyas **103**

CATTLEYA AURANTIACA & OTHER RED AVENUES

The strong orange color of *Cattleya aurantiaca* and its hybrid progeny is another avenue to colors approaching red and is based on the same pigment chemistry previously outlined. The flowers are generally smaller owing to the *C. aurantiaca* influence, but an intensity and depth of color is achieved that is difficult to describe. *C.* Chocolate Drop (*aurantiaca* x *guttata*) has long been a favorite display plant, despite its sometimes overlarge stature, since it has magnificent clusters of bronzy red blooms of intermediate size. Keeping quality is also exceptional. We have seen a series of very successful *C.* Chocolate Drop hybrids produced over the last few years. Among these are *Brassolaeliocattleya* Dennis Kone (x *Blc.* Painter's Brush) and *Laeliocattleya* Miva Royal Chocolate (x *Lc.* Royal Emperor), which is notable as its parent *Lc.* Royal Emperor is of the yellow x lavender type, cherished for its deep, wine red color.

Plants that satisfy both the connoisseur and the gardener are guaranteed a place in the "Orchid Hall of Fame." Sometimes such

The influence of the bifoliate cattleyas, C. aurantiaca *and* C. gutatta, *is evident in the waxy texture of the flowers of* Blc. Dennis Kone 'Lakeview' HCC/AOS.

plants are the result of hard work, sometimes caprice. *Cattleytonia Why Not* (*Broughtonia sanguinea* x *C. aurantiaca*) is a great example of the latter. When the hybridizer asked his manager if he could or should make this cross, the response was "Why not?" Certainly only average examples of either parent were used. As the seedlings began to bloom, only a few years later, the growers were astounded by the overall high quality of the cross, which gained the coveted Award of Quality from the American Orchid Society, given only to those hybrids or seed-raised populations demonstrating high overall quality. Many were cloned, some were selected for further breeding, and one plant in particular went to Hawaii, where it was found to be a chance tetraploid. Now we have an entire race of free-growing and free-blooming red orbs on very compact plants, all the result of a fortuitous "Why not?"

The round cheery flowers of Ctna. Why Not are popular with hobbyists and breeders alike. The clone 'Adkin's Firesign' received an HCC/AOS.

Ctna. Why Not makes a wonderful specimen plant. Shown here is the clone 'Crownfox Ruby' CCM/AOS.

Red, White & Blue Cattleyas **105**

POTINARA SUSAN FENDER

In the process of orchid breeding, particularly in the more difficult to achieve color ranges, happy chance often takes a hand. *Potinara* Susan Fender 'Cinnamon Stick' AM/AOS (*Pot.* Caesar's Head x *Laeliocattleya* Mary Ellen Carter) has a great story, for which we are indebted to the owner for sharing. Both parents of this cross come from the complex breeding of the yellow with the lavender type and show strong coloration, including, in the case of *Lc.* Mary Ellen Carter, a bold picotee petal edging of red. The gift of four seedlings from the originator to the namesake of the cross produced an orchid of exceptional quality, 'Cinnamon Stick'. While quality is sometimes elusive in these lines of breeding, and "growability" can also be suspect, apparently all four seedlings were good growers with high-quality flowers. But one stood out for its beautiful blooms and heady fragrance. Under some cultural circumstances and some lighting, the red petal and sepal overlay nearly coalesce into a glowing red that is beyond compare. Under other conditions, the red overlaying the yellow background color forms a picotee edging and netting of equally unique character.

Pot. Susan Fender 'Cinnamon Stick' AM/AOS stands at the peak of this particular line of breeding today. We can be thankful that the owners are dedicated nursery people whose business goal includes providing the highest quality plants to the most possible people. Too often are sensational orchids displayed and awarded, only to vanish "on the desert wind" into a private collection, never to be seen again. When good-quality—of both flower and plant habit—orchids are made commercially available, everyone benefits.

Often blooming more than once a year, Pot. Susan Fender 'Cinnamon Stick' AM/AOS can produce flowers that vary in color depending on the temperature and light conditions of the blooming season.

STANDARD WHITE CATTLEYAS

Blc. *Redland Rio Blanco 'Crystelle' AM/AOS sets a new standard for white cattleyas.*

Unlike more exotic colors, a very high standard in white cattleyas was reached shortly after World War II with the introduction of *Cattleya* Bow Bells, *C.* Estelle Alba 'Cynosure', and *C.* Joyce Hannington. Indeed, the "typical" white cattleya was of such high quality that some called for a cessation of their judging, as "they just aren't getting any better." To a jaundiced eye, perhaps, but shape, size, texture, productivity, and season can always stand improvement. And, no, not all whites are alike. Is the texture flat or matte, or is it sparkling with diamond dust? Are the flowers carried well on the stem, above the foliage, on a strong inflorescence that

needs no staking? Does the shape consist of two overlapping equilateral triangles, as in the ideal *C. trianaei* shape? Is the lip full, frilly, and trumpet shaped? Is there a dark, egg-yolk yellow color in the throat, or is it nearly pure white? The list of possible improvement is nearly endless. There is simply nothing to compare with the beauty of a fine white cattleya. Both *C.* Sierra Blanca and *C.* (Old Whitey x *gaskelliana*) exemplify just how good modern white cattleyas can be.

One of the more difficult goals in the breeding of better white cattleyas was the attempt to add the better points of *Brassavola* (now *Rhyncolaelia*) *digbyana*. These include improved substance, beautifully fringed lip and a sweet citrus perfume. Pink "brassos" (Brassolaeliocattleyas and Brassocattleyas) of high quality were relatively common but when crossed with white cattleyas, invariably gave all pink progeny. That is, until the almost simultaneous introduction of *Brassocattleya* Deesse and *Brassolaeliocattleya* Nacouchee, both of which would prove to give some white flowers among their progeny that would, more importantly, prove to breed as true as white parents. We take this all for granted today, but the introduction of plants such as *Blc.* Burdekin Wonder and the very new *Blc.* Redland Rio Blanco show the great advances achieved in this field by persistent breeders.

Below: C. *Sierra Blanca 'Mount Whitney' AM/AOS.*

Blc. Donna Kimura is a parent of Blc. Burdekin Wonder 'John's Pride' AM/AOS, which also has pink flowers.

BIFOLIATE WHITE CATTLEYAS

Bifoliate white cattleyas have long been mainly the provenance of cut-flower growers. A few of the older hybrids such as *C. Claesiana* (*C. intermedia* x *C. loddigesii*), *C.* Henrietta Japhet (Eucharis x *loddigesii Alba*) and *C.* Wendy Patterson (Helen P. Dane x *intermedia Alba*) are occasionally seen, but even these are held onto more for the occasional cut-flower need more than any display quality. Still, occasionally, a breeder will "rediscover" the multiple good qualities of this type or come up with a fresh approach, and plants will again become popularly available, like the use of *C. walkeriana Alba* to produce semidwarf plants and

In the 1950s Cattleya Henrietta Japhet was such a popular corsage orchid, often used in wrist corsages, that any white "cocktail orchids" were known as Japhets by florists.

flowers, such as in *C.* Victorian Lace 'Janet' HCC/AOS (Moon Festival x *walkeriana*).

"Out of sight, out of mind" surely applies with this type. For when new crosses are shown, especially the *C. walkeriana*-based hybrids or *C.* Angelwalker hybrids, buyers clamor after the plants. And no wonder, since what could be more satisfying for display than heads of purest white, often fragrant blooms, with outstanding, lasting qualities? An added attraction to these is that they are made more vigorous by breeding them from plants that are close in proximity of species. This gives them all the charm of a species with none of the finicky nature when it comes to potting or growing. Bifoliate whites will flower more than once a year, with a main blooming season in late spring or early summer, followed by another bloom in late summer or early fall as the summer growth matures. For true beauty, these are tough to beat.

Some say that the large flowers of Cattleya Wendy Patterson are among the most beautiful white cattleyas.

Cattleya *Victorian Lace 'Janet' HCC/AOS shows the influence of the* C. *walkeriana parent in the open lip and round petals.*

Red, White & Blue Cattleyas **111**

One of the attractions of using Bro. sanguinea *Alba* for creating white hybrids is the sparkling, or "diamond dust," texture.

BROUGHTONIA-BASED WHITE HYBRIDS

The true test, however, of the great appeal of white cattleya types has been the universal acceptance of Broughtonia-based white hybrids. This interest was first stimulated with the introduction of *Cattleytonia* Maui Maid (*C.* Hawaiian Variable x *Broughtonia sanguinea Alba*), whose heads of round, pure white blooms were much like an improved *Bro. sanguinea Alba*. These were improved in many ways, including flower substance, keeping quality, size, and ease of culture. When backcrossed to *Bro. sanguinea Alba*, *Cattleytonia* Jet Set resulted, an even more floriferous example of the type.

But it is in the Caribbean homeland of *Bro. sanguinea* that some of the greatest strides are being made. The finest cultivars are available here and grow to perfection in the favorable climate. One breeder in particular has concentrated on *Bro. sanguinea* and its close allies such as *Laeliopsis domingensis*, a combination of which resulted in the lovely pure white *Lioponia* Kingston 'Elizabeth' HCC/AOS. A backcross to the *Broughtonia* parent led to the outstanding and shapely *Lpna.* Hamlyn's Masterpiece.

Where conditions are right, or where the grower can emulate the airy, tropical environment from which they originate, *Broughtonia* and related hybrids are difficult to beat as display

Liponia Hamlyn's Masterpiece 'Mem. Claude H. Hamilton' HCC/AOS *is a fine example of advanced* Broughtonia *breeding that still retains the charm of the species.*

plants. Plants are generally quite small, less than six inches, and thanks to their short rhizomes can be accommodated in relatively small pots. In many cases, they will grow even better mounted on cork or grown in an open-slatted teak basket. The grower will be rewarded with multiple, often branching, inflorescences of sparkling white orbs that last a good length of time. *Broughtonia* hybrids seem to be more forgiving than the species and can be grown on a windowsill or under lights. Allow the plants to thoroughly dry between watering while keeping the humidity high.

SHADES OF BLUE

A beautiful and rare color form, C. loddigesii 'Blue Sky' AM/AOS.

Blue is one of the most elusive colors in orchids, especially so in the cattleya alliance since no "true blue" pigments exist. Instead, we must make do with the so-called coerulea forms of the various species, which have a color that may be called cyanotic or, in some cases, gray or even lavender. We refer to all these colors, though, as "blue" and recognize them with the term coerulea. Within cattleyas, the intensity of the blue color varies inversely to the size of the flower. In other words, the smaller flowered bifoliate species, such as C. bowringiana, C. intermedia, and C. loddigesii, have the more intense blue color, while the labiate, or unifoliate, species, such as C. gaskelliana, C. jenmanii, C. labiata, C. lueddemanniana, and C. mossiae, have a paler, more pastel color to their larger flowers. Many of the cattleya-like large-flowered laelias also have blue forms, such as L. purpurata and L. perrinii, as does the Mexican L. anceps. The larger-flowered blues generally have lips with much more intense blue color for contrast. The mechanism behind this is such that, in a photograph, the representation of its color is less than adequate. For example, the famous C. trianaei Coerulea 'Blue Bird' never photographed well, appearing more pink than blue.

With the introduction of improved forms of many of the Latin American cattleya species have come vastly improved coerulea varieties as well. Some of the older blues were difficult in the

Line breeding of select species can produce superior offspring like
C. lueddemanniana *Coerulea 'Coromoto' AM/AOS.*

extreme to grow and had flowers that were not of the best quality, often with poor substance and inability to last. One of the most amazing of the more recently introduced species is the early winter-flowering *C. jenmanii* Coerulea, which has a blue color of greater than expected intensity. Thanks to its silver-blue color similar to so-called blue roses, *C. loddigesii* Coerulea 'Blue Sky' AM/AOS is a personal favorite. While this cultivar has been cloned for a broader market, it remains somewhat rare, as it is not the

easiest plant to grow well, since its roots can be especially sensitive to damage when being repotted.

For slightly later in the winter, *C. lueddemanniana* Coerulea 'Coromoto' AM/AOS shows exceptional quality, with good color saturation and extraordinary petal breadth and carriage. Both the *C. jenmanii* Coerulea and *C. lueddemanniana* Coerulea are great examples of the value of propagation from the orchid's range country. Formerly exceedingly rare, these fine plants can be made available to a wider audience, among them aspiring hybridizers, who will use this fresh genetic material to advance the state of blue hybrids beyond what was once a dream to early breeders.

Red, White & Blue Cattleyas **115**

attaining good blue color as were those striving after red. The smaller the bloom, the richer the color; the larger the bloom, the paler the color. Some of Colman's best work involved breeding on from *C.* Ariel Coerulea (*bowringiana* x *gaskelliana*) in an attempt to capture richer color in larger and shapelier flowers. His legacy remains today in such hybrids as *C.* Sir Jeremiah Colman, utilizing his Ariel with the rare *C. walkeriana* Coerulea, and the other important progeny stemming from *C.* Ariel, *C.* Sapphire (x *labiata*), and *Laeliocattleya* Blue Boy (x *Lc.* Elegans).

Two modern blue species, both blooming in spring, one after the other, that show considerable improvement over the older varieties

Cattleya mossiae *Coerulea 'Von Scholl' AM/AOS.*

One of the most dedicated early breeders of blue cattleyas was Sir Jeremiah Colman, of Colman's mustard fame. He, like those who followed him, was beset by the same problem in

are *C. mossiae* Coerulea 'Von Scholl' AM/AOS and *C. gaskelliana* Coerulea 'Katarina's Blue' HCC/AOS. For many years, the standard blue *C. mossiae* was Reineckiana 'Blue Lip', with a richly blue-veined lip offsetting the soft blue color of the petals and sepals. It was so known because its fragrance seemed to show a closer link to the semi-alba Reineckiana type than to the lavender forms. This is a tenuous connection, admittedly, but we are talking about horticulture and not botany here. Sadly, its form, carriage, and substance were all rather poor, with the blooms often displayed sloppily on the stem and not lasting very long. Neither was the well-known *C. gaskelliana* Coerulea 'Blue Dragon' of any particular quality beyond its blue color. The flowers were large, but substance was thin, and the flower parts were not proportionately full. So while neither of the more recently awarded cultivars have flowers whose shape rivals that of their more traditionally colored siblings, they both represent significant advances. *C. mossiae* Coerulea

C. gaskelliana *Coerulea 'Katarina's Blue' HCC/AOS.*

'Von Scholl', particularly, has a classic *C. mossiae* shape, not full but flat and very well held. Indeed, some prefer this slightly more open form, if accompanied by flatness as it gives a less perfect, more natural lock in keeping with something of nature's creation, as opposed to the circular, artificial look of so many hybrids. This is

ironic, of course, as most of these newer, improved species have never seen the inside of a jungle; they are produced, rather, from the process of selective breeding. In a conservation sense, this is a

good reason why man-made species will probably never serve to repopulate natural habitats. Artificial selection by people is different from natural selection in the wild.

Blues have always had a minor following by those who eagerly search out the newest, best, and most unusual cultivars. However, this market segment has not proven to be sufficiently large to warrant any great concentration on the regular production of blue cattleyas, new or otherwise. Nor are most blue hybrids sufficiently uniform in quality to "cross over" and be desirable to those not specially looking for blues. An almost offhand remaking of the famous primary *Lc.* Canhamiana with blue parents, *L. purpurata* Werckhauseri 'Blue Lyre' x *C. mossiae* Coerulea, gave a population of blue cattleyas of high uniform quality and created a demand still unmet, despite the cloning of several select/awarded cultivars. When the breeder is surprised, so is the public, because in the case of this hybrid, neither parent was known to be as reliable or as high quality as they turned out to be. The *C. mossiae* Coerulea came from existing stock and was not remarkable in any way. *L. purpurata* Werckhauseri 'Blue Lyre', on the other hand, was exceptional and quite distinct in its depth of blue color, with darker blue petal venation, but these favorable attributes were offset by what can only be described as deficient shape. The resulting plants were extraordinary from the start. They grew well and rapidly, something often characteristic of a primary hybrid, and all

began to flower within the first couple of years of approaching flowering size, rather than the more typical stretching out over a period of three to four years. If the grower is quick-thinking, he or she can reap great benefits from this, both by marketing the cross effectively and by selecting potential cloning subjects from a good cross-section of bloomers.

Sadly, not all happy circumstance is well utilized. Clones were made of some of the best *Lc.* Canhamianas, including 'Azure Skies' AM/AOS, and further breeding was done in the years immediately after the first blooming of the seedlings. *Lc.* Alarcon Coerulea (x *C.* Dupreana), a remake of another ancient hybrid, gave an equally even-growing population thanks to the very vigorous primary *C.* Dupreana (*warneri* x *warscewiczii*), but the momentum had by this time been lost. The nursery essentially faltered in its marketing and plant-selection processes.

For all the seeming general disinterest in blue cattleyas, it is productive to muse on those cultivars that have, for a combination of reasons, caught the public's fancy and gone on to orchid fame. *Lc.* Mini Purple Coerulea (*L. pumila* Coerulea x *C. walkeriana* Coerulea) is an example of the right orchid at the right time. It is also an example of a hybrid whose making might never have occurred except under the most extraordinary of circumstances.

Following Page: The remake of this popular hybrid using Coerulea parents has revived interest in Lc. Canhamiana *'Azure Skies' AM/AOS.*

Following Page Opposite: Lc. Alarcon *has delicate Coerulea flowers.*

and improved forms of the species and for its significant role in modern minicatt breeding. One of the finest of all blues, *C. walkeriana* Coerulea has the "silver" blue akin to that of *C. lcddigesii* and can impart this color in progeny, such as *C.* Sea Breeze (x *warneri* Coerulea). More importantly, the species' flowers are relatively large for the size of the plant. In breeding, it reduces plant size but not at the expense of flower size, which can equal or occasionally exceed that of the larger-flowered parent. With coerulea, alba, semi-alba, and lavender varieties, *C. walkeriana* is one of our most important modern cattleya parents.

Among the "other" blue cattleya alliance species is *Laelia anceps* Vietchiana. The importance of *L. anceps* as a parent is far more than its compact and full-star shape or its long, strong inflorescence. In Southern California, *L. anceps* is the "king" of cymbidium companions, those plants that make happy garden subjects to grow alongside the ubiquitous garden cymbidiums. Early cut-flower growers made extensive use of *L. anceps* for its

Neither parent is common, neither parent is easy to grow, nor is either parent known for exceptional flower quality. What is baffling is that any breeder might even have both plants, let alone flower them at the same time, with one of the two plants strong enough to carry a seedpod. The standard lavender-colored *Lc.* Mini Purple is a very popular and widely distributed plant. The flowers are about what would be expected in such breeding, an average of the parents. However, and for whatever reason, *Lc.* Mini Purple Coerulea is of much higher than expected flower quality, with plants that grow substantially better than either parent.

C. walkeriana, a dwarf-growing bifoliate from Brazil, is a good case study both for the current craze for the introduction of new

season and the strong stems. While many of these early hybrids have been lost because of grower indifference and indifferent quality, enough remained into the 1950s to spur a resurgence of breeding with this species for outdoor growing in areas that also suit cymbidiums. Because the blue form of *L. anceps* was available, and because a famous Southern California nursery was growing hybrid seedlings for a breeder obsessed with blues, quite a few hobbyists got their start with blue outdoor cattleyas. I am one. My first orchid was a plant of *Lc.* Blue Kahili (*L. anceps* x Blue Boy) obtained as an unlabeled plant at a ten-dollar sale. It was quite a performer and made a lovely showing mounted on a schefflera tree in my backyard. I still regret not taking the plant with me when we sold that house.

A very similar hybrid of equal merit is *Lc.* Wrigleyi (*L. anceps* x *C. bowringiana*). First registered in 1899, this hybrid has been remade in recent years in both lavender and

blue forms. Either make very satisfactory display subjects with multiple good qualities. The temperature tolerance of the *L. anceps*

Top: One of the parents of the preceeding hybrid, C. walkeriana Coerulea. *Pictured clone is* C. walkeriana Coerulea *'Canaima's Caerulea' AM/AOS.*

Right: C. bowringiana *is from Central America and has a Coerulea form that is a valuable parent used by breeders.*

parent, coupled with the robust *C. bowringiana* parent, gives it the fine vigor of a hybrid. First and foremost, plant habit is superb, with plants remaining under thirty inches tall at maturity and tolerating a wide range of cultural conditions. It would be difficult to find a better beginner's cattleya, no matter whether the beginner was growing in a sunroom, under shade in a frost-free area, or moving plants grown under lights outdoors in the summer. The strong, not-too-tall inflorescences can hold a well-spaced cluster of blooms of six or more. And you can have your choice of brilliant lavender or pastel blue. Cattleyas are certainly worth considering as garden plants, under the right conditions.

The round full shape of C. bowringiana Coerulea has been used to create a whole family of fall-blooming blue Cattleya hybrids.

Left: Lc. Wrigleyi has a tall sturdy inflorescence due to the influence of the L. anceps parent.

Red, White & Blue Cattleyas **125**

THE MANY FACES OF LAELIA PURPURATA

Brazil, the largest nation of South America, is home to a significant portion of our planet's remaining virgin rain forest and, consequently, a staggering amount of biodiversity.

Aside from the many implications that such an important legacy carries, including responsible stewardship of an increasingly endangered and irreplaceable resource, Brazil also has one of the richest orchid flora anywhere. So rich, indeed, that the true depth and breadth of its countless species may never be known. However, considering how many beautiful species orchids are part of the everyday scene to Brazilians, it is of no small note that the most popular orchid in Brazil, its national flower, is none other than *Laelia purpurata*. And no wonder. None of Brazil's many species are as majestic, and few, if any, can match the sheer variety of color forms. There are orchid societies in Brazil devoted entirely to the cultivation of this magnificent plant in its many incarnations.

Some of these varieties were imported into European collections in the early days of the orchid business, and some of these made their way into collections outside of Europe and England. The most beautiful and distinct formed the basis of our modern laeliocattleyas, brassolaeliocattleyas, and potinaras. However, as interest in species waned, many of these fabulous clones were lost. Not in Brazil, though. Enthusiasm for *L. purpurata* remained high, and the very best were closely held, propagated for the enjoyment of a few cognoscenti, and never to be seen outside of the confines of Brazilian collections. Until direct trading with Brazilian orchid nurseries began to be the norm in the latter part of the twentieth century and pent-up demand for new and spectacular varieties of well-known species provided the impetus for wider propagation, these and other fine cultivars remained only a dream to American hobbyists and nurserymen. With the introduction of select seedling populations from the best Brazil had to offer, cultivars of the quality of *L. purpurata* Rosada 'KG's Purpurtrator' AM/AOS began to appear in the 1990s.

Above: A grouping of a few of the many color forms of L. purpurata *that make it so appealing to collectors.*

Left: A mature plant of L. purpurata *may produce several inflorescences of four to five flowers and be easily accommodated in an eight-inch pot. Pictured here is* L. purpurata *Rosada 'KG's Purpurtrator' AM/AOS.*

LAELIA PURPURATA VAR. CARNEA

American nurseries were propagating *L. purpurata* prior to 1990, of course. The few plants that were occasionally available found favor with cattleya lovers as well as those looking for a great display plant around Mother's Day, the prime season for *L. purpurata*. Ironically, though, the Tipo, or type, form was not often seen. The salmon-pink-lipped form of *L. purpurata*, known as Carnea, was the most popular and available. With its ivory white sepals and petals offset by the highly unusual lip color, fans were not in short supply.

Originally imported by B. O. Bracey in the late 1940s and first propagated by him, it is fairly safe to say that most, if not all, of the many carneas seen in the United States until very recently came from this one plant. Initial selfings gave way to sibling crosses of the best, until plants displayed a very high average standard. Growability, which can suffer as a result of continued inbreeding, did not seem to be adversely affected, though the plants were generally not free-branching, giving at most one or two leads in a reasonably sized pot. Rhizome length was not unacceptable, though the lack of branching was. However, with few, if any, alternatives to grow or against which to judge, growers tolerated the rather large plant size as part of the package. *L. purpurata* Carnea is, along with *Paphiopedilum delanatii*, an outstanding example of the value of nursery propagation in the preservation of a valued horticultural subject based on only a single, original plant. It is also a great argument for allowing the importation of a limited amount of fresh material collected from the wild by responsible nurseries to add to the availability of ethically propagated stock, which would help reduce demand by the general nursery trade for collecting more wild plants.

The *"Carnea"* form of L. purpurata *has a lip of a pink color seldom seen in orchids.*

LAELIA PURPURATA VAR. VIRGINALIS

As the 1990s wore on, the initial trickle of new *L. purpurata* seedlings from Brazil became a flood wave. This was in response to a demand that grew based on the quality of the first to bloom from the earliest shipments. Initially, the trade was in selfings and siblings of pure varieties, that is, such types as Alba (or Virginalis), semi-alba, Coerulea, Sanguinea, and so on. (The lack of consistency in the naming conventions of these types is a result of their being purely horticultural terms, as opposed to botanical terms, which are ruled by an international authority.) Early growers were quick to exhibit their new plants, often obtained on trips to Brazil, at shows and judgings. The quantum leap in quality standards led to a spate of awards to the species, previously considered at a sort of

plateau. The awards led to more publicity which led to more demand. As the demand grew, and the potential for profit (not to mention American dollars) became apparent to Brazilian growers, many changed from their traditional marketing through U.S. nurseries to visiting orchid shows and selling directly to the customers previously serviced by the U.S. nurseries.

These new seedling populations held many surprises for growers beyond the hope and expectation of improved flower forms. Of course, improved flowers were a result, but the real

A flowering plant of L. purpurata *commands attention to its stately appearance. Flower stems are strong, held erect, and generally need no staking.*

shocker came in the vastly improved growability and overall growth habit of the plants. Where previously *L. purpurata* had been rather notorious for straight ahead, rarely branching growth, the new seedlings showed a freedom of growth and propensity to break multiple leads that to date had simply not been seen. In addition to their freedom of branching, many also tended to flower a year or two sooner than did the better-known and longer-cultivated varieties. Where only one or at most two flower stems were the norm for a reasonably sized pot of *L. purpurata*, growers were now thrilled to see three, four, even five inflorescences on moderately sized plants (at least moderately sized for the species)! This created a whole new aspect of *L. purpurata*, the display plant for Mother's Day, and created a new market that previously had not existed.

Above: The rare L. purpurata Alba, *also known as variety "Virginalis."*

LAELIA PURPURATA (FLAMMEA X STRIATA)

A flared parent crossed with a veined parent created this attractive "purp."

The next step in the growth of this emerging market was the trend for Brazilian breeders to take the best of the L. purpuratas, regardless of the variety, and cross them together. Formerly pure breeding lines of particular color forms were combined in an effort to not only create new color forms but also to attain new heights in plant vigor and rapidity of growth. L. purpurata had truly become a horticultural (as opposed to speciality) subject with this step. Strains that had been more difficult to grow but had very exotic color patterns or markings were crossed with more prosaic but more vigorous strains to improve strength and potentially recover the more exotic colorations in some proportion of the progeny, at least for breeding on. Such crosses as L. purpurata (Flammea x Striata), a striking variety with lip-colored petal tips crossed with a strongly veined type, gave not only outrageous color combinations but also a degree of cultural ease that neither parent possessed on its own. One of the earliest of these attempts was a cross of two pink-lipped forms, Russeliana x Carnea.

Vigor was a given, but the range of colors from this cross was nothing short of astounding. This included everything from large, pure white blooms ('The King'), to bold semi-albas ('Treasure of

Carpinteria' AM/AOS), to type (ivory sepals and petals flushed rose with a dark lip), to the expected pink-lip types. A more typical sibling cross was the California-bred L. purpurata (Semi-alba 'Treasure of Carpinteria' x Sanguinea). This population was one of the nicest yet seen in terms of overall uniformity of plant growth and flower production. Interestingly, the first to flower were a combination of the two parents, resembling a nice Tipo. The later to bloom, sometimes two years later, more resembled the difficult and slow Sanguinea, with great intensity of near magenta petal flushing and striation to match the dark magenta lips.

Breeding between previously pure strains has led to new and exciting color forms of L. purpurata.

LAELIA PURPURATA VAR. WERKHAUSERI

A new day, it seems, is dawning for *Laelia purpurata*. Increasingly popular in the United States, both with hobbyists and gardeners, its somewhat large size is now mitigated by a more branching growth habit. Growers are finding, too, that it is not a demanding subject if care is taken to pot at the season when new roots are flushing out. It is also quite temperature tolerant, being equally at home in Florida shade houses, California cymbidium gardens, sunrooms, and conservatories, as well as traditional greenhouses. Despite the fact that a mature plant really needs an eight-inch pot to accommodate it properly, it is much easier to justify the space when such a plant can produce several flower heads as opposed to just one. Many varieties are sweetly fragrant, too.

Nor is there danger of *L. purpurata* becoming old hat. Certainly, we can expect many of the more commonly seen varieties in good quantities; even some of the formerly rare types such as Flammea and Sanguinea may eventually become more readily available. But with such wonderful novelties as Trilabelo (three-lipped) entering the trade, even the most jaded aficionado can expect something new right around the corner. With the added attraction of a great tropical connection through being the national flower of the fun-loving Brazilians, as well as a heritage plant much utilized in hybridization, *L. purpurata* will never again nearly fade away as it once almost did. For this we can be grateful.

Top: There are other nearly "blue" color forms of L. purpurata, *but the well-known variety,* Werkhauseri, *has a elusive overall slate blue color with a darker lip.*

Right: Although not for everyone's taste, this nearly peloric L. purpurata *Trilabelo may prove to be a useful parent in creating other novelty forms of the species.*

MINIATURE BRAZILIAN LAELIAS

The genus Laelia is widespread and quite variable, most likely as the result of its being developed artificially.

That is, it is comprised of four very distinct groups that do not constitute a "natural" genus, in the strict botanical sense of the word, but are lumped together for convenience's sake. Some would split them into separate genera, some would lump them into other, existing, genera, and some would simply let them be, which is the path followed here. We have touched upon the cattleya-like group in our focus on *L. purpurata*, mentioned the Mexican laelias with *L. anceps*, and now we will see some examples of the two groups of "miniature" laelias: the hadrolaelias and the rupicolous laelias.

The hadrolaelias are a very distinct group and are probably more closely related to *Sophronitis*, especially if their flowering habit is taken into account. Their flowers, relatively large for the size of the plants, emerge sheathless from the developing new growths. *Laelia pumila* is the best known of the group and comes from a slightly higher, cooler location and so requires temperatures consistent with cymbidiums; i.e., cool summer nights are needed for long-term success with this plant. Thankfully, Hawaiian breeding has given us some plants that are more tolerant of warmer temperatures, so even those in South Florida, where 'KG's Hot Ticket' HCC/AOS was awarded, can succeed with the right plant. *L. sincorana* is a more recent introduction, at least in any quantities, and is rather similar to *L. pumila*, though with larger flowers on stronger stems

that stand clear of the foliage. *L. sincorana* generally also has several flowers, as opposed to the usually single blooms of *L. pumila*. *L. sincorana* is also more temperature tolerant, which explains its use in hybridizing, the results of which are often very similar to those when using *L. pumila*, and it has the advantage of a wider potential "success zone." Two of its best-known hybrids are *Laeliocattleya* Love Knot (x *C. walkeriana*) and *Sophrolaelia* Isabelle Stone (x *Sophronitis coccinea*), one of which received a FCC/AOS for its almost unbelievably large red blooms. Neither

L. pumila nor *L. sincorana* will generally exceed six inches in plant height, and their relatively large blooms give a great show.

Above: L. pumila *'KG's Hot Ticket' HCC/AOS. The species is typified by glowing color and a darker velvety trumpet-shaped lip.*

Opposite: Flowers of L. sincorana *can measure more than four inches across, while the plants are only two to three inches tall. The beautiful full form of* L. sincorana *'Sierra Rose' AM/AOS is the result of line breeding select clones of the species.*

LAELIA LUCASIANA

Entire Brazilian orchid societies are devoted to the lovely and diverse rupicolous laelias. Rupicolous, because they are truly "rock dwelling," inhabiting some of the most unlikely and rugged of all

landscapes, where their roots have a tight hold in nooks and crannies where moisture and detritus collect. The botanically correct name for this group is Parviflorae, but the popular name rupicolous seems to serve best in this case. To a much greater extent than similar groups who love *L. purpurata*, the rupicolous laelia growers have as wide a palette of colors, shapes, and sizes as could ever be desired. Rose, lavender, yellow, orange, red, and near-white flowers are available, and plants range from less than two inches tall to those that may, with good culture, reach more than eighteen inches. The inflorescences appear well held above the foliage in most cases, enabling the flowers to be seen to their best advantage.

Laelia lucasiana is a wonderful representative of the lavender tones shown in some members of this group, having soft rose-lavender blooms offset by an unusual and highly contrasting yellow lip. Plants of *L. lucasiana* may range from as short as three inches to more than five inches with the strong spike often reaching twice the height of the plant. The heads of three to five or more blooms are produced in May and June. Little breeding has been done with this species, but *Laeliocattleya* Tiny Treasure (x *C.* Porcia) illustrates the potential of this line, especially with its bold yellow lip contrasting with the deep magenta blooms on very compact plants. Other lavender-toned species in this group are the very dwarf *L. ghillanyi*, with shapely deep magenta booms on very small plants, and *L. rupestris*, a taller plant growing to twelve inches or more with sparkling rose blooms appearing well above the foliage.

Above: This habitat photo of L. lucasiana *in the Serra da Caraça of Brazil shows how these miniature laelias grow on rocks.*

Right: Pretty pink flowers with a contrasting gold lip make L. lucasiana *unique.*

LAELIA SANGUILOBA

Owing to the often somewhat remote and inaccessible nature of their habitat, many of the rupicolous laelias have only recently been discovered. Those that have been known for some time are still not commonly represented in collections or in the trade. The legendary difficulty growers have in keeping plants alive for any length of time probably has a lot to do with this. Thankfully, some hobbyists are beginning to learn the methods necessary for success with this group, so we may begin to see them a bit more frequently than we do now. The "trick" seems to be to give the plants a very airy potting media that does not break down easily. Some of the modern aggregate products are proving very satisfactory. If the same care is paid to potting when roots are

active, as with many other seasonal orchids, growers can expect some degree of success.

One of the newer species in this group, whose exact habitat is still under debate, is *Laelia sanguiloba*, one of the few really reddish-orange species. This lovely orchid has been confused with the vegetatively similar *L. flava* when out of bloom. The shades of rich orange found here have great potential for further breeding in these popular shades. Another true orange member of this group is *L. cinnabariana*, which has been more common in cultivation owing to its easier care. However, as it originates at higher elevations where cooler temperatures prevail, growers in areas with cooler summer nights, as in coastal Southern California, have had more success. Nevertheless, the potential for *L. sanguiloba* may be in its tolerance of warmer conditions, allowing it to impart these characteristics into hybrids similar to those initially made with *L. cinnabarina*, such as *L.* Coronet (x *harpophylla*), *L.* Icarus (x *flava*), and *Sl.* Psyche (x *Sophronitis coccinea*).

Above: Growing among tall grasses, plants of L. sanguiloba *are difficult to find when out of flower.*

Right: Only described in 1990, the pure orange color of L. sanguiloba *may eventually lead to its use as a parent in breeding brightly colored miniature hybrids.*

LAELIA MILLERI

Every group of orchids, it seems, has a member that attains mythic proportions. Often, this is the result of two or more circumstances, usually color and rarity. The rupicolous laelia that fills this place in orchid history and hybridization is *Laelia milleri*, the red laelia. The plant created a sensation and was probably first seen in the United States in the 1960s when it came to a Southern California nursery in a shipment of *L. flava*. The plants of *L. milleri* were initially named *L. flava* var. *aurantiaca* until the differences in plant habit and flower shape were finally sorted out. The relatively tall six-inch to twelve-inch inflorescence bears three to six fire-engine-red blooms up to two inches across. Of course, red is one of the most sought-after of all cattleya alliance colors, so it was not long before hybrids began to appear. One of the earliest was *Sl.* Jinn (x *Sophronitis coccinea*), a true red dwarf cattleya with all the good qualities of the cooler growing *Soph. coccinea* in a plant that grew easily under intermediate conditions. A plant of *Sl.* Jinn was my first AOS award, 'The First' HCC/AOS. Other important hybrids from this parent are the previously discussed *Brassolaelia* Richard Mueller (x *Brassavola nodosa*) and *Laeliocattleya* Pink Favorite (x *C. walkeriana*).

Sadly, iron-ore mining critically endangers *L. milleri*'s habitat in the mountains of Serra de Moeda, southwest of Belo Horizonte. Plants may be found growing fully exposed to the brilliant tropical sun or among debris piles on the crags of this mountainous area. Here is another example where responsible nursery propagation of this beautiful and possibly soon-to-be-extinct orchid is becoming an imperative.

L. milleri *created quite a sensation when it was discovered in a shipment of laelias from Brazil. It was the first truly red* Laelia *to be found.*

LAELIA BRIEGERI

most important reasons for *L. briegeri*'s widespread use in breeding is the simple fact that breeders have been successful in growing plants with which to breed. The same cannot be said for many of the plants of this group.

Not only has *L. briegerii* been widely used in breeding, its progenies have been widely distributed in the trade, and quite a few of them have gone on to be important parents in their own right. Breeders have produced more than 275 hybrids and five

Horticultural value is difficult to assess. Is it the species itself and the effect it has as a plant on the market, or is it the species' value as a parent? In other words, is beauty enough, or does utility play a part? In the case of *Laelia briegeri*, we have an orchid that has not only great beauty and intrinsic appeal but also has seen extensive use in hybridizing. Plants of *L. briegeri* are quite short, often under four inches, and the flowering stems are of moderate length, up to twelve inches, with, occasionally, as many as eight flowers but more commonly three to five. The brilliant canary yellow of the generally full-formed two-inch blooms is what has drawn the interest of breeders and hobbyists alike. In addition, *L. briegeri* may also have subtle "chip" flaring at the tips of the petals, which is passed along in breeding. In a very pragmatic sense, one of the

generations to date. Two of the more important, if measured by their further use in breeding, are *Brassolaeliocattleya* Love Sound (x Bouton D'Or), beautiful in its own right and a fertile as well as successful parent and *Laeliocattleya* Tokyo Magic (x Irene Finney). Both *Sophrolaeliocattleya* Mine Gold (x Jewel Box) and *Slc.* Orglade's Early Harvest (x Hazel Boyd) are popular potted plants in

shades from brightest yellow, through orange, to red. All have deep red lips and terrific shape for type, as well as being compact.

Opposite: Most plants of L. briegeri *have flowers of full form and symmetrical starry shape.*

Opposite bottom: Blc. Sunday 'Quest' AM/AOS *shows chips of color on the petals and sepals resulting from using* L. briegeri *as a parent.*

Below: Blc. Love Sound *has proven to be a valuable parent in its own right.*

LAELIA LILIPUTANA

Collectors are drawn to extremes. The rarest, the brightest, the most expensive, the largest, and the smallest of anything are worth collecting. Along with *Laelia kettiana*, *L. liliputana* is the smallest of an already small-growing group of plants. At an average of one inch tall, "cute" is the word that comes most quickly to mind. One or two flowers emerge from the developing growth and barely clear the foliage on a strong stem. Its color ranges from pale lavender with a butter-yellow lip to more intense lavender and egg-yolk-yellow lip. Photographers love subjects that can be fit into some sort of proportionate scale, and orchid photographers are no different. A favorite image is of a hand holding the diminutive plant. Naturally, such small plants are favorites for people who grow orchids under lights and on windowsills. Plants of a very small stature such as this are able to fit more readily into a limited area. *L. liliputana* is a perfect choice for these situations.

Above: The flowers of L. liliputana *are bigger than the plant! Appropriately named after the mythical island of Lilliput.*

Right: Flowers of the species can be dark or light colored and have a sparkling texture.

BULBOPHYLLUMS

The "beauty" of orchids is in the eye of the beholder, the human beholder. Orchids, of course, have not evolved their extravagant and colorful floral displays for the good of people.

Though we perceive many flowers as "beautiful," far more important is how they are "seen" by their pollinators. This, after all, is the main and only reason for flowering plants to flower—to attract pollinators, be pollinated, and perpetuate the species. The orchids that we perceive as beautiful tend to be pollinated by animals that we find somehow beautiful as well: birds, bees, moths, butterflies, and so on. There are many more (very many, as anyone who has visited the tropics will tell you) small flying creatures attracted to what we would consider bizarre colors and unpleasant odors than there are lovely, flitting, large, anthropomorphically pleasing animals. These potential pollinators are attracted to objects that resemble their food sources or objects of sexual desire. For this reason, there are far more orchids with peculiar shapes, odd color combinations, and putrid fragrances than those that meet our sense of beauty.

Bulbophyllum medusae is a strangely lovely species and is exemplary of a habit within *Bulbophyllum* that is so odd as to be beautiful. The heads of many smallish individual blooms combine to give the impression of a shaggy rag mop. Large, well-grown plants will produce multiple heads from the many leads, and the overall effect, particularly when the penetrating fragrance is added, is overwhelming. Growers who can provide the high humidity, light

shade, and space that this fine orchid demands are rewarded with

a blooming spectacle. Owing to their somewhat rambling growth

habit, the best plants will be grown on mounts or in slatted teak

baskets under warm to intermediate conditions.

Above: When examined close up, the flowers of Bulb. medusae *have attractive details.*

Opposite: Growers of Bulb. medusae *have the pleasure of watching the curious heads of flowers unfold.*

BULBOPHYLLUM ECHINOLABIUM & BULBOPHYLLUM RECURVILABRE

The pros and cons of wild-collected orchids will be debated for the foreseeable future. The main question is whether it is better to grab one while the grabbing is good (after all, they've already left their habitat, haven't they?) or to wait for ethically propagated plants, to

discourage those who would simply denude a habitat to get all of a newly discovered orchid species. This debate has been particularly intense in the case of Bulb. echinolabium. When this highly desirable, large-flowered plant first entered the trade, it was

in the form of specimens of dubious provenance. As more and more began to flower in cultivation, more and more hobbyists simply had to have one. And more and more commercial folks went to greater and greater lengths to provide for their demanding clients. It was a slippery slope. Visitors to the native habitat told of all plants being stripped, leaving none to continue to grow and repopulate the area. The enormous—often to over fifteen inches in vertical spread—bloom with its curious scent seemed to draw out the worst in orchid collectors. Thankfully, the plant has proven to grow rather easily under shady intermediate conditions, preferring to be mounted, so we can hope that commercial growers have seed-grown populations on the way.

Bulb. echinolabium and Bulb. recurvilabre are both large-flowered species in a generally small-flowered genus. Bulbophyllums are among the rising stars for true orchid lovers these days, and new discoveries are made quite often, since these are relatively common inhabitants of some of the areas of high biodiversity now being opened to human development.

Above left: The lip of Bulb. recurvilabre *has an interesting warty texture. Pictured is* Bulb. recurvilabre *'JEM' CHM/AOS.*

Right: Bulb. echinolabium *is a recently introduced species with large attractive flowers that have a fishy smell.*

BULBOPHYLLUM SUMATRANUM & BULBOPHYLLUM POLYSTICTUM

Bulbophyllum lobbii has been around and widely cultivated for many years. Several select cultivars are known to grow well and flower freely. Being another of the larger flowered members of the genus, it is popular among orchid growers in general, and not just with the connoisseur. *Bulb. lobbii*'s light yellow blooms, held on strong stems above the relatively compact plants (rhizomes are about one-and-a-half inches), have a "rocking" lip that, when triggered by the pollinator's landing (or a curious viewer), rocks

The colors and markings of Bulb. sumatranum *'Borneo' CHM/AOS make it attractive to even nonspecialists.*

back, trapping the pollinator against the column. In recent years, as Borneo and its surrounding areas have become better explored, more of *Bulb. lobbii*'s relatives are coming into cultivation.

Two of the best are *Bulb. sumatranum* and *Bulb. polystictum* *Bulb. sumatrana*, especially, is notable for its brilliant red netting over the yellow background. Some feel that it is simply a color

variant of *Bulb. lobbii*, while others think that it is a true species in its own right. Such questions, while best left to experienced taxonomists, often arise in a group like *Bulbophyllum* for several very good reasons. The genus is thought to be largest in the Orchid family and is quite cosmopolitan, ranging over the entire tropical and subtropical Old World, even into Africa. Plants range from among the very smallest to quite large, as do the flowers.

Bulbophyllum, like *Laelia*, is probably an artificial construct, and will

Many bulbophyllums have a hinged lip to leverage the pollinator upward to receive the pollinia. Pictured is Bulb. polystictum *'A-doribil' CHM/AOS.*

eventually be broken down into several constituent genera. In addition, it is still rapidly evolving, with new species coming into being at a relatively fast rate, as with *Bulb. sumatrana*, which certainly began as a color variant of *Bulb. lobbii*, and is now on its way to being its own, true-breeding species.

BULB. ORTHOSEPALUM, BULB. PHALAENOPSIS & BULB. ARFAKIANUM

The complex of species related to *Bulb. phalaenopsis* are some of the biggest and most curious of the genus. It has been named not for having blooms that in any way resemble the lovely moth orchids, *Phalaenopsis*, but for the large, pendant, glaucous leaves that top the rounded pseudobulbs. Because of the large size and pendant leaves, these truly tropical plants do best on mounts or in baskets, where their leaves can grow down unimpeded and undamaged. A mature plant of any one of these species provides a year-round talking point, simply owing to its massive aspect and overall attractiveness. Some shade is necessary, since the broad leaves can sunburn easily if care is not given.

It is the flowers, however, that really start people talking—and sometimes running. As with *Bulb. echinolabium* and some others in this genus, the flowers' scent can only be called foul. "Stench" is not too strong a word, for rotting meat is what attracts its fly pollinators to the bizarre, waxy blooms. Borne on short stems fairly close to the bulbs, the sometimes hairy, red-meat-colored blooms have the substance and texture of the wax lips popular at Halloween. And beware the friend who asks you to smell one. Whew! Nevertheless, these plants are highly sought-after by collectors. Sadly, most are wild-collected and can suffer quite a bit in transit owing to their large and fleshy leaves. Also, since the plants often are quite similar between species, the consumer doesn't always know exactly which species they are getting. Efforts are being made at seed culture, but the resulting plants, often from low germination, are slow-growing to the extreme and very difficult to bring to flowering size in a reasonable time, the result of which is cost that remains high.

Opposite: Long fleshy leaves make Bulb. phalaenopsis *a conversation piece even when not in flower. However, it is the flowers, fragrant of carrion, that elicit the most response—even from a distance!*

Right: The flowers of Bulb. arfakianum *'JEM' HCC/AOS have a beautiful tapestry-like pattern.*

Below: Looking much like a nest of baby birds, Bulb. orthosepalum *'A-doribil' CHM/AOS is closely related to* Bulb. phalaenopsis.

DENDROBIUMS

No one who visits a "Big Box" retail center today can go away without seeing phalaenopsis and dendrobium orchids in flower, for a quick sale or a stunning, long-lasting display.

With blooms that last for weeks in perfection, under less-than-ideal conditions, flowering orchid potted plants simply provide a better value than the more traditional "mums" or a bouquet. With the modern orchid industry increasingly, and almost totally, becoming stratified, offshore production of young plants allows the quick turnaround necessary to compete. One of the staples of this market is hybrid dendrobiums.

Dendrobium is the second-largest orchid genus, after *Bulbophyllum*, and offers a commensurately enormous variety of shapes, sizes, colors, and forms in its many species. However, it is in the hard cane evergreen types, bred from a relatively few species, where the highest pinnacle of achievements are seen. Flower color can be almost black and ranges from purest white, through all shades of yellow, green, blue, and lavender to red and orange. Plants that are most commonly seen include several canes, or pseudobulbs, that average eighteen inches with fifteen-inch flowering stems of eight to ten blooms. Great strides are being made in the miniature types, originating from *Dendrobium bigibbum* Compactum. These extraordinary plants are often small enough to fit in a teacup and give long-lasting pleasure with their lavender or white colors. Additionally, consumers may have better luck in reflowering the small-statured plants in a bright window or

sunroom. Literally tens of thousands of these plants enter the marketplace each year, and they were the starting point for the new flowering orchid potted-plant business that has lately gone over to the production of not only dendrobiums but also millions of phalaenopsis.

Above right: Den. *Mini Diamond is a typical miniature "pot plant"* Dendrobium.

Left: Den. *Quique Ramirez 'Karen's Delight' AM/AOS is a good example of just how dark modern* Dendrobium *hybrids can be.*

DENDROBIUM IMPACT SPLASH 'IMPACT' & DEN. BURANA EMERALD 'BURANA'

Despite the incredible popularity of potted-plant dendrobiums, they have not lost their appeal to hobbyists in warmer areas, such as Florida, where their cultural needs are better accommodated. Breeders in areas like Thailand turn out hundreds of crosses every year as well as dozens of new tissue-cultured (mericloned) cultivars to meet the need not only here in the United States but also in other potted-plant-hungry markets in Japan and elsewhere. Vibrant colors and unusual patterns, as with so many other flowers, sell. Flowers with splashes of color against contrasting backgrounds seem to jump off the sales table into waiting customers' arms. Nor are orchid judges immune to the charms of these highly bred beauties. Whether or not the plants get any award is ultimately secondary to the "award" of consumer confidence, marked with their purchase.

However, and in contrast to phalaenopsis, dendrobium potted plants are not so likely to rebloom for their owners, unless some care beyond that which is ordinarily available in the home can be given. For example, if plants can be grown in a sunny window

during colder months, kept in adequate humidity, and not overwatered or overfed (which would force weak growth unlikely to flower), consumers can then place the plants outdoors during warmer months (where night temperatures do not go below fifty-five or sixty degrees) to take advantage of the higher humidity and better quality of light. Dendrobiums tend to have highly seasonal growth in any case, so encouraging strong summer growth with adequate water and fertilizer can lead to matured canes producing inflorescences in late summer and early fall, just in time to come indoors for the cooler months. Of course, those growers in southern states blessed with frost-free nights year-round can do admirably in screen houses and under shade. Greenhouse culture is always appropriate, as well.

Above: Den. *Burana Emerald 'Natasha' HCC/AOS is an interesting variation on the theme of potted-plant hybrid dendrobiums.*

Opposite: Den. *King Dragon has been used to create many large-flowered hybrids with interesting petal flares, such as* Den. *Impact Splash 'Impact' HCC/AOS.*

DENDROBIUM ODOM'S HARVEST GOLD & DENDROBIUM DANDY DAME

While many of the most commonly seen dendrobiums are heavily influenced by *Dendrobium phalaenopsis* and *Den. bigibbum*, with their "traditional" orchid look, many more modern hybrids have more exotically shaped species in their background. Almost equally popular in warmer climes are the hybrids stemming from the Antelope-type dendrobium species. Corkscrew-twisted sepals and petals may have one twist or a series, always rotating through the bloom. Color combinations are equally wild, ranging from nearly concolor yellows and greens to striped and veined flowers. Another of the big attractions to this type of hybrid is the propensity to make several spikes per cane, often over a period of two or three years, which, on larger plants, can give a fountain of long-lasting blooms second to none. Many plants of this type are grown in warm climates where, during the summer, they are kept on a patio or in a screen house. Where the expense of heating during winter is not an issue and where truly big, mature plants can be accommodated, spectacular displays are the norm.

In any discussion of the culture of larger orchid plants, the sheer size of the mature plant is an important issue. Does the plant take up more than its share of room—room where several smaller plants might give an overall more satisfactory and cost-effective display—or does it really present a showy display, as you would like it to? Especially with dendrobiums, where plants will tolerate overpotting, plant space is different than bench space. Many commonly grown dendrobium hybrids, of the sort discussed here, make very large plants if given time. They do not want a pot that is sized for the mass of the plant. The root system is surprisingly limited for such large plants, and the plant can be quite top-heavy. Clay pots and a heavy medium, such as one of the increasingly common aggregates, will help this situation. Most importantly, the large top when supported by a small root mass must not be roughly treated and must have the "help" of good humidity to prevent overtaxing the roots' ability to take up water.

Above: Den. *Dandy Dame 'Lynn' AM/AOS exhibits the typical "corkscrew twist" petals that give antelope dendrobiums their name.*

Opposite: The clear yellow-green color of Den. *Odom's Harvest Gold 'Elly's Golden Princess' HCC/AOS makes an attractive and unusual "antelope type" hybrid.*

THE CALLISTA GROUP: DENDROBIUM LINDLEYI & DENDROBIUM JENKINSII

Den. jenkinsii has fewer flowers per inflorescence and looks like a miniature version of the closely related Den. lindleyi (far right).

The early postwar years were the heyday of wild-collected orchid plants. Newfound prosperity and modern transportation conspired to open new markets for species orchids previously only available to a few. No country was more aggressive in the export of its wild-collected plants than was India. India is a vast country, encompassing a wide variety of climates, from sea-level tropics to Himalayan cloud forests. Its orchid flora is just as varied and of great interest to orchid lovers. *Dendrobium* is well represented in the

Indian flora, and many of the showiest species have the advantage of traveling well, establishing easily, and flowering freely. The Callista group of *Dendrobium* was especially popular, and spring orchid shows of the '60s and '70s, even into the '80s, were full of fine flowering and bare-root plants of *Den. lindleyi* (popularly still known as *Den. aggregatum*). These plants were easily grown in the intermediate house and, if given a dry winter rest, rewarded the grower with showers of golden circles, whose prominent round lip was highlighted by a darker golden-orange center. Because these plants were best grown on slabs or in baskets, the flowers could be allowed to cascade naturally around the plant, giving a really spectacular show. While the inflorescences of *Den. lindleyi* carried twelve or more blooms in a dense, almost foxtail-like appearance, the closely related *Den. jenkinsii*, often considered simply a variety of *Den. lindleyi*, had single booms on the stems. Either one flowered from multiple nodes along the cigar-shaped pseudobulbs.

Today, we see far fewer of these plants. Those that are in cultivation are highly prized, far from their formerly very inexpensive status. India is no longer an "easy" source from which to obtain orchids, and not unlike Mexico, few of its best orchids are widely

propagated from seed. Plants of *Den. lindleyi* and *Den. jenkinsii* are

seen at spring shows but more often in the displays of nurseries

and orchid societies, and the few plants that may be available are

of select varieties and priced accordingly. This does not stop eager

Den. lindleyi, *long known as* Den. aggregatum, *has been a perennial favorite among orchid collectors and prized for its pendant sprays of round golden flowers.*

buyers from quickly purchasing those few that may be offered

for sale.

THE CALLISTA GROUP: DENDROBIUM FARMERI

Dendrobium lindleyi and Den. jenkinsii are the smaller of the Callista group, which also includes the somewhat larger Den. farmeri. The fifteen-inch pseudobulbs are topped by five or six broad leaves, from whose nodes the slightly pendant stems of up to twenty sweetly fragrant blooms are borne in late winter and early spring. This species appears across Southeast Asia. The blooms range in color from white to pink and are often offset by a golden disk in the throat. While the flowers do not last long, a mature plant will give many inflorescences, blooming over a period of weeks, and so is a worthwhile subject.

Like many other orchids from areas whose climate is dominated by the monsoon, Den. farmeri and other members of Callista have seasonal needs that profoundly affect their flowering. Tropical and subtropical areas have flora that have adapted to making most, if not all, of their season's growth when moisture and the attendant nutrients are available. Such plants begin their growth as days lengthen (or nights shorten) in expectation of the coming rains, and they grow almost unbelievably rapidly, topping out in late summer and early fall. When they don't seem to be growing, hold back on water and fertilizer. When they are growing, it is difficult to overwater or overfeed. Stop fertilizing, especially high nitrogen fertilizers, before the plant slows growth. Watering may remain heavy, and this will help to flush out any additional, unneeded nitrogen and thereby help to encourage flowering on the maturing canes.

Above left: Den. farmeri *is found over a wide range in Southeast Asia and is an easy-growing subject for the orchid beginner.*

Right: Some plants of Den. farmeri *produce flowers that have a pink cast.*

THE CALLISTA GROUP: DEN. SULCATUM

This lesser-known member of Callista is often grown as much for its curiously flattened pseudobulbs as for its yellow blooms. Looking all the world like a *Dendrobium lindleyi* that was smuggled, flat, in a suitcase, the pseudobulbs never really "plump up," growing upright at first then becoming pendant as they mature. Nor are the plants really green, tending more toward a yellow-green that can also give the appearance of being unhappy. Nevertheless, when well grown, plants of *Den. sulcatum* are conversation pieces year-round.

Too many would-be orchid growers, it seems, overlook the pleasure of a well-grown plant. Particularly with plants such as *Den. sulcatum*, the plant itself can be a source of pleasure. Orchid growing is a hobby that is meant to be relaxing and enjoyable. If the grower is always tense and concentrating on the flowers, 90 percent of the potential enjoyment is lost. The plants are out of flower far longer than they are in flower. Those who learn to participate in the growing of the plants are often those who get the best blooms while sincerely appreciating the plants when they have no flowers. Plants whose needs are tended to appropriately throughout the year simply do better.

Den. sulcatum *is an easy plant to identify even when out of flower because of its curiously flattened pseudobulbs.*

DENDROBIUM PARISHII

Dendrobium parishii and the similar, but more robust, *Den. superbum* (more properly known as *Den. anosmum*, popularly called Hono Hono in Hawaii), are sensational and showy plants for basket culture, where their slender, bare, deciduous canes bear several blooms at each node. Both come from higher elevations, where a decidedly cool and dry rest signals the plants to drop their leaves and initiate the late-winter flowers. Plants that do not receive a rest seldom flower, and this condition is indicated by the failure of the leaves to fall. Well-grown specimens will have a cascade of semipendant canes up to fifteen inches or more. As with so many of this monsoonally influenced type, the growth, initiated in spring, is extremely rapid when adequate humidity, moisture, and fertilizer are supplied. The best flowering comes from plants that are allowed to grow quickly during the season and ripen with a rest period. The lovely, cattleya-like blooms are variable in color, ranging from medium rose through white with a darker lip. The center of the bloom often fades to white, contrasting with the deep-rose lip. Flowers smell richly and sweetly of raspberry, creating a lovely overall presentation.

Both species are excellent subjects for a variety of situations, owing to their tolerant nature in general. Outstanding plants are seen in the spring in areas as diverse as Southern California, Hawaii, and Florida. Because both plants are best in baskets, due to the somewhat pendant nature of their canes, they may be hung from the roof of the growing area, preserving precious bench space. As with the members of the Callista section, however, the previously seen wild-collected plants are far less common today. Mostly select varieties, propagated by discerning and patient growers, are offered in today's marketplace. Thankfully, this is ameliorated to an extent by both species' habit of freely producing keikis (Hawaiian for "baby"), which are offsets from the cane and which may be potted up as individual plants when rooting is seen.

The distinctive sweet fragrance of Den. parishii *makes it a favorite orchid among species collectors. There is also a semi-alba form with white flowers and a raspberry-colored lip that is sometimes known as* Den. rhodopterygium.

DENDROBIUM FORMOSUM
& DENDROBIUM CRUENTUM

The so-called Nigrohirsute dendrobiums form a distinct group characterized by their upright canes often covered with a light layer of black hairs. *Dendrobium formosum* comes from higher elevations in Southeast Asia, where it grows in open forests. Growers have long coveted the long-lasting white flowers of *Den. formosum* and the related *Den. infundibulum*, and a range of hybrids is available that makes the most of the large, white, cattleya-like blooms. Because they originate at higher elevations, plants may not flower in warmer locations, needing cool nights to perform at their best. It is reported that the larger-flowered *Den.*

The brightly colored lip of Den. cruentum *has an interesting granulose appearance.*

Den. formosum *has pristine white, paper-thin flowers that are long lasting despite their lack of substance.*

formosum Giganteum comes from lower elevations and is more adaptable to lowland tropical areas. Plants appreciate high light when growths begin to mature and harden in late summer. Flowers appear in clusters of two or three from the nodes of the leaves on the upper portion of the pseudobulbs. Despite the sometimes crepe-like, fragile looking flowers, they remain for several weeks.

A smaller member of this group is *Den. cruentum*, which has been very important in the hybridizing of miniature Nigrohirsute types that will flower in a variety of conditions. Because the species comes from lower elevations in Thailand, it is able to impart the ability to flower where some of its cousins might not. Indeed, in more tropical areas, such as Hawaii or South Florida, *Den. cruentum* and its hybrids may be almost continually in flower. An interesting side note to *Den. cruentum* is that because it was considered endangered in Thailand, it ended up on CITES (Convention on International Trade in Endangered Species of Wild Flora and Fauna) Appendix I. This means few, if any, wild-collected plants are in the trade, and it is extensively grown from seed.

DENDROBIUM JUNCEUM

Dendrobium junceum is a curious orchid from the Philippines. Growing slightly above sea level, it is subjected, nevertheless, to very high temperatures and high humidity throughout the nearly seasonless year. Very bright light is a must, as is indicated by the terete leaves, which in strong sunlight help reduce the chance of heat buildup and subsequent burning that a broader leaf surface would endure. This species' only seasonality is influenced by the heavy seasonal rains of its native habitat, which can push the very rapid growth of this relatively tall plant to over forty inches in height. Under many conditions, the tall, reedlike pseudobulbs can become

Opposite: The terete "pine-needlelike" foliage of Den. junceum make it an interesting addition to any orchid collection.

pendant under their own weight. The small yellowish-white blooms are borne from tufts of bracts emerging near the terminus of the canes.

Like *Den. sulcatum*, the overall aspect of the plant is so charming and distinct that it would be a welcome addition to almost any collection. Perhaps better than a pot is a mount or small slatted basket, particularly where high humidity can be maintained—the plants' roots can get overstressed. In such conditions, the species grows freely and is displayed to its best, whether in its brief flowering season or as a foliage plant. The blooms, when they do appear, are sprinkled among the leaves and are nicely perfumed.

Left: In warm climates, Den. junceum *will quickly grow to specimen size and produce flowers in flushes throughout the summer.*

DENDROBIUMS FOR THE BIRDS: DENDROBIUM VICTORIA-REGINAE & DENDROBIUM GONZALESII

Den. victoria-reginae *is a favorite "blue" orchid among growers who have cool greenhouses.*

We are much more accustomed to seeing and thinking about orchid flowers that are pollinated by insects. Cattleyas, phalaenopsis, many dendrobiums, cymbidiums, and paphiopedilums all display characteristic insect-pollinated flowers.

All come from areas where insects can be expected to be active during at least part of the year, or even part of the day, when it is warm enough for their metabolism. What about plants that grow at higher elevations, where it is cooler, or where insects may otherwise not be present? Many of these exhibit bird-pollination syndrome, which encompasses different colors—often reds and oranges—that offer more distinct, attractive "targets" around the lip or column area and, since pollination may be a chancier occasion, blooms that are either longer lasting or occur over a longer period of time.

Den. victoria-reginae comes from mossy forests at higher elevations in the Philippines, while the similar *Den. gonzalesii* occurs at somewhat lower elevations. Both can flower sporadically more than once a year, though a main season in late spring is common. Because of the cooler, moister, and somewhat shadier nature of the habitat, neither plant particularly needs any sort of rest, although, as with most orchids, when not in active growth, both water and fertilizer should be lessened if not withheld. *Den. victoria-reginae*, with its white blooms richly veined in blue, is the more desirable of the two, but can be the more difficult to grow. While *Den. gonzalesii* is far easier for the hobbyist to cultivate, its flowers can lack the richness of hue of its cousin. Both are relatively compact. As the plants mature, plantlets will form on the aging canes, giving an unkempt appearance but tempered with more flowering potential.

The closely related Den. gonzalesii *comes from the lower elevations of the Philippines and will grow in intermediate, even warm conditions.*

Dendrobiums **175**

DENDROBIUM LAWESII

More has been done with *Dendrobium lawesii* in the past few years than with almost any other of its group. Growth habit has improved. The range of flower color, formerly limited to vibrant purple, now includes cultivars that have emerged and been propagated that range from mauve, salmon, yellow, red, and white to orange. Some forms may be bicolored, and many will have white-tipped petals. The often-white lip forms a clear target for pollinators. From a plant that until recently was relatively seldom seen, originating from a remote area of Papua New Guinea, this species has become a relatively widely grown and highly appreciated horticultural subject. In its mossy, shady habitat, plants may often be seen growing from the underneath of overhanging limbs, resulting in a species that does not appreciate overstrong light conditions. Unlike many dendrobiums, *Den. lawesii* should be kept evenly moist most of the year, with a slight lessening of watering when plants are least active.

Den. lawesii has other agreeable habits, chief among which is its very compact growth. The slender upright pseudobulbs have persistent leaves, which are only shed after several years, and the older canes continue to produce clusters of up to eight brightly colored blooms over a period of some years. A very nice plant can be accommodated in a relatively small pot, especially as, like most dendrobiums, oversized pots are not recommended and can cause a decline in the plants health. It is imperative to always size the pot for the size of the root mass, underpotting rather than overpotting. In this way, the grower can give plants the frequent waterings they prefer without danger of allowing conditions to get soggy or sodden. Additionally, the mix in underpotted plants does not seem to decompose quite as quickly as it otherwise might under high humidity, high moisture conditions. The grower needn't fear repotting back into a similarly sized pot.

Opposite: *The curious lip of* Den. lawesii *have a demon-like appearance in close-up.*

Den. lawesii *is a variable species with flowers in colors ranging from pink through red to purple and orange.*

DENDROBIUM OBTUSISEPALUM

Of all the many recent and relatively recent *Dendrobium* introductions from the remote Papua New Guinea highlands, none has been more spectacular than *Den. obtusisepalum*, the "Candy Corn Stealth Bomber." What an odd name for such a fabulous plant, yet how appropriate. The colors are certainly those of the old Halloween favorite, candy corn, rich orange with a thick yellow stipe along the base of the sepals. And of what else would the shape remind one but a delta-winged stealth bomber! I remember the first time I saw this plant in the flesh—it was one of the most staggering moments of my orchid career. The fifteen-inch-tall plant—they can reach over thirty inches tall at maturity—held clusters of the one-and-a-half to two-inch blooms throughout the framework of canes and was simply astonishing.

The first plants imported seem to have come through Japan, although seedling flasks of select siblings were quickly in domestic production. The mother plant, which I first saw, went to the Japan Grand Prix International Orchid Festival in the hopes of garnering the coveted, for the sheer monetary value, Grand Champion. Surely another plant as profusely flowered to perfection as this one was could not be. But the Japanese are master growers, and the prize is on their home turf. Little surprise then that the American plant was not even among the top three largest of those displayed! Growers seem to have little trouble with this species under conditions that suit its other relatives, that is, high humidity, moderate temperatures year-round, and even moisture. Mature plants can be a tangle of roots, canes, keikis, and flowers. What a great new species this is!

The large candy-corn flowers of Den. obtusisepalum *always elicit a gasp when seen in person for the first time.*

DENDROBIUM SMILLIAE

So far, the members of this type that we have seen are smaller growing and more suitable to areas with cooler temperatures. However, there are some perfectly good species that are extremely amenable to warmer climates and make a commensurately larger show. *Den. smilliae* could be called the "Fireworks Orchid." It is easy to see why. The strong-growing, leafy, upright canes often reach nearly forty inches and have been seen to grow much larger. Showy heads of many creamy blooms are flushed with rose. Individually, the tubular blooms have a very dark green "spot" as a target for pollinators. *Den. smilliae* comes from Northern Australia into New Guinea and is a lowland species, hence its more forgiving and adaptable nature. To do their best, plants require very strong light most of the year, with heavy watering and fertilizing during the summer months to approximate the seasonally available moisture of their habitat. A winter drying to the extent where plants lose a few leaves will ensure best flower production. As with many dendrobiums, older canes will continue to produce flowering heads for several years, long after the last leaves have fallen.

This type of larger orchid, adapted to some climatic extremes, makes an excellent patio subject in frost-free areas, where the flower heads may come just about any time of year, except winter. Experienced growers have noted how "tough" this species is, which compensates for the habit of dropping leaves after the first year.

Opposite: The watermelon-colored heads of flowers of Den. smilliae *make it a favorite display subject at spring orchid shows.*

Below: Den. smilliae *is found in low elevation areas of New Guinea and northeastern Australia. It prefers intermediate to warm conditions.*

DENDROBIUM BULLENIANUM (SYN. TOPAZIACUM)

This showy lowland species comes from near sea level in the Philippines, where it is subjected to high humidity and moderate to heavy rainfall all year. Between rain showers, light is brilliant through the clear air, only slightly mitigated by a thin canopy. As a result, this is a truly tropical subject that will not do well under windowsill or artificial light conditions. However, it is a favorite in warmer summer areas like South Florida, where it is grown outdoors, enjoying the frequent rain and strong light. The upright canes can reach twenty-four inches under ideal circumstance, though somewhat less is more common. The leaves are deciduous on mature canes, and the clusters of two to three dozen blooms come from nodes along the tops of the stems. Flowers are waxy yellow and often have darker red to amber stripes for a stunning color combination.

A drawback to this and others of its type is the habit of newer canes emerging around the base of the previous year's growth—which on young plants is often smaller—and eclipsing the flower clusters that are produced down in what has become the center of the plant. As plants mature, this becomes less of a problem, especially as the older canes continue to produce flower clusters for a period of some years, adding to the floral display year by year. *Dendrobium bullenianum* has proven to be another excellent patio orchid in warm summer climates and gives satisfactory performance for a long time with minimal care.

Left: Den. bullenianum *is still known by many as* Den. topaziacum.

Right: Flowers of Den. Builenianum *can range from yellow to vibrant orange and have attractive red striping. Many of the dendrobiums in this color range are thought to be pollinated by tropical hummingbirds.*

DENDROBIUM GOLDSCHMIDTIANUM (SYN. MIYAKEI)

Originally collected in both Taiwan (then Formosa) and the Philippines at mid-elevations of around a thousand feet, some authors consider *Dendrobium goldschmidtianum* to be a mystery species, preferring instead to go with *Den. miyakei*. It is as *Den. miyakei*, of course, that this species is well known and loved. As the habitat is usually cloudy, and moisture is constant with some slackening in midwinter, plants do best if kept shadier than most similar types and moist year-round, with a bit of drying when growth is mature. Slender canes are deciduous and range from as little as twelve to over thirty-six inches. Growth can be upright, or, under the weight of the stems, pendant. The bright purple to magenta blooms are often striped with darker color, giving a wonderful display of clusters along the bare canes. As with so many similar species, the clusters appear along both old and new canes.

While the climate of its habitat would not seem to indicate such, growers report that a winter rest, particularly in cooler climates with dull days, may help to initiate better flowering. In warm summer areas, this may occur naturally as the hurricane season passes and drier, brighter conditions ripen the canes nicely. Like most dendrobiums, *Den. goldschmidtianum* does not tolerate stale

Left: Den. goldschmidtianum, *also known as* Den. miyakei, *usually has a drop of sweet nectar at the base of the flower column. Although probably bird-pollinated in nature, we have seen honeybees attracted to the flowers in our Florida garden.*

Below: The flower color of Den. goldschmidtianum *can range from dusty pink to bright fuchsia. A low elevation species, it is well suited to temperatures from intermediate to warm.*

conditions at the roots. For this reason, and because the canes will almost always eventually become pendant, a mount—where humidity can be kept high—or a smallish, slatted basket that can be hung gives the best results, both for culture and display.

DENDROBIUM BRACTEOSUM

The high elevation dendrobiums from Papua New Guinea are among the most desired in the world. Unfortunately, they are rare and can be very difficult to cultivate in many warmer areas. *Den. bracteosum* is a low-elevation orchid found from sea level to two hundred feet or so, with most of the sought-after characteristics of its higher-elevation cousins. And thanks to a prominent Hawaiian nursery, we now have good availability of both the standard brilliant rose to red forms as well as the distinctive alba variety. Flowers are somewhat variable in color, ranging from white to greenish, to yellow, rose, purple, and red. Plants stay compact, with slender upright canelike pseudobulbs, usually less than twenty inches in length. Glossy green leaves are deciduous on bulb maturity, revealing the node-borne clusters of smallish blooms subtended by showy bracts. A well-grown plant can literally be covered with flowers, although to a greater extent than with *Den. bullenianum*, the encircling newer leads may eclipse the older smaller canes where flowers occur. Once the plants become well established, this is of little consequence, as the older canes continue to produce flowers in the autumn over a period of some years. *Den. bracteosum* shares with its higher-elevation cousins the characteristic most loved by growers: flowers seem to last forever in perfection, up to six months or more. As a result, for patio basket culture in warm summer areas, this member of the Pedilonum type is an outstanding candidate for both hobbyists and commercial growers.

Opposite: Most species in the Pedilonum section of the genus Dendrobium bloom in the spring, and the flowers last for about a week. Den. bracteosum blooms during the hottest part of the summer, and the paper-thin flowers can last for well over a month.

Above: The flower color of Den. bracteosum ranges from light pink, though deep fuchsia to white.

PAPHIOPEDILUMS

No one can deny that paphiopedilums, also known as paphs and popularly known as slipper orchids, are an acquired taste.

Not everyone appreciates the sexual nature of the flowers, the sometimes melancholic color combinations, or the unmitigated weirdness that some impart. On the other hand, no other group of orchids has quite the rabid following as paphiopedilums, nor do any other orchids command the same exorbitant prices, often well into five figures. There has been a great deal of debate as to why this is. Two contributing factors are certainly that neither the hybrids nor the species can boast of uniformly high quality, making good examples rare. In concert with this goes the current impossibility of reliably cloning the best plants, as can be done in most other orchid genera, so high quality material stays rare. However, a good paphiopedilum retains its value, as shown by such plants as *Paphiopedilum rothschildianum*. Even though seed-raised populations are relatively common today, high-quality plants still command prices starting at thousands of dollars.

Until quite recently, the true habitat of *Paph. rothschildianum* was in essence unknown. Roughly thirty years ago, and coinciding with the first large-scale seed populations coming to market, it was rediscovered on Mt. Kinabalu in Borneo and plants began to be illegally collected from the wild. Despite being a gamble as to flower quality, they commanded very high prices if only because they were so very illegal. Indeed, the slow growth and reluctance to flower of some of the originally collected plants led to the equally slow growth and poor flowering of most of the early hybrids. Today, thanks to the contribution of a few of the wild-collected plants and thoughtful use of existing cultivars, plants of this stately species grow reasonably quickly and well, flowering from seed in an acceptable length of time (under ten years). Recent *Paph. rothschildianum* hybrids are showing the same promise.

Paph. *Prince Edward of York 'Everglades' HCC/AOS* (Paph. roth-schildianum x Paph. sanderianum) *is one of the popular hybrids of* Paph. rothschildianum. *The influence of the* Paph. sanderianum *parent is evident in the long, twisted petals.*

PAPHIOPEDILUM SANDER'S PRIDE & PAPHIOPEDILUM PAUL PARKS

The mystery "twin" of *Paphiopedilum rothschildianum* is *Paph. sanderianum*, whose habitat was also lost until quite recently. However, unlike *Paph. rothschildianum*, we had only illustrations of *Paph. sanderianum* and its few hybrids to remind us of its long-

petalled glory. For *Paph. sanderianum* is truly the stuff of legends. It has the longest petals of any orchid, reaching an amazing thirty-six inches in some superior clones. The first plants out of the newly discovered habitat were particularly sought after, also because they were classified as an endangered species and a risk as well as a promise. The first of these species to flower in cultivation caused a

sensation; they were every bit as spectacular as the early botanical prints led us to believe. Hybrids were made, or remade, as the case more truly is, of past crosses that existed only on paper. These, too, were eagerly awaited and coveted.

Paph. Prince Edward of York (*sanderianum* x *rothschildianum*), *Paph.* Sander's Pride (*sanderianum* x *stonei*) and *Paph.* Michael Koopowitz (*sanderianum* x *philippenense*) were among the first to bloom. When introduced, they created an uproar among cognoscenti, and prices were outrageously high. As time went on, more and more of the hybrids began to reach market, while *Paph. sanderianum* itself, although also raised from seed, remained rare because of difficulties with the successful culture of the seedlings. In retrospect, it can fairly be said that, when compared with the hybrids bred from its "twin" *Paph. rothschildianum*, *Paph. sanderianum* hybrids have been a bit of a disappointment. They lack the vibrant color and "snap" of a good *Paph. rothschildianum* hybrid, and some growers have found themselves with expensive plants they couldn't resell for enough to recoup their costs.

Above left: Paph. *Sanders Pride 'Belle Glade' AM/AOS.*

Right: The dominance of Paph. sanderianum *has been used to produce hybrids with petals than can reach a foot or longer.* Paph. *Paul Parks 'Krull-Smith' AM/AOS (*Paph. adductum x Paph. sanderianum*) is a recent hybrid exploiting this trait.*

PAPHIOPEDILUM WIERTZIANUM & PAPHIOPEDILUM JAN RAGAN

Both the staying power of older *Paphiopedilum rothschildianum* hybrids and the continuing rush to make more, are living testaments to the true "King" of paphiopedilums. Although some of the older hybrids can still be difficult to bloom, when they do produce flowers, as shown by *Paph.* Wiertzianum (*rothschildianum* x *lawrenceanum*), they are majestic. The lightly checkered foliage is an added attraction stemming from the *Paph. lawrenceanum* parent. Happily, many of these older hybrids have been remade with newer, more floriferous and faster-growing *Paph. rothschildianum* plants, so the only reasonable objection to growing them will soon fade.

What will the future hold for *Paph. sanderianum* hybrids? The paucity of flowering plants of the species in general circulation will mitigate against any run-up in numbers of hybrids being made. But, in a larger sense, will it prove to have value beyond mere novelty? The new hybrid, *Paph.* Jan Ragan offers some clues. It is a hybrid of *Paph.* St. Swithin (*rothschildianum* x *philippenense*), arguably the best overall *Paph. rothschildianum* hybrid, crossed with *Paph.* Michael Koopowitz (*sanderianum* x *philippenense*), also one of the finest of its type. *Paph.* Jan Ragan is a fine example with massive character that will surely draw attention. But is it the *Paph. rothschildianum*, *Paph.*

sanderianum, or *Paph. philippenense* that makes it what it is? Two doses of *Paph. philippenense* can make any hybrid good, some might say.

Above: Paph. *Jan Ragan 'Crystelle' AM/AOS.*

Opposite: Paph. *Wiertzianum 'Ken' HCC/AOS.*

PAPHIOPEDILUM DELROSI & PAPHIOPEDILUM LYRO SUNCATCHER

The majestic elegance of multiflora paphs, species, or hybrids, is impossible to deny. Yet there are always breeders who are looking for something with different color, different form, or simply different. An avenue often pursued is the crossing of multifloras, especially *Paphiopedilum rothschildianum* and its hybrids, with the fuller-formed Brachypetalums like *Paph. bellatulum* or *Paph. godefroyae*, or with the Parvisepalums best represented by *Paph. delenatii* and the new *Paph. micranthum*.

Paph. Delrosi (*rothschildianum* x *delenatii*), in shades of pink and white on tall stems, is one of the most beautiful of all paphiopedilums. It may also be one of the most widely remade, in different forms with different cultivars of the two parents. Unfortunately, it can also be among the most recalcitrant to bloom. Many growers have never seen one in flower in person, though

many have tried. If a secret to blooming this fine hybrid has been discovered, it has yet to be publicized, and the chance occasional blooming simply whets the appetite. In the future, we may see easier-to-bloom populations using some of the more modern *Paph. rothschildianums*.

Thoughtful breeders also breed with *Paph. rothschildianum* hybrids. However, there is the same gamble of breeding with *rothschildianum* itself, insofar as blooming goes. We can be grateful when we see something the quality of *Paph.* Lyro Suncatcher (St. Swithin x James Bacon), a near primary Brachypetalum hybrid of *godefroyae* and Conco-bellatulum). This flower has so much of what is desired in this type that the prospect of easier-blooming members of this particular line of breeding is eagerly anticipated.

Above right: Paph. *Delrosi 'T.O.P. Choice' AM/AOS uses the beautiful species,* Paph. delenatii *to create a delicately colored hybrid with the stately influence of* Paph. rothschildianum.

Right: Paph. *Suncatcher 'T.O.P. Choice' AM/AOS.*

PAPHIOPEDILUM MEM. LARRY HEUER

As trade opened up with Vietnam and China, horticulturists waited with baited breath for the wonders to be introduced from these countries that were previously out of bounds. What would be the beauty to come out of what should be prime orchid habitat? First were the Chinese paphs, brought to market by herb collectors and exported to a waiting world. The earliest to flower, *Paphiopedilum armeniacum*, was a miracle of brilliant yellow, with size and form far beyond what anyone had seen or hoped to see. It was a quantum leap in beautiful slipper orchids. I was a judge on the team that awarded the FCC/AOS to the first to be exhibited in the United States. Many have argued about it since, but I stand behind the award, deserved simply for its incredible beauty.

As more and more new species made their way into the Western World, hybrids were inevitable. Among the first to bloom was a fine cross of the large green *Paph. malipoense* with the china white *Paph. emersonii*. As in the earliest days of hybridizing, when little was known about the genetics of orchids, growers waited anxiously for each flowering, so as to enable them to begin assessment of the strong and weak points of these late arrivals. In the case of *Paph.* Memoria Larry Heuer, the result was not so surprising, being intermediate between the two parents as is expected of primary hybrids. What was a happy and unexpected result was the hybrid vigor that resulted in robust plants and flowers nearly exceeding the size of either parent.

The soft colors of both parents create the watercolor subleties of Paph. Mem. Larry Heuer 'T.O.P. Choice' HCC/AOS.

PAPHIOPEDILUM FANATICUM

In nature, when populations of two related species overlap, there is potential for natural hybrids to result. Flowers appear that do not quite match either species. Often, these are named as entirely new species, simply by overeager taxonomists who want to see their names in print. Usually, though, cooler heads eventually prevail, and the hybrid nature of the "new" species becomes accepted. However, until someone actually remakes the putative hybrid and proves by flowering similar results in the artificial remake, the origin of such hybrids remains speculation. Two of the most "fanatic" slipper growers did just that, remade the hybrid of *Paphiopedilum malipoense* with *Paph. micranthum*, thereby proving the hybrid nature of the naturally occurring plants. In orchids, such hybrids are still registered with the International Registration Authority but are differentiated from the natural hybrid by being capitalized: *Paph.* Fanaticum for the artificial hybrid versus *Paph. xfanaticum* for the naturally occurring hybrid. An alternate method for proving the hybrid nature of an orchid is to self-pollinate the flower. If the plant is indeed a species, the flowers will come true from seed; if not, the progeny will assort themselves in the classic Mendelian 1:2:1 ratio. That is, overall in the population, one part will look like one parent, two parts will look like the hybrid, and the last part of four will most resemble the other parent.

Primary hybrids utilizing the Chinese paphs have a lot to offer to the home grower. Their foliage is simply fabulous, richly marbled and patterned, and is not too large for the average windowsill. The flowers are generally borne on strong, not-too-tall stems, and the color combinations are exotic and unusual. Additionally, they have a splendid hybrid vigor that often renders them easier to grow and flower than either parent. Some are even fragrant, which is rare to the extreme for slipper orchids. Almost all will grow happily in a standard paph mix (whichever you happen to prefer) in a relatively small pot and, if kept evenly moist in a fresh mix, will be among the more rewarding plants in your collection, even when not in flower, thanks to the lovely foliage.

Paph. *Fanaticum 'Crystelle' AM/AOS shows the soft "puffy" lip of both parents as well as beautiful netting on the petals.*

PAPHIOPEDILUM MAGIC LANTERN

Paph. *Magic Lantern is one of the most successful hybrids of recent years and has received dozens of awards. A fine example is* Paph. *Magic Lantern 'T.O.P. Dream' AM/AOS, which is commended for its rich color and full, symmetrical shape.*

Every so often a hybrid comes along that simply works, that has everything. In slippers, *Paphiopedilum* Maudiae, *Paph.* St. Swithin, and *Paph.* Vanda M. Pearman come to mind as exemplary of fine, timeless horticultural subjects. When one of these hybrids appears, it is often so fine, so far ahead of others of its type, that standards need to be rewritten. Judges and growers alike are taken by surprise, rewarding what later turn out to be average cultivars with high awards and higher prices. *Paph.* Magic Lantern (*delenatii* x *micranthum*) is just such an orchid.

Plants are exceptionally beautiful and vigorous, with jewel-like foliage marbled and patterned with checkerboard markings. The flowers have the best of both parents, glowing soft pink offset by a deeper pink tessellation and a shapely bowl-like lip of solid pink. Shape and texture are exceptional, with the texture being almost like velvet: soft and lustrous. The hybrid has been made many times by many breeders, and some versions are better than others. Some crosses out of Japan have been particularly fine and uniform. As more and more of the parent species are flowered from wild-collected plants, surely more exceptional progeny will result and we can expect a long life for the popularity and appeal of *Paph.* Magic Lantern—it even has a catchy name.

Above: Paph. *Magic Lantern 'Everglades' AM/AOS*.   Below: Paph. *Magic Lantern 'T.O.P. Light' AM/AOS*.

It is important to note that in slippers, as in other horticultural subjects, success is not just measured by the popularity of the moment. Plants that stand the test of time in collections and in the marketplace are those that will endure. Unfortunately such plants are all too rare, especially in paphs, where meristemming (cloning) is not possible and exact parents may not survive to remake a given good version of a hybrid. Indeed, paph fanatics have, in general, not proven to be driven by anything more than a desire to see something new, something superior. The intentional remaking of proven hybrids is rarely practiced in paphs nor orchids in general for that matter. Rather, the experimental is far more attractive to the passionate orchidist. Is it any wonder that orchids have been so slow to catch on with gardeners?

Paphiopedilums **201**

PAPHIOPEDILUM BELLATULUM ALBUM

There are many ways an orchid can achieve legendary status. Beauty, rarity, size, bizarre character, market acceptance, and others are among the "status makers." Some orchids achieve their status by a combination of factors. In the case of *Paphiopedilum bellatulum* Album, it is a legend because it is both rare and beautiful. Unfortunately, it is rare because so few can keep this species alive for any length of time. Plants are horribly expensive, and the risk is great, because even a standard spotted *Paph. bellatulum* often seems to have an incurable death wish, dying slowly or quickly, but dying just the same. Aberrant color forms, such as white albums, are that way from population isolation and the resultant inbreeding. Good characteristics are passed along with bad, and the negative aspects often manifest as poor vigor. Recently, which in terms of paphiopedilums means in the last twenty years or so, assiduous breeding has led to a population of this sublimely beautiful species that seems to grow, at least for a while, for the experienced grower. *Paph. bellatulum* needs to be kept warm, but not too warm; moist, but not too moist; in a small pot in a fair amount of shade. Sound inexact? It is. The culture of this species is truly mastered by few. For this reason, it is also of a class of orchids that people seem to love to buy, fairly secure in the knowledge that they are going to "kill another one." The chances are against their success, but they are always trying. Happily, the same growers who worked toward developing growable Album forms are breeding more vigorous standard members of the species. So, in the future, there will be another reason for hobbyist growers to make another attempt, by buying a responsibly propagated plant.

Paph. bellatum *Album 'J.E.M.' AM/AOS represents a rarely seen color form of the species. It received a high award for its pristine beauty.*

PAPHIOPEDILUM FRANCISCO FREIRE

Primary hybrids (species crossed with species) are made for many different reasons, ranging from "they were both in flower at the same time" to the effort to impart good qualities from a more difficult subject to an easier one. *Paphiopedilum godefroyae*, related to *Paph. bellatulum*, is only marginally less difficult to grow though every bit as round and beautiful. *Paph. sukhakulii*, the other parent of *Paph.* Francisco Freire, is more distantly related but has extreme vigor and is known for imparting this vigor as well as exceptionally broad petals. Not so long ago, *Paph. sukhakulii* was the high-priced "new kid on the block" but today has been extensively propagated from seed, reaching a very high pinnacle of success. *Paph.* Francisco Freire is a happy mix of both parents and maintains the good vigor so desired in *Paph. sukhakulii* progeny. With such hybrids, less experienced growers can have the "look" of a more difficult species without sacrificing its ability to thrive. Primary hybrids usually have the charming species "look" about them that is so attractive to species lovers, as opposed to more complex hybrids that may be shunned by some for their artificial appearance.

The textural details of Paph. *Francisco Freire 'T.O.P. Shelf' AM/AOS add interest to the pleasing form and subtle coloration.*

THE MAUDIAE PAPHIOPEDILUMS:
PAPHIOPEDILUM BOB NAGEL

Over the years, countless words have been written singing the praises of an orchid that has truly transcended time, the *Paphiopedilum* Maudiae (*callosum* x *lawrenceanum*). If the breeder, who first registered this hybrid in 1900, could have only known the impact this plant, in its dozens (hundreds?) of iterations, what might he have done differently? What, in those distant days, could he have done? Plant patents at that time were a thing of the far future; even now they are still in their infancy for orchids, despite breeders' success with roses and other horticultural subjects. The same can be said about trademarks. The parents were in wide circulation, so exclusivity was not an option. For better or worse, the same questions confront today's breeders. If they know how they are about to affect orchid development, how can they effectively capitalize on their success?

Paph. Maudiae was originally made in the alba form: greens and whites. The good-sized, attractively formed blooms were proudly held above strikingly marbled foliage and were exceptionally long lasting. The best of the type have made great cut-flowers for nearly a century. But it was as a subject for flowering potted plants that their greatest success would be seen. There is simply no other orchid that can match a potful of *Paph.* Maudiae or one of its many hybrids as a stunning display plant. The foliage is lovely and decorative year-round. The flowers are long lasting—two months is not out of the question—and often appear more than once a year. Nor have breeders stood still in the production of "improved" Maudiaes. *Paph. sukhakulii* has broad, horizontally held petals, and *Paph.* Bob Nagel is a wonderful example of improving on perfection.

Paph. *Bob Nagle 'New Horizon' AM/AOS is a much improved* Paph. Maudiae–*type hybrid.*

PAPHIOPEDILUM BLACKLIGHT

It wasn't too long before a colored form of *Paphiopedilum* Maudiae appeared. These would be, by and large, similarly colored to their species parents, in tones of rose, mahogany, and white, and known as Coloratum. There would be cultivars that would set the standard for this type, much as there were in the green range. Two well-known examples from the early days were *Paph.* Maudiae Coloratum FCC/RHS and 'Los Osos' AM/AOS. No other cultivar name would be given to early award winners beyond their award designation, and FCC/RHS remains in cultivation as an example of an extraordinarily large representative of the type. However, 'Los Osos' AM/AOS, thought to originate from an English collection, is still a standard by which the quality of Coloratum types are judged. Large, with especially rich coloration and a flat, broad dorsal sepal, it has retained its value for many years.

In the late 1960s, a new type of *Paph. callosum* entered the scene, probably from Germany. In 1969, *Paph. callosum* 'Sparkling Burgundy' received its FCC/AOS as an entirely unique, wine-colored variety of the species. Unfortunately, it was as hard to grow as it was beautiful, remaining rare to this day, if it is even still alive. The first round of progeny began to be offered in the 1970s, and no one could have foretold that a revolution was afoot. Joined by the similarly dark *Paph. callosum* 'JAC' AM/AOS, a new kind of Maudiae type bloomed and came to be designated as vinicolor, "wine colored." These were, and still are, a sensation. Breeders rushed to obtain plants to enjoy and with which to breed. One plant, *Paph.* Maudiae 'Diamond Jubilee' FCC/AOS, was touted as the $50,000 orchid. As breeding continued through several generations of color concentration and out-crossing to other species, distinctive results like *Paph.* Blacklight appeared. Are black orchids possible? Are they attractive? Are they any more than curiosities? You be the judge.

Vinicolor Paph. hybrids have their own following of collectors who prize them for their rich color and round dorsal sepal. Paph. Blacklight 'J.E.M.' AM/AOS demonstrates these qualities.

PAPHIOPEDILUM MYITKYINA

Dark red Maudiae types had, of course, been a goal since the inception of hybridizing. Indeed, the first artificially produced hybrid slipper, *Paphiopedilum* Harrisianum (*villosum* x *barbatum*), received its First Class Certificate from the Royal Horticultural Society in 1869. What age can orchids attain? No one really knows, but *Paph.* Harrisianum, divisions from the original plant, is still in cultivation today. The rich coloration and vigor of this cultivar continue to be paragons for breeders to strive toward. *Paph.* Redstart, another seminal red breeding clone and an unknown hybrid thought to stem from *Paph.* Bingleyense, is also presently in cultivation and used for breeding.

What is the significance of all this? If one is to look closely at *Paph.* Myitkina (Maudiae x Redstart), first registered in 1943, one cannot help but see a slightly darker version of *Paph.* Harrisianum.

This particular iteration was bred using a modern vinicolor Maudiae and was exhibited by the modern version of an old-time English nursery, but have we really come so far? In a way, it is comforting to know that old standards still hold true, but it could as easily be said that orchid judges, too swayed by novelty, simply did not see or realize the historical link. Certainly there are hybrids from the early days of breeding—Charlesworth's *Odontoglossum crispum* and hybrids come to mind—that modern breeders would give a great deal to have. But when a "modern" hybrid simply reaches a previous level, should recognition follow? There is no arguing the beauty of such flowers, and the market will measure their desirability, but a true advance in standards must have history as its judge.

Paph. *Myitkyina 'Midnight' AM/AOS. As hybrids improve and flower size and substance increase, stems are not always adequate to support the flower and need staking at least during bud development and for transport to judging.*

PAPHIOPEDILUM SATCHEL PAIGE & PAPHIOPEDILUM PETULA

The purpose of the introduction of a species orchid into hybrid breeding is, obviously, to take advantage of very specific characteristics. *Paphiopedilum sukhakulii* is valued for its flower carriage as well as the broad, horizontally held petals. The species' petals are also heavily warted with black, and these "warts" can coalesce in its hybrids to form the appearance of nearly solid black. It is so black that light seems to fall into the petals, with no reflection or sheen, and the novelty value is inarguable.

Another of *Paph. sukhakulii*'s valued traits is the tendency to give plants that grow freely and routinely produce multiple leads, which results in multiple flowers at any given time. The closely related and somewhat more rare *Paph. wardii* can give the same

results, though the flowers are often not of the immense size imparted by *Paph. sukhakulii*.

Paph. Satchel Paige (*wardii* x Vintner's Treasure) was one of the first to be seen of newer *Paph. wardii* hybrids. *Paph.* Vintner's Treasure was one of the very first hybrids to bloom from *Paph. callosum* 'Sparkling Burgundy' and, along with the vinicolor *Paph.* Maudiae, has figured in dozens of new hybrids. The flowers bred from *Paph.* Vintner's Treasure are often slightly smaller than when Maudiae is used, but the intensity of color is just as often greater. *Paph.* Satchel Paige is among the darkest flowers of this type yet seen. Comparing this with an individual of the similar *Paph.* Petula (*wardii* x Maudiae) is unfair, because there are certainly plants of *Paph.* Petula with greater depth of color. However, this particular *Paph.* Petula does amply demonstrate the potential display one can attain with a little patience.

Left: The almost black petals of Paph. Satchel Paige 'Janet' AM/AOS *caught the judges' attention.*

Right: Paph. Petula 'Ponkan' CCM/AOS *demonstrates the beauty of a well-grown orchid.*

PAPHIOPEDILUM TRYON

Today we have a wide range of Maudiae types incorporating the best of new forms of species combined with the finest breeding from yesteryear. In perhaps no other group have the older breeding clones persevered to the same extent as in paphiopedilums. Despite the fact that paphs are not always the easiest to grow, and despite the vicissitudes of more than a century of cultivation, the ups and downs, the wars, and the deaths and disinterest of owners, these plants have endured. The novelty of such advanced "species-like" breeding has grown in popularity to eclipse other types. The assiduous combination and recombination of species' influence gives us flowers like *Paph*. Tryon that has been influenced both on and below the surface. In the end, however, exactly what species influences which trait is academic to most and cared about by even fewer. What really matters is the beauty of the flower, its lasting quality, market appeal, and vigor of growth. For, as popular as paphs might seem to those who love them, or to those who follow the awards system, they remain a fairly minor group in the larger marketplace.

Paph. *Tryon 'Mendenhall' AM/AOS.*

BULLDOGS OF THE ORCHID WORLD

In almost direct opposition to the continuing love of the "species-like" look of the maudiae types are the standard paphs, or "bulldogs." Long known as standard paphs because they were so much more popular and developed to such a high degree of perfection, what set them apart was their sheer difference from the species with which they originated. Early breeders were clearly operating mostly in the dark when it came to genetics.

Nevertheless, they knew a superior flower when they saw one. *Paphiopedilum insigne* 'Harefield Hall', now known to be a naturally occurring chance polyploid, not only created a sensation in and of itself (I still consider it to be one of the best of all orchid species) but also proved to be the entrée into polyploid improvements in the creation of bigger and rounder slipper flowers. Interest in the bulldogs waxes and wanes to the extent that when the public

Paph. *(Hoopla x Mazalin)* 'Chilton' HCC/AOS.

wakes up to the many fine qualities of the type, breeders are caught with low supplies and cannot meet the demand.

There have always been, and probably will always be, those who swim against the tide and breed to their own agenda. These breeders continue to make and grow hybrids, even when the public has to be convinced to buy them. They quietly continue to advance the cause. Today there is another periodic upswing in the popularity of bulldog paphs. Some growers are prepared and have the proven breeding programs—or the simple good luck—to supply this demand. Big, round, spotted, and heavy, the appeal of a standard paph never diminishes for some and is rediscovered by the many, to their delight.

Paph. (Valwin x Buena Bay) 'Penny' HCC/AOS

PAPHIOPEDILUM MYSTIC KNIGHT

Persistence is nearly as important as luck in the creation of new types. *Paphiopedilum* breeders need both. When something new appears, something that could be a stepping-stone to the creation of a truly superior population of a desired color range, good observational powers must be coupled with just a bit of courage. All these factors came into play when *Paphiopedilum* White Knight burst onto the scene some years ago. White standard paphs of the quality of other colors in the type had been but a dream to many breeders. *Paph*. F.C. Puddle was a good parent, but progenies were small-flowered and seed was not always easy to obtain. *Paph*. White Knight is not only a good flower in its own right but also gives copious seed and breeds on to produce populations of reliably white progeny of high average quality. The originator of this plant has been able to answer some of the hypothetical questions that could have been posed to the originator of *Paph*. Maudiae. How to capitalize on the success of a new type? If you have developed something new, from parents you hold, and have exclusive use of the proven best breeder, you may charge whatever the market will bear. In the case of slippers, it will bear quite a lot.

Paph. Mystic Knight (White Knight x Elfstone) is an outstanding example of this breeding line. Additionally, it utilizes another breeding line developed by the same breeder for large green flowers. When large green standard paphs—often with a broad white border to the dorsal sepal—are crossed with proven white parents, some of the very best overall results are obtained. Have these types reached a point where they are available to the everyday grower? Not yet, but with the average generational time for orchids shrinking all the time thanks to improving technology and technique, it is only a matter of time. With paphs, patience is not only a virtue, it is a necessity.

Even non-fanciers of the type cannot help but admire Paph. *Mystic Knight 'Florida Snow' AM/AOS for its near perfection of form and subtle coloration.*

PHRAGMIPEDIUMS

Slipper orchids, as an entirety, are very cosmopolitan. They occur in both subtropical and temperate zones, at sea level and in the mountains, in bogs, fields, forests, and mountainsides.

The temperate zone cypripediums are well known to wildflower lovers as inhabitants of bogs and fields but are unfortunately rather difficult to cultivate as a group. Paphiopedilums, the tropical Asiatic Slippers, are the most important group to horticulture. However, we cannot ignore the New World Slippers, the phragmipediums. These water-loving plants often grow where moisture is nearly constant, such as in or near flowing streams. As such, they need constant moisture in cultivation and are very intolerant of hard water. Indeed, some of the best growers recommend that plants actually sit in pans of water, which is a distinct "never" in most types of orchid culture.

If there is a reason why this group has never been as popular with the orchid growing public as have their Asiatic cousins, it is their often-subdued colors and general "sameness" of flower shape and appearance. A closer look, though, readily demonstrates that this is simply not the case. The great majority of the most commonly cultivated phrags are "classics" and are based on a relatively small group of species. However, they are "classics" because they have endured, and some have been constantly grown for many decades. A more recent hybrid, *Phrag.* Sorcerer's Apprentice (*longifolium* x *sargentianum*), is what a "typical" hybrid phrag can look like. Exotically shaped blooms appear in mossy shades of green, brown, and rose, successively along a tall inflorescence over a period of months. This longevity of bloom along with the glossy green foliage is what attracts growers to these plants—they stay in bloom for months on end and remain attractive even when not blooming.

Phrag. *Sorcerer's Apprentice 'Caldwell' HCC/AOS. Most new world slipper orchids have different cultural requirements than their old world counterparts and must be kept evenly moist at all times.*

PHRAGMIPEDIUM GRANDE & PHRAGMIPEDIUM PENNS CREEK CASCADE

Before the rediscovery of *Paphiopedilum sanderianum* wrested its title of longest-petalled slipper, *Phragmipedium caudatum* and its allied species were grown simply for their massive quality and exceptionally long petals. Their petals have the curious habit of reaching maximum elongation when and if their growth is uninterrupted by contact with a surface. In other words, if the petals hit something during their growth, they stop growing. *Phrag. caudatum* is a wonderful example of the paradox of water-loving orchids. Ample water is a must, but too much will lead to rot. Unless watering is coupled with good air circulation, the plants are too easily lost. *Phrag.* Grande (*longifolium* x *caudatum*) is probably the classic phrag, the plant most people associate with the genus and the plant they are most likely to have in their collection. The happy combination of features from both parents is the likely reason. The *Phrag. longifolium* parent adds vigor, compactness, and a successive flowering habit, while the *Phrag. caudatum* gives long petals and massive character. With the glossy green foliage underneath the moderately long stems of several immense, long-petalled beauties, it is easy to see the continuing popularity of this hybrid. Additionally, West Coast cymbidium growers find that this plant will do well outdoors with additional shade.

The occasional hybrid will come along in the attempt to unseat the reigning popularity king. *Phrag.* Penns Creek Cascade is a relatively recent hybrid of *Phrag.* Grande crossed with *Phrag. wallisii*, a near relative of *Phrag. caudatum*, the parent of *Phrag.* Grande. This is a happy marriage, giving very large blooms with all the character of the two long-petalled parents and the vigor of the *Phrag. longifolium* grandparent.

Opposite: Phrag. *Grande 'Krull Smith' AM/AOS is a good example of this long–popular hybrid.*

Below: Phrag. *Penns Creek Cascade 'Crownfox' AM/AOS.*

PHRAGMIPEDIUM BESSEAE, PHRAGMIPEDIUM JASON FISCHER & PHRAGMIPEDIUM NOIRMONT

There is nothing like the discovery of a new species, particularly one with yet unseen color, to jump-start interest in a neglected group. And it was the discovery in the later part of the twentieth century of *Phragmipedium besseae* that did just that for New World slippers. Even more exciting was the prospect of an entirely new range of colors that might result from the intense orange of *Phrag. besseae*. Much speculation centered on just why the species was not unearthed sooner. Perhaps the look was too common. Visitors to Machu Picchu in Peru often see dots of orange along the cliffs and crags in and around the various trails and temples of the monument. These are not *Phrag. besseae*, but a rather common begonia, whose color and flower presentation almost precisely mimic *Phrag. besseae*'s.

Primary *Phragmipedium* hybrids were often sterile, threatening further development of a

Right: Phrag. *Jason Fischer 'Miami Beach' FCC/AOS is yet another clone of the hybrid that has received a high award.*

Above opposite: Phrag. *Noirmont 'A-doribill' FCC/AOS.*

Below opposite: Phrag. besseae *opened a whole new palette of color to* Phragmipedium *breeders.*

line of hybrids including *Phrag. besseae*. Thanks to the artificial induction of polyploidy in several *Phrag. besseae* primary hybrids, notably *Phrag.* Eric Young (*besseae* x *longifolium*), we are now graced with an entirely new complex of orange-based *Phragmipedium* hybrids. The popularity of this type is abetted by orchid judges' love of orange, and the old racing adage of "win on Sunday, sell on Monday" is applied to the awarding of the many new *Phrag. besseae*–derived hybrids such as *Phrag.* Jason Fischer (*besseae* backcrossed to its hybrid with *sargentianum*) and *Phrag.* Noirmont (Eric Young backcrossed to its parent *longifolium*).

PHRAGMIPEDIUM ERIC YOUNG
& PHRAGMIPEDIUM SERGEANT ERIC

Another aspect of the success story of *Phragmipedium besseae* is its rapid deployment into European breeding. Growers of early *Phrag. besseae* hybrids found that the plants grew exceptionally rapidly, reaching flowering size in a fraction of the time expected of other slippers. Fast growth equals quicker bench turnaround, and this is the making of a new type of potted plant. The bright color and successive blooming over a period of weeks did not hurt the cause, either.

While these plants were strictly intended for potted-plant consumption in the huge market of the European Union, American growers were quick to seize the advantage and import these reasonably priced young plants for their waiting clients. The result was an unusually rapid saturation of the market for a new slipper. This did not stop either the Europeans, who continued to produce hybrids for their potted-plant market, nor did it really slow down U.S. activity in the group. However, a result may be that the limited market for slippers could lead to a lack of interest in orange tones and a decline in demand. Does this diminish the appeal of what is really quite a good orchid? For those who follow trends, the answer might be yes. But for the many people who simply want to grow an adaptable plant that easily bears beautiful, striking, and bright flowers, it could be the beginning of a new general horticultural type, as any surplus is siphoned off into garden centers and wider acceptance is encouraged.

Above right: Phrag. *Eric Young 'Ronald Lee' AM/AOS.*

Right: Phrag. *Sergeant Eric 'Mercerful' AM/AOS.*

MASDEVALLIAS

Higher-elevation plants often have to rely on birds for pollination. The elevation and attendant cooler temperatures make insects less active and, hence, less reliable as pollinators.

The brilliant coloring of the goblinlike flowers of Masd. veitchiana *serve to attract bird pollinators in the species' high elevation habitat.*

Birds, with their higher metabolic rate, are not as common as insects, so the flowers must be brightly colored and long lasting to ensure that a potential bird pollinator, when it happens by, is attracted. *Masdevallia veitchiana*, from the area around Machu Picchu in Peru, is an example of one of the very showiest of the genus. It also amply demonstrates the value of mimicry, since its color and shape suggests several other, more commonly seen, local flowers. *Masd. veitchiana* was once quite common around the ruins of Machu Picchu, and we can be sure that the original residents held it in high regard. Sadly, collectors have reduced it to the occasional sighting around Machu Picchu, where the plants that flower in the main season are quickly removed. However, there are areas where plants that flower in odd seasons still exist, and the dedicated observer, with the right guidance, can still experience the thrill of seeing a showy orchid in its natural habitat. I have seen flowers from some of these "hidden gems" that equal, if not surpass, long-cultivated clones such as 'Prince de Gaul' AM/AOS.

Because of their relatively compact size and brilliantly colored flowers, species like *Masd. veitchiana* and *Masd. ignea* from Colombia are highly prized

by orchid growers. Especially in cooler climates, plants thrive in semishade and easily produce good size clumps of upright leaves, resulting in a bounty of tall-stemmed blooms that last for weeks. Growers in cooler areas are even more drawn to these high-altitude types as the cost of energy makes the heating of a greenhouse more and more dear. Windowsill growers are equally happy with masdevallias for the same reasons.

Successful cultivation of high-elevation species such as Masd. ignea *requires a cool greenhouse that simulates a cloud forest.*

MASDEVALLIA HIRTZII
& MASDEVALLIA LIMAX

The flowers of masdevallias are relatively unusual for orchids, with the fused sepals making up the real show and petals and lip hidden deep inside the often tubular flower. The degree to which the flowers form a tube varies greatly from the open *Masd. veitchiana* to the more tubular *Masd. hirtzii* and the closely related *Masd. limax*. Tubular need not imply that the flowers are not showy. Quite the opposite: when flowers are as richly colored on the outside as on the inside, a fine display results. Both *Masd. hirtizii* and *Masd. limax* are good representatives of another great quality of many masdevallias: they grow to under six inches, but are prolific in their flowering.

While masdevallias have long been popular with growers, several events have conspired to make them both more widely grown. As the previously inaccessible high forest of South America became more widely explored in the latter part of the last century, amateur taxonomists and orchid lovers alike combed areas for new novelties. Many new species of masdevallia were uncovered on these expeditions and entered the literature, if not cultivation, as habitat information was lost or obscured to protect the new discoveries from predatory collectors. Some of the discoverers, though, had formed alliances with reliable, reputable nurseries back in the United States and shared small propagations with them so that they might attempt the production of seed-raised populations.

The flowers of Masd. hirtzii *clearly show the sepaline tails distinctive to the genus.*

Above right: Many of the smaller masdevallias are best appreciated when allowed to grow to specimen size. For these small plants, this generally means a four-to-five-inch pot.

Right: The closely related Masd. limax *is named for its fanciful resemblance to a slug.*

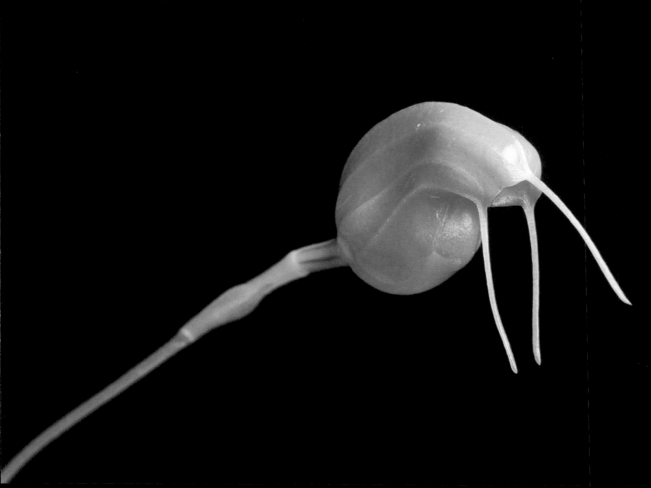

MASDEVALLIA TOVARENSIS
& MASDEVALLIA AGASTER

Not all masdevallias are orange. All colors are represented in the palette of this variable and widespread genus. Some, like *Masdevallia tovarensis*, have the happy characteristic of producing multiple flowers—up to five—on each inflorescence, which may then bloom again in ensuing years. *Masd. agaster*, with its multiple long-tailed blooms nestled in typical *Masdevallia* foliage, is less well known but clearly represents a desirable horticultural subject.

The size and variety of *Masdevallia* is a fascinating case study of evolution in action. In a fractured environment of soaring peaks and deep valleys, where each valley may harbor its own unique flora and fauna, orchids are forced to adapt to differing pollinators and selective pressures. While orchid seed may be carried far and

wide by the wind, unless there are appropriate pollinators where it ultimately lands and grows, it is a dead end. Plant groups with the ability to quickly change and adapt to such vicissitudes will survive, while others may not. Each valley or gorge may have its own unique group of orchids adapted to the available pollinators. On the one hand, the diversity gained in this way is a wonderful thing and fills the coffers of horticulture with a constantly changing array of new and different subjects. On the other hand, a plant that is stripped from such a limited habitat may not occur elsewhere and could be lost forever, or it may be found just over the next ridge. Responsible maintenance of existing cultivars of never-to-be-refound species is the only answer. A network of those willing to undertake their preservation through propagation has to be cultivated and preserved as well.

Above: Masd. agaster *is found in a very limited area of Ecuador at high elevations. During cool damp periods, faded flowers can become moldy, which can result in infection of the plant itself. Cutting off faded flowers is the best prevention. This applies to many of these species, which produce an abundance of bloom from the base of the plant.*

Left: Masdevallia tovarensis *has been sought by collectors since Victorian times. This cool-growing species is found in the coastal mountains of northern Venezuela near Colonia Tovar.*

MASDEVALLIA STROBELII,
MASDEVALLIA STRIATELLA
& MASDEVALLIA GLANDULOSA

This lovely trio of masdevallias shares little in common aside from their prolific habit and a preference for cooler conditions. *Masdevallia strobelii* is native to the Andes of Ecuador at elevations of five thousand feet or more and is notable for the hairy interior to its orange and white blooms. Because *Masd. striatella* is more widespread than many of its cousins, ranging from Costa Rica to Venezuela at moderate elevations, this rose-striped white beauty may prove to be more tolerant of a wider range of temperatures than many. *Masd. glandulosa* is named for the glistening glandular interior

of its richly colored, kite-tailed blooms. All three of these plants give a profusion of flowers on stems slightly shorter than the leaves, lending the impression of a collar of flowers around the foliage.

How can plants that come from so close to the steaming equator be so cool growing? Cool-growing orchids come from higher elevations near the equator, such as in the Andes, or, in the Old World, the Himalayas. As one ascends in altitude, it is like moving away from the equator. Thus, we can have orchids living at elevations approaching twelve thousand feet that, in cultivation,

Left: The fuzzy texture of Masd. strobelii adds interest to the flowers. Found in Ecuador at about 4,500 feet.

Right: Masd. striatella is found from Costa Rica to Venezuela at elevations between 1000–2400m. Its wide geographic and altitude ranges indicate that it may be tolerant of a wider range of conditions than its cooler-growing relatives.

require temperatures seen only in areas like Seattle.

Cool growing does not mean that temperatures must always be uncomfortable for people, though they may on occasion. Rather, cool-growing orchids are unused to extremely high temperatures, preferring more the even temperature regime given by their often cloudy, shady environment. It is quite difficult for residents of the southern United States to match these requirements. Also, plants from higher elevations tend to be constantly moist in their habitat, with roots immersed in moss kept damp by condensation and mist. This results in their intolerance of any sort of dissolved solids in their irrigation water. People living in arid areas of the Southwest, unless they have special water filtration, will also find difficulty with these plants. Temperatures will be tolerable, but their roots will not flourish if water quality is poor.

Found at moderate elevations in Peru, Masd. glandulosa is named for the warty appearance of the lip interior. The flowers can be slightly fragrant.

Above: Using a bit of imagination, one can see how Masd. salatrix is named for the Latin for "woman dancer." From high elevations near Medellin, Colombia.

Right: The goblinlike flowers of Masd. setacea can reach five inches tail-to-tail. This species was discovered in 1975 and is found in Ecuador, Colombia and Peru at high elevations.

MASDEVALLIA SETACEA, MASDEVALLIA SALTATRIX & MASDEVALLIA REGINA

Clowns, as most adults come to recognize, are not always happy and cheery. More often they are creepy, spooky, and more than a little scary. The clownlike faces of these masdevallias may evoke ghosts and nightmares. *Masdevallia setacea* has goblinlike blooms that can reach more than five inches from the tip of the dorsal sepal's tail to the ventral sepals. Ghostly white color is offset by a central reddish stripe. Plants are relatively small, often three inches or less. Hailing from higher elevations in Ecuador, this is another species that requires cool conditions. The gaping "mouth" of the tubular bloom of *Masd. saltatrix* is odder yet. Sepalline tails are held at the apexes of an equilateral triangle, adding to the bizarre nature of this curious species. Red color outlined in yellow heightens the illusion of something otherworldly. On the other hand, *Masd. regina* (Latin for "queen") is a stately bloom that can be exceptionally large when the vertically held tails are measured. In some cultivars, the tails are swept behind the flower, but in the best, the stance is entirely upright and tall.

It would be easy to get the impression that all masdevallias are somehow "pretty." But many are not and can best be described as odd. Yet collectors still prize them, searching out the most unusual, which may only be of value owing to their distinctive and different character.

Tail-to-tail, the flowers of Masd. regina *can exceed six inches. Described in 1988, this attractive species is found in Peru.*

MASDEVALLIA TIGER KISS & MASDEVALLIA AUREOPURPUREA

In any group of fast-growing floriferous plants there are bound to be attempts at hybridizing. In masdevallias, the attempts have been sporadic over the last century or so, not the least because not everyone can hit the hard-to-find "spot" to affect pollination. Nevertheless, the undeniable attraction of the group has led to a great many hybrids over the past few decades, not a few of them very successful and widely grown. Probably the best of these for overall horticultural interest has been *Masdevallia* Copper Angel (*veitchiana* x *triangularis*). Somehow, this combination has resulted in a happy marriage of the very best both parents have to offer, not the least of which is extraordinary floriferousness. Plants quickly reach specimen size in as small as a three-inch pot and can produce a multitude of brightly colored, good-sized blooms with little special care. Indeed, this may be the only hybrid from this genus that has any chance of succeeding as a potted plant. Many have tried to duplicate the success of this hybrid, but none have really succeeded to their satisfaction. Even the Dutch, masters of both marketing and growing, have not achieved their goals. Certainly they have grown benches and benches of potential subjects, but the market has not materialized.

There is assuredly a specialty market ready to be met, and hybrids like *Masd.* Tiger Kiss are exemplary of some of the best results. Masdevallia hybrids, even more complex ones like *Masd.*

Tiger Kiss, are selected not only for flower quality, but for plant quality, resulting in great vigor and floriferousness. As more diverse species, such as *Masd. aureopurpurea*, enter the breeding pool, we can be sure of many exciting introductions to come.

Right: Although the small flowers of masdevallias can be challenging to pollinate, when successful, spectacular flowers such as Masd. *Tiger Kiss 'Sol de Tazajera' AM/AOS can result.*

Below: From low to moderate elevations of Colombia, Masd. aureopurpurea *is suitable for intermediate temperatures in cultivation.*

MASDEVALLIA FLORIBUNDA &
MASDEVALLIA GUTTULATA

So many of the masdevallias are high-altitude plants, fussy about temperature and water quality, and thus nearly ungrowable for a good portion of their potential audience. There are, though, members of the genus from lower elevations that can also make admirable specimen plants in small pots, with flowers of great charm, if not quite as showy as some of their cooler cousins. Perhaps one of the most satisfactory for warmer climate growers, or, for that matter, anyone who cannot provide uniform moderate temperatures, is *Masd. floribunda*. Originating at lower elevations over a broad area from Mexico south into Costa Rica, *Masdevallia floribunda* has shown itself a perfect performer even in South Florida, if kept shady and moist with good air circulation. While the individual flowers, variable in color from pale cream to shades of

Masd. floribunda is a variable species found throughout Mexico, Guatemala, Belize, Honduras, and into Costa Rica, growing in damp forests at low elevations. Although small, the flowers can be produced in profusion, making this species a good subject for growers with warmer conditions.

rose, are not especially showy, they are cute and when produced en masse give quite a satisfactory display in a small pot.

Masd. guttulata is another good subject for warmer areas, though not as reliable for South Florida as Masd. floribunda. The small creamy, white flowers are heavily spotted and are produced over a long period of time, individually, on spikes that will continue to give flowers over a period of years. The sight of the small kite-like blooms hovering over medium green leaves is one that will cheer the heart of anyone who sees it.

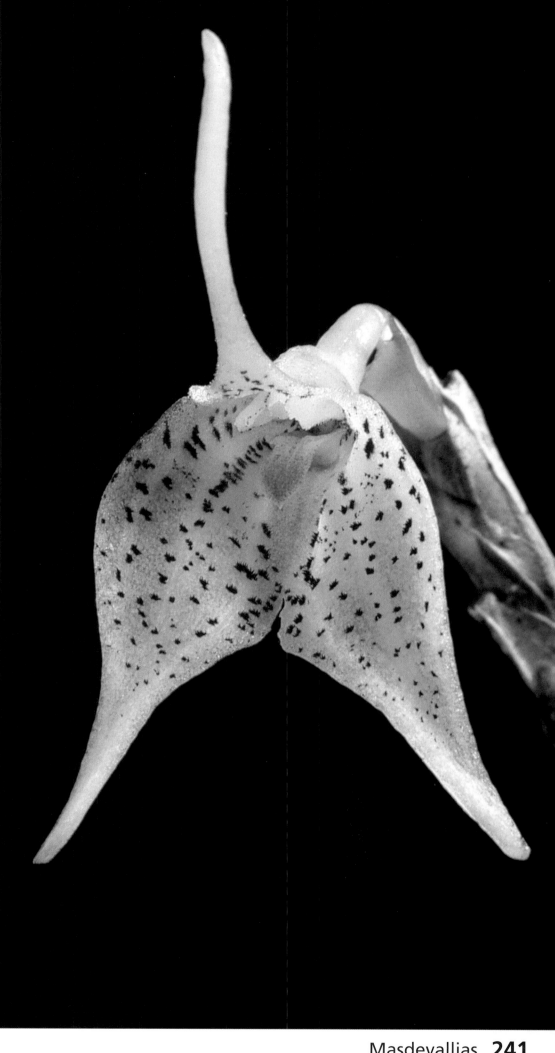

Masd. guttulata is a species from lower elevations of Ecuador making it suitable for warm to intermediate conditions. Flowers range in color from pink to cream and have many small dark spots.

MASDEVALLIA INFRACTA & MASDEVALLIA SPRUCEI

Hailing from lower elevations near Rio de Janeiro, *Masdevalia infracta* is a satisfying substitute for those who cannot grow the cooler types of this genus. The largish blooms, variable in coloration, are often a quite nice grape purple, though variations through white to near yellow are also seen. The long-tailed, tubular flowers are borne singly on tall stems, in succession, giving a floral display that is quite long lasting. South Florida growers report some success with this species, so it can safely be said to be more temperature tolerant than most. The key in warmer areas seems to be smallish pots that allow rapid drying in between the frequent waterings. Sphagnum moss used in clay pots may also be a factor to keeping a moderate climate, as evaporation from the porous surface of the pot provides some evaporative cooling.

Masd. sprucei, found at low elevations in Amazonian Brazil and Venezuela, is another good subject for warm areas. Yellow blooms are produced in profusion and stand proudly on strong stems just above the attractive foliage. Blood-red "cheeks" in the center of the blooms add a delightful contrast to their kitelike shape.

Left: Although not the showiest of the masdevallias, Masd. infracta *makes up for its shortcomings with ease of culture. The variable flowers can range in color from a grapy purple to almost white to a golden yellow. Flowers are produced in succession on the same flower inflorescence, so do not cut stems until they dry.*

Below: Found at only a few hundred feet elevation in Amazonian Venezuela and Brazil, where few other pleurothallids grow, Masd. sprucei *is an attractive subject for those with warmer-growing conditions.*

"OTHER" PLEUROTHALLIDS

Who says taxonomists have no imagination, no sense of humor? When it comes time to naming a genus, and the name selected is *Dracula*, you just know that there is some thought behind it.

Draculas were once considered part of *Masdevallia*, but their growth and flowering habit, as well as their more open flowers often displaying a prominent white lip, led to the name change. Draculas can have some of the largest of all orchid flowers, some being nearly twelve inches from tip to tail. The trouble is, so many of them prefer cool climates, are sensitive to low humidity, and have blooms that hang that they are almost never seen at orchid shows or judging. I remember nearly thirty years ago, attending a judging with a friend who was bringing in a dracula to exhibit. Despite transporting the orchid in an ice chest, the flower collapsed anyway. Draculas are most often grown in open baskets to allow their descending flower stems to hang freely. The horizontal blooms are displayed such that a viewer must look up at them from underneath, providing a wonderful spectacle.

Dracula erythrochaete is one of the smaller-flowered of the group, but does have the advantage, owing to its lower-elevation habitat from Costa Rica south into northern South America, of being somewhat warmer growing. This results in a plant that is more accessible to more growers. Despite this tolerance, good air circulation and as even a temperature regime as possible will suit this species best. The fungus gnat pollinators of this genus are said to target the white lips of these species as a fruiting fungal body suitable for their eggs. Certainly, many draculas that look like fungus could be growing from them.

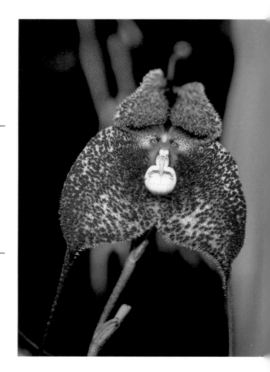

Right: Draculas are among the most whimsical of orchids. It is easy to envision the face of a gnome in the flower of Drac. Chimaera.

Opposite: Draculas have hinged lips that to their pollinator, resemble a fungus. Drac. erythrochaete *is more temperature tolerant than most members of the genus.*

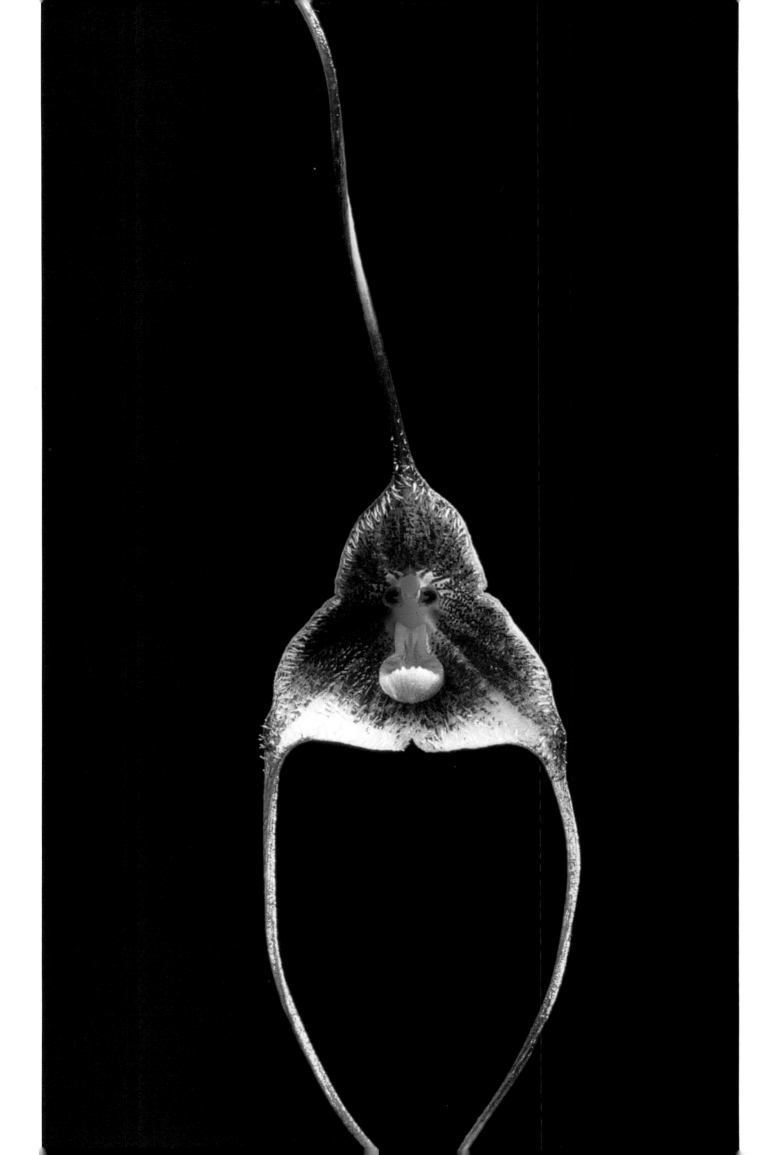

PLEUROTHALLIS GROBYI

An entire book could be written about the widespread and diverse genus, *Pleurothallis*. Like its Old World counterpart, *Bulbophyllum*, *Pleurothallis* relies on the many small flying creatures of the forest to pollinate its small, often insignificant flowers. The range of flower colors and shapes that have evolved to accomplish this feat are every bit as bizarre as those of *Bulbophyllum*. In addition, as is beginning to happen with *Bulbophyllum*, there is a significant group of collectors who live to see and obtain the newest and most unusual members of this large New World genus.

However, for every pleurothallis lover, there are many more who just want to grow satisfying orchids. For many such folks, *Pths. grobyi* is all they need or want to know about the genus. Small, tufted plants originate from a wide area in the tropical Americas, resulting in a wide variety of similar, but different, plant habits and flower appearance. Some speculate that what we call *Pths. grobyi* is a swarm of related species. Few miniature orchids that are so easy to grow can provide the charming display that this species will in just a short time. If given proper shade and even moisture, *Pths. grobyi* will in a few years produce a clump of foliage that will be covered with stems of small, yellow to white blooms. The best results are often attained with mounting the plants on wood or treefern, where the plant quickly overgrows the mount, leaving just a ball of foliage and flower stems. This is a small-flowered miniature orchid with that certain something to appeal to just about any plants-person.

Right: Pths. grobyi is widespread throughout the tropical Americas, suggesting that it may actually be a swarm of related but different species. There is considerable variation in the size and coloring of the flowers, but all are miniatures.

Below: Pths. grobyi is best grown on a small piece of moisture-retentive material such as tree fern or osmunda. Eventually the plant will cover the mount, making a pleasing ball of flowers when in bloom.

PLEUROTHALLIS CARDIOTHALLIS

Every orchid genus has its surprises. Every so often flowers that dwarf the plant that produces them surprise us. Far more seldom is the reverse true, if only because orchid species with such a habit (and there are many) simply do not make it into horticulture, and the general public are not given an opportunity to see the flowers. However, in *Pleurothallis*, there is a group of species with quite large, heart-shaped leaves not unlike an *Anthurium* or water lily, whose flowers, while large for the genus, are almost inconsequential against the foliage. *Pths. cardiothallis* from Central and northern South America, is such an orchid. In the case of this species, at least, the flowers are rather large—up to nearly an inch,—and have a distinctive oxblood color that stands out against the backdrop of the glossy light-green leaf. The real attraction here, though, is the foliage. The large leaves appear well above the top of the media and seem as if to float on an invisible surface. It is a display that lends interest and beauty year-round. The unusual oxblood-red blooms are borne right in the center of the leaf as if framed. Sadly, these are not often grown from seed, and they are rather difficult to import owing to the large, soft leaves that are subject to damage and water stress. Another difficulty in their cultivation is keeping them upright in the relatively small pots that seem to suit them best.

There is much variation of floral and vegetative characteristics among the pleurothallids. The large leaves of Pths. cardiothallis *make it an attractive houseplant even when out of flower.*

RESTREPIA CUPREA

Restrepia cuprea is a fine representative of this good-sized pleurothallid genus. The species comes from moderate elevations in Colombia, where it enjoys even moisture and intermediate temperatures. Restrepias in general are excellent miniatures for a variety of situations, including growing them under artificial lights or on the windowsill. Greenhouse growers also enjoy their almost ever-blooming habit. Upright growths have single, thin, ovoid leaves on what are technically ramicauls (types of stem). From the base of the leaf, flowers emerge singly over a long period of time, giving the plant some flowers at almost all times. Small pots are best for these plants, which will also enjoy fresh mix, since any breakdown of the medium will be attended by a sour condition that will kill the roots.

Right: Restrepia *is a rather widespread genus ranging from Mexico well into South America.* Rstp. cuprea *is a good example of why some growers of miniatures specialize in this genus.*

Below: Restrepias *often sprout "keikis" (plantlets) at the old flower stems. Leaves with these keikis can be removed and potted up as new plants.*

ONCIDIUMS

Gazing at a truly beautiful, wonderfully exotic bloom, it is often difficult to conceive of the complex maze of happenstance that had to occur to reach such a pinnacle.

In the case of 'equitant oncidiums," or tolumnias as they are now properly known, it is the story of a complex of Caribbean island species, rather weedy and nondescript in their natural state, raised to a high degree of quality largely by the vision and work of one man. It is ironic that the species upon which the genus *Oncidium* was founded, *Oncidium variegatum*, is a member of this group now split off from *Oncidium* as a distinct genus, *Tolumnia*.

Equitant refers to the overlapping, somewhat succulent and triquetrous (three-sided) leaves that form the characteristic fan shape of the plants in this group. The plant habit and leaf shape are adaptations to the high light and windy conditions prevalent in their native habitat.

Consequently, equitants demand good air circulation, high light, frequent watering, and rapid drying. For this reason, most plants are grown on mounts or in very small (two-inch) clay pots with little or no medium.

W. W. Goodale Moir, a widely traveled businessman in the sugar industry, is generally regarded as one of the truly visionary orchid breeders of all time. His forte was working with previously underexploited, or unexploited, groups of orchids and literally in many cases making "something from nothing." This is surely the case with equitants. After nearly thirty years of working with these plants, Moir had not only reached some conclusions about what made a good hybrid in the group. Others, mainly Hawaiian breeders, became interested and followed in his large footsteps. These later-generation breeders have continued to use Moir's principles to advance color, size, shape, and vigor to the high level of today.

The broad frilly lip of oncidiums has given them the popular name, Dancing Ladies. Pictured here is Tolu. Dorothy Oka 'Rocky' AM/AOS.

TOLUMNIA GUIANENSIS

Even today, with their vast array of color patterns and combinations, equitants are not widely cultivated. There are some mass-market growers who raise beautiful populations for distribution in the Gulf States, and fine plants are often seen in spring orchid shows in these areas, but many potential growers have either had problems with these plants themselves or "know someone who has." Thus, a myth of them being difficult to grow developed despite the wealth of information available to help in the successful cultivation of these rewarding plants.

It is easy to see how confusion might continue to reign as just the names of the species can be confusing. *Tolumnia guianensis* was, for a long time, known as *Oncidium desertorum*, familiar in a variety of color phases, from pure yellow, to yellow and red, and to red and white. Interestingly, the various color forms of the species do not seem to breed true—I have seen all three color forms come out of the same seedling flask. Taxonomists then declared that the proper name was *Onc. guianense*. With the shift of the entire group to *Tolumnia*, the specific name shifted from *guianense* to *guianensis*. This is one of the five "building block" species necessary, according to Moir, to the quality of today's hybrids. The proportionately broad petals contribute greatly to the fine, round shape of the orchids we see today in the best of the breed.

Left: Tolu. guianensis *is a twig epiphyte from the island of Hispanola.*

Right: The flowers of Tolu. guianensis *give the appearnce of having three lips.*

TOLUMNIA PULCHELLA
& TOLUMNIA TETRAPETALA

All wildflowers are beautiful in situ, best viewed where they grow. This is as true for orchids as it is for poppies and wild mustard. Wildflowers are often less imposing when placed into a more artificial construct, like an orchid collection or garden setting, even though they retain a simple charm that continues to appeal. *Tolumnia pulchella* is, in its most natural state, one of the most beautiful of this group, even in orchids as a whole. The strong, arching stems of round one-inch pale pink to rose-lavender blooms are exceptionally fine. Since there is habitat overlap in many of the *Tolumnia* species, and as a fairly recently evolved and still evolving group, natural hybridization occurs with some frequency. For this reason, "pure" *Tolu. pulchella* is thought to be rather rare in nature. Many of the more attractive (and hence more likely to be selected by growers) forms are the natural hybrid, *Tolu.* x *Hartii* (*Tolu. pulchella* x *Tolu. concava*). A variety of ramifications arise from this situation, not the least of which is the continuing variability of progeny arising from selfed and sibbed populations of the "species," *Tolu. pulchella.* Another potential "breakdown" is in the registration system. Registration is usually so accurate for the majority of orchid hybridizing, but problems arise when it is impossible to ascertain whether *Tolu.* x *Hartii* is the actual parent or *Tolu. pulchella*, and we can never truly know with certainty the contribution of the minor species, *Tolu. concava*.

However, just because a member of this group is considered "minor"—relatively unimportant to hybridizing—it doesn't mean it sn't beautiful and worthy of cultivation. Indeed, many *Tolumnia* species such as *Tolu. tetrapetala* deserve space in any orchid collection, where they will flower over a period of weeks or months.

Above: Tolu. pulchella *and* Tolu. tetrapetala *are closely related species that are variable and can produce flowers that resemble each other.*

Opposite: Tolu. pulchella *is a building block for equitant* Oncidium *hybrids. It is valued for its full form and good color.*

TOLUMNIA TALISMAN & TOLUMNIA POPOKI

As in any popularly hybridized group of plants, there seem to be certain parents that are used again and again. Whether owing primarily to availability, productivity, or, as might be hoped, quality of progeny, breeding success varies from group to group and parent to parent. There are parents that are used simply because they reliably give seed. Others are used because they are widely distributed. Still others, often long in cultivation, are known to produce fine progeny. Breeders knowledgeable in equitant hybridizing generally agree that for a parent to be of value in this group, or a hybrid to give worthwhile progeny, there must be a balance between the two groups into which the five main important species segregate: *urophylla*; *pulchella* and *triquetra*; and *guianensis* and *henekenii*.

Tolu. Talisman shows the influence of probably the most important parent, *Tolu.* Golden Sunset. While of what might be considered rather "typical"—with a large skirted white lip suffused and dotted with darker color, and very dark petals and dorsal sepals—its coloration is more intense, its size larger, and its shape fuller. The result is a flower of superior quality and beauty.

Tolu. *Talisman 'Big Joe' AM/AOS shows the random spotting that is a feature of these hybrids.*

Tolu. Phyllis Hetfield is also considered one of Moir's creations necessary to the breeding lines as we know them today. In *Tolu.* Popoki, we see what is essentially a highly improved *Tolu. pulchella*, with color so intense as to approach red. An increase in flower count and larger flowers of fuller shape, borne on more compact inflorescences, complete the picture of a wonderful modern equitant.

Right: *The rich red color of* Tolu. Popoki *has made it a popular hybrid in the trade, making plants of this floriferous miniature easy to find. Pictured here is* Tolu. Popoki 'orchidworks.com' HCC/AOS.

TOLUMNIA CALYPSO BAY

An oft-overlooked aspect of hybridizing is the presentation of the flowers, both individually and as a whole, on the inflorescence. There is no "perfection" per se, only an available range of characteristics that combine to make the final product either pleasing or not. In equitants, several factors need to be considered. First is stem length coupled with the distance to the first flower. If the stem is too long in proportion to the distance to the first flower, an unbalanced presentation results, often with a general weakness that can only be countered with staking. How far apart are the flowers? If too close, they appear bunched and the individual flower cannot be appreciated. If too far apart, the overall look is one of separation and not an entirety. How strong is the ovary, the individual flower's stem, especially in regard to the size of the bloom? If the ovary is too short, the flower cannot be presented well in relation to the inflorescence; if too long, it may not support the weight of the flower, instead bending down in a "sloppy" way. Of course, there are a variety of combinations of stem, flower spacing and size, and pedicel length that can result in a proper display of blooms.

One of the characteristic displays seen in equitants is demonstrated in *Tolu*. Calypso Bay. The inflorescence is arching, slightly cascading, with the large blooms carried in a way where each flower is well presented individually but the whole is greater than the sum of the parts. The flowers are close enough together and arranged such that no stem is seen between each, forming a nicely shingled display. Taking into consideration that the starting point is a yellow-flowered species with a rangy, open inflorescence, the importance of balance in breeding is ably demonstrated.

Tolu. *Calypso Bay is a* Tolumnia *hybrid that has received a number of awards for its large, broad-lipped flowers. The clone 'Boca Chica' HCC/AOS typifies these qualities.*

TOLUMNIA PELICAN ISLAND

Tolumnia triquetra is one of the smallest of the five important breeding species in equitants. What it lacks in size, it more than makes up for in several important ways. The inflorescences are erect and strong, with flowers fairly well presented starting about two-thirds of the way to the tip. Color, in the best varieties, is strong and contrasting in shades of rust red. The important characteristics of the species in breeding include compact flower stems, red color, and a heart-shaped lip. Additionally, it seems to be the source of at least some of the lip spotting that is so prized. Lastly, the inflorescence branches freely after the initial flowers fade, giving a long-lasting display and added value.

Because of their relatively small flower size, generally under one inch, equitants really must have attractive overall flower presentation. Another style of effective presentation is demonstrated in *Tolu.* Pelican Island, where the *Tolu. triquetra* influence can be seen in the shorter, slightly stiffer floral display. Evidence of an emerging secondary spike is further evidence of the strong influence of the species. The brilliant red color of the shapely lip contrasts well with the dark, horizontally held petals, which form a significant framework for the lip. In a group where the lip is often the primary feature, flowers with this improved balance are a wonderful advancement in hybridizing.

The sum is greater than the individual parts with equitant Oncidium *hybrids, and* Tolu. *Pelican Island 'O'Whimsey' AM/AOS shows how beautiful an inflorescence can be.*

TOLUMNIA LOST REEF

Orchid breeders, especially breeders in more esoteric groups, are too often "lost" in attempting to produce flowers that, while beautiful, have features that would exclude them from a broader horticultural audience. Orchid judges, it must be said, can share this same myopia. And this is not entirely a fault. Orchid judging is based on a set of criteria that develop based on "improvement in type." Simply, is it good for what it is? Also, orchid judging takes place at a specific moment in time. There is no provision for how the flower(s) might have been yesterday or a week ago, or how they might be tomorrow or in a month. This system only takes into consideration how an orchid is on a specific day, and it admirably does what it was designed to do.

An aspect too often overlooked by many amateur breeders, and impossible for orchid judges to consider, is performance and beauty over a longer term. Additionally, certain floral features, if strongly and pleasingly enough expressed, can overcome other, negative attributes that might otherwise render the flower/plant unacceptable from a horticultural standpoint. In the "orchid world" this is not necessarily bad and is considered part of the territory. However, it is also a good reason for each grower to be his or her own "judge."

Tolumnia Lost Reef is an outstanding example of its type and breeding, well worth the high award it was given. It might not be so satisfactory from an overall horticultural standpoint, however, owing to the somewhat nodding flowers held at the end of a long spike. Although a good plant for orchid growers, it is somewhat less so, perhaps, for plant lovers. When considering plants, so much more than flower quality must be taken into account.

Intense, contrasting markings set Tolu. Lost Reef 'Smuggler's Cove' AM/AOS apart.

TOLUMNIA MEMORIA RALPH YAGI

Tissue culture, synonymous with meristemming or cloning, is a wonderful thing. It enables many to enjoy the fruits of successful breeding, often also ensuring the longetivity of particularly pleasing and satisfactory cultivars. The basic process involves taking the emerging growth of a selected plant and peeling it down like an onion to reach the undifferentiated meristemmatic tissue, the site of true growth in a plant. This tissue, suitably cleaned and sterilized, is cultured in specifically designed media that encourages multiplication, eventually ending in a population of exact duplicates, or clones. Cloning has long been a fact of life in horticulture and agriculture, having been originally developed to help propagate virus-free potatoes. Scientists aware of the work on this problem believed that it could also be used for orchids, in which viruses are also an incurable scourge. As the process developed, it has spread from orchids into almost every aspect of the culture of plants, giving a reliable method to rapidly produce exact replicas of desirable types.

In orchids, meristemming continues to be an avenue through which highly prized new and old cultivars can be profitably distributed. As with any process, there are caveats. In much the same way that a tool distributed by the original developer must be the most accurately produced and the "knockoffs" increasingly less accurate the further from the source they get, orchid meristemming has its limits. Those limits, when exceeded, result in products inferior to the original. Meristemming is responsible for the propagation and distribution of such popular cultivars as *Tolumnia* Mem. Ralph Yagi, a very superior example of equitant breeding. The boldly marked lip, with its prominent sidelobes adding to the overall fullness of the bloom, and the proportionately sized petals and dorsal sepal framing it, give one of the nicest of its type. Newer varieties have come and gone, but *Tolu.* Mem. Ralph Yagi, thanks to tissue culture, remains as a standard of the industry.

Tolu. *Mem. Ralph Yagi 'Palolo' AM/AOS has been a popular hybrid since it was introduced in 1989.*

TOLUMNIA FIRECRACKER

This group of hybrids stands at a pinnacle, one reached by the efforts of a few persistent pioneers. *Tolumnia* Firecracker, the product of one of the best, but least known, of these pioneers, represents so much of what is good about equitants. Round, colorful, and contrasting blooms produced from very compact plants are modern requirements, and *Tolu.* Firecracker fulfills this proudly. The pioneering orchid breeder, Moir, would be pleased with the progress in what were once known as "Moir's weeds."

However, equitants remain a relatively minor group of orchids, beloved by a few knowledgeable growers. Their beauty will certainly result in continuing attempts to bring them to the masses.

Dedicated breeders persist in their efforts to combine the best traits of the group. Overseas markets, long a popular outlet for many terrific varieties never seen in the United States, will continue to drive the best hybridizing. New enthusiasts will enter the fray with fresh ideas and new products. As the potted-plant market continues to grow, breeders may begin to more carefully assess growability, vigor, and horticultural desirability as part of their programs. Once a greater number of orchid hobbyists discover that they can indeed successfully cultivate these lovely plants, a new era of beautiful potted plants will be led by equitants, plants whose vigor has been aided by the work of astute breeders.

The dark red mask makes a focal point for Tolu. Firecracker 'Roman Holiday' AM/AOS.

PSYGMORCHIS PUSILLA

How long do orchids live? How quickly do they grow? These are two of the most frequently asked questions about orchids. While orchids can and do live for decades, at least, a corollary question might be regarding whether or not they have a set "life span." This, of course, would tie in nicely to just how quickly they might reach maturity and flowering before receding into senescence. A particular class of orchids known as "twig epiphytes" is relatively common through the New World tropics. One of the best known is *Psygmorchis pusilla*, previously considered an *Oncidium*. These plants grow at the outer part of the forest canopy, on the twiggy growth. In Central America, they are even present growing on orange trees. Sometimes, plants are found on leaves, which have a much more limited life than the woody parts of the trees. This translates to plants that have adapted to growing quickly in an ephemeral environment, flowering, setting seed, and often perishing, all in the time it might take another orchid plant to simply flower for the first time.

Such plants present a unique cultural challenge. Because they come from marginal environments, it would be natural to assume that they were somehow hardier and easier to grow than most. They are not. Constant air movement, frequent watering, and rapid drying are the watchwords for these quick little plants. Indeed, a gimmick used by some nurseries in the marketing of *Psygmorchis pusilla* is to grow individual plants in flask, which will flower and grow in their miniature terrariums quite happily. Rarely do these fan-shaped plants live more than a few years in cultivation, leading many growers to continually renew their stock from seed. Some have reported long-term success, but these growers are famous for being among the best anywhere. Otherwise, if the grower is prepared for the eventual death of the plant, these small-growing species make showy additions to the collection, their bright yellow blooms borne over a long period of time.

Psygmorchis pusilla is an ephemeral species often found growing in orange groves in Belize. The small fan-shaped plants usually last only a few years.

PSYCHOPSIS MEMORIA BILL CARTER & PSYCHOPSIS PAPILIO ALBA

Who knows what course the orchid hobby might have taken had not the Bachelor Duke of Devonshire, William Spencer Cavendish, taken such delight in *Psychopsis papilio* (then *Oncidium*), the orchid that started it all. It is easy to see why this butterfly-like flower, so different from other flowers, indeed other orchids, would catch his attention. Growers today continue to be fascinated by this species and its few hybrids. The limited amount of breeding that has been done with *Pyp. papilio* and the closely related *Pyp. kramerianum* has largely been with the intent to improve the individual species as well as to propagate more uncommon color forms such as the albino yellows. This continued inbreeding has resulted in flowers that are significantly larger than the wild-collected species. The tall, often flattened inflorescences bear their showy blooms individually and sequentially over a period of months.

Unfortunately, not everyone finds these easy to grow. There are those for whom the plants perform wonderfully, growing rapidly and profusely, flowering with a towering display of the giant butterfly blooms. For others, the plants languish, diminishing in size until they fade away. Is there a secret? If there is a particular cultural trick that will make successful growers out of failures, it has yet to be widely circulated. So, yes, there must be a secret.

Left: Most hybrids using Psychopsis *parents such as* Pyp. Memoria Bill Carter 'John's Pride' AM/AOS *resemble the parent.*

Right: The beautiful yellow clones of Pyp. Papilio *are much in demand.*

ONCIDIUM AMPLIATUM, ONCIDIUM SPHACELATUM & ONCIDIUM SARCODES

The true "nature" of oncidiums, the best known and loved by the most people, is as display plants, often in the landscape, bearing multitudes of golden-yellow blooms. It is not by accident that many are known as "golden showers." *Onciudium ampliatum* bears a somewhat more formal presentation of blooms than many, with upright arching and branching sprays of brilliantly yellow-skirted blooms above the odd, turtle-shell-like pseudobulbs. It will do equally well potted, in a basket or on a mount, but should be grown in a way that enables the grower to position and place the plant to best display the magnificent stems of long-lasting blooms. Cattleya conditions suit it well.

It is *Onc. sphacelatum* and other closely related types that really personify the "Golden Shower" orchids. The robust, slightly flattened and furrowed pseudobulbs have upright, attractive bladed leaves that can reach over thirty-six inches. The inflorescences, two or three per growth, extend to six inches or more and are extravagantly branched,

showing the one-inch bright yellow blooms to their best advantage. Many grow this in baskets in the garden or even as quasishrubs around the base of trees in semitropical gardens, where the true grandeur of the orchid is shown.

Onc. sarcodes shows another side to the spray oncidium experience, with its deep golden flowers richly marked and spotted with glowing mahogany. The upright flower stems are not as highly branched as some, but the slightly larger size and contrasting color scheme more than make up for any shortfall of blooms.

The large and wide-ranging group of orchids formerly included in the genus *Oncidium* is only now being split up into more manageable and natural groupings. Taxonomists are scrutinizing heretofore suspected and unsuspected relationships in the light of clearer knowledge and remaking the group that includes not only *Oncidium* but also *Odontoglossum*. This will inevitably result in new names and name combinations that will be confusing to even the best-informed aficionados. Thankfully, these are among the most important horticultural groups today, and so many retain some sort of uniformity of nomenclature, even if only in the popular trade.

CYMBIDIUMS

From just after World War II until the latter part of the century, *Cymbidium* Trigo Royale and similar pastel types were the "face" of cymbidiums.

Their full shape and mild, if any, fragrance, combined with a rather limited pastel color palette and generally boldly marked lip, made cymbidiums a popular and useful garden subject in mild climate areas like the West Coast of the United States. Many plants were originally grown as spring cut-flowers, for which cymbidiums are ideally suited as they are exceptionally long lasting. The large-scale production of cut-flower types fueled the potted-plant market from the surplus of plants produced. Basically, growers of cut-flower cymbidiums could sell 30 percent or more of their stock each year as potted plants, while maintaining the same level of mature, bearing cut-flower plants.

All of this was made possible by a few chance tetraploids bred in England in the period between the two World Wars. *Cymdidium* Alexanderi 'Westonbirt' FCC/RHS was especially influential in siring a race of progenies that were superior to anything yet seen. As a result of tetraploids being bred, unwittingly at first, with diploids, triploids (4N x 2N = 3N) of extraordinary vigor and productivity became the norm throughout the industry. The only drawback to these types was the pastel color range, which, since pastels were in vogue at this time, was no bad thing.

Many people's first experience with growing orchids came from *Cymbidium* garden plants. In areas where summer night temperatures do not often exceed the midsixties, cymbidiums make outstanding garden subjects, where their tall, strong inflorescences are proudly presented in midspring. Whether in large pots of fine fir bark or in raised ground beds, a beautiful and long-lasting show was almost guaranteed, especially where light levels were kept high by ensuring that the tree canopy did not get too thick.

Colorful lip details provide an attractive contrast to the pale flowers of Cym. Trigo Royale 'Ridgeway' HCC/AOS.

CYMBIDIUM VIA VOLCANO

The preponderance of pastel flowers in the early days of cymbidium development did not mean that breeders weren't struggling to come up with brighter and more exotic colors, or that consumers weren't asking for them: quite the contrary. Since the earliest days of *Cymbidium* hybridizing, "high color" types have been bred. Unfortunately, the species used to impart richer color were often weaker growers, with relatively poorer shape and substance. Bright yellow, deep green, brown, orange, and red hybrids were available, but quality and uniformity were not the same as for the more common pastel types. Low yield and low quality meant that the few "good ones" were kept in short supply. Seemingly, the only way to improve quality was to breed with the pastel tetraploids, which, since the high-color types were almost entirely diploids, carried the risk of loss of color intensity.

The breakthrough came with the artificial induction of polyploidy to a few choice parents, as well as the discovery of chance polyploid mutations in tissue-cultured populations of older, better known, high-color cultivars. Advances did not come quickly or all at once. The best parents were closely held, and seedling populations were not widely distributed. As generation followed generation and improvements began to be significant, more and

more of the new breed of high-color types became available to the public at large. Sadly, an increased interest in raising plants of new high-color seedlings seems to have come too late to save many of the more established breeders. Today, there are very few breeders who can claim to have a genuine breeding program, where they are using parents developed by them, perhaps over a period of two or more generations. While hybridizing in any genus is speculative to some extent, it is almost always tempered by a long-term knowledge of the attributes of the parents being used. Such knowledge is increasingly uncommon in the world of cymbidiums.

The large round flowers of Cym. Via Volcano 'Flash' *exemplify the ideal for standard cymbidiums.*

CYMBIDIUM ENSIFOLIUM

Asian growers have treasured the graceful foliage and delicately scented blooms of *Cymbidium ensifolium* for hundreds, if not thousands, of years. In China and Japan, this reverence has led to the best or most unusual varieties being kept sequestered in private collections, only rarely to be seen by the public. Indeed, the supply of the most highly prized cultivars is kept intentionally limited, which further adds to their value and rarity. *Cym. ensifolium*, even the typical types, has a lot to offer to Western growers. While Eastern and Western sensibilities remain distinct, Westerners are coming to appreciate the grace of the foliage and flowers—which remain in wonderful proportion to each other—as well as the enchanting perfume. Additionally, growers are finding that *Cym. ensifolium* is much more tolerant of, even preferring in some cases, warm summers. It is quite happy in South Florida and similar areas, where it shows its contentment by blooming during the very hottest summer months. A significant shortcoming of *Cym. ensifolium* is that the flowers last only a few weeks, as opposed to the six to eight weeks or more of the more traditional "standard" cymbidiums.

With the increasing availability of products from Asian suppliers, we are seeing a substantial increase in interest in *Cym. ensifolium* and other Asian cymbidiums. This type is often grown in Oriental-style pots, which, unlike more commonly used containers, are much taller in proportion to the width. The tall pots, usually attractively styled, again unlike most nursery containers, show off the fine, grassy foliage of the plants very nicely. Many hobbyist growers further enhance the presentation with elegant ceramic pots. Upright inflorescences of five to eight rather starry, vertically elongated blooms come in summer and early fall. Color is typically "woodsy" in browns and tans over a lighter background, but color varieties abound, and soft-green alba cultivars are readily available. Strong light and even moisture are the rule, as they are for the more commonly grown types.

Cym. ensifolium has been revered in China and Japan for centuries. The ice-green form, 'Iron Bone', has a sweet citrus fragrance.

CYMBIDIUM GOLDEN ELF 'SUNDUST'

While the spring season for most cymbidiums is a naturally good one, efforts to extend this season earlier into the winter and fall and later into the summer have been a part of breeding from almost the beginning. The introduction of influence from both earlier and later blooming species is the primary method by which this can be accomplished. And while today we think more of *Cymbidium ensifolium* as beautiful in and of itself, with worthwhile attributes beyond season, it was initially used in an attempt to pull the season into early fall. The first successful attempt was *Cym*. Peter Pan (*ensifolium* x Miretta), a bronzy green miniature with a bold red-banded lip. Unfortunately, it was sterile and only became an important parent some years later with the induction of polyploidy. Also, especially at first, other colors were needed to round out the palette. Too many of the hybrids ended up green.

Nearly twenty years later, a similar hybrid utilizing an even older parent than Miretta came to light with *Cym*. Golden Elf (*ensifolium* Album x Enid Haupt). Apparently the best of the cross was the surprising 'Sundust'. Surprising because it seemed to be a pure color yellow, devoid of any red, anthocyanin pigments. Later, it would turn out that it would breed some pure color progeny. The original form was sterile, and only when a chance tetraploid showed up in a population of clones were breeders able to begin exploring the range of new colors and types available to them through this new parent. Whether diploid or presumptive tetraploid, *Cym*. Golden Elf 'Sundust' HCC/AOS has many charms, not the least of which are the brilliant concolor golden-yellow blooms with their heady fragrance. The very compact plants easily bear multiple flower stems of five to eight medium-sized blooms. In warmer areas, the diploid form may be almost in continuous bloom. I have seen plants with old flower stems, stems in bloom, and new stems emerging. What a rewarding plant!

Cym. Golden Elf 'Sundust' HCC/AOS was a breakthrough hybrid offering rich color in a temperature-tolerant Cymbidium.

CYMBIDIUM CARPENTER'S GOLDEN ANNIVERSARY, CYMBIDIUM GOLDEN VANGUARD & CYMBIDIUM GLITTERING GOLD

Cymbidium Golden Elf, it turns out, has many fine attributes as a parent, the most important of which may be its tolerance of warmth and its early season. Its compact growth habit, attractive foliage, and possibility of multiple bloomings per year in warmer climes make it an attractive parent for a variety of new hybrids. A good number are quite beautiful but do illustrate the need to intelligently select the mate in such hybridizing. As with *Cym.* Peter Pan, many of the early hybrids, and the most successful to date, have

Orchid hobbyists seem to have an attraction for those plants that they cannot grow. Cym. Carpenter's Golden Anniversary 'Green Pastures' HCC/AOS is a warmth-tolerant hybrid that can even be grown in Florida.

Above: Cym. Golden Vanguard 'New Horizon' HCC/AOS takes Cym. Golden Elf a step further toward perfection with its large colorful flowers of heavy substance.

Left: Cym. Glittering Gold 'Mothe Lode' HCC/AOS is another fine example of a temperature-tolerant hybrid Cymbidium.

involved parents that tended to continue this line resulting in populations that were primarily in shades of yellow and green. This is analogous to the situation in early Cym. Peter Pan breeding. As we see the next generation of Cym. Golden Elf hybrids being used in further breeding, the color palette is considerably wider.

A first-generation Cym. Golden Elf hybrid, Cym. Milton Carpenter (x Via Ambarino), is the subject of an interesting test at one of the largest mass-market suppliers in the United States. Trials are now under way to determine the suitability of Cym. Milton Carpenter and, by inference, others of its type, as mass-market flowering potted plants. Will the tissue-cultured plants grow quickly and easily enough, flowering at a precise time, to be a viable new horticultural type? Only time can tell.

CYMBIDIUM STRATHDON & CYMBIDIUM LAST SUPPER

Cym. *Strathdon* 'Cooksbridge Noel' AM/RHS offers erect sprays of color-ful flowers on compact plants that bloom in winter.

Standard cymbidiums, particularly the long-popular triploid cut-flower types, have a distinct drawback in plant size. A mature plant can be unwieldy, requiring up to a fourteen-inch pot and weighing almost more than can be lifted. Thankfully, they are good garden plants where space is not at such a premium, but they are not houseplants—too big, too demanding of light, and intolerant of house temperature regimes. As with other horticultural types, attempts to "miniaturize" cymbidiums were not long in coming. H. G. Alexander registered the first "miniature" cymbidium immediately after World War II, but it was not until a Southern California nursery was joined by several aspiring hybridizers that "minicyms" were truly born. Beginning with Cym. *Flirtation* in the mid-1950s, a stream of hybrids utilizing the Japanese species Cym. *pumilum* came out of California and revolutionized the hobby. It quickly became apparent that the first-generation Cym. *pumilum* hybrids, while attractive and popular, were not the final answer for making an ideal potted plant.

Unfortunately, in many cases, these hybrids would turn out to be a final answer of sorts, as they were too often sterile. Many attempts were made—with other *Cym. pumilum* hybrids, with standards, and back to *Cym. pumilum* itself—but failure was commonplace.

Advances were made as time went on and breeders began to discover parents that would breed. Through the 1970s and 1980s, flower color and spike habit were refined, in both the larger "polymins" and in more compactly sized plants, until a set of standards began to be recognized for what would characterize a "good" miniature cymbidium. (Note: "Miniature cymbidium" technically means a hybrid with a miniature species as a parent. Most of what we see and know as "miniature cymbidiums" are more properly "novelty cymbidiums," where a miniature species is in the immediate background. Exactness is not as important in horticulture as it is in science.) *Cym.* Strathdon is notable for its very restrained growth habit and tendency to make multiple spikes in a small (five-inch) pot. As can be seen in *Cym.* Last Supper, standards have leveled off somewhat in the past few years, after having reached a plateau where further advancement would be difficult.

Cym. *Strathdon 'Cooksbridge Noel' AM/RHS.*

CASCADING CYMBIDIUMS: CYMBIDIUM CANALICULATUM

Much of what most think they know about cymbidiums is predicated on only a very small number of species from what is a large, widespread, and diverse genus. Cymbidiums range from Australia, up through Malaysia and India, across the Himalayas into China and Japan, from sea level to moderately high elevations. Many are terrestrial, but some of the more tropical members are epiphytic. This habit is fairly common, and plants have adapted in a manner of ways to the periodic drought of an epiphytic habit. One of the chief methods is by having thicker leaves, giving them their name of coriaceous cymbidiums. Generally, such plants are found in very open areas of the forest, often in the crooks of trees, where the bright light may be slightly tempered and there is accumulation of debris to help nourish the plant as well as provide a more even source of moisture.

Perhaps the most desirable of the coriaceous cymbidiums is the Australian *Cym. canaliculatum*. As is too often is the case, though, it is not easy to obtain or maintain. Collectors have a difficult time successfully removing the plants from their roosts.

Nor is the species easy from seed, being very slow and prone to rot-related diseases. Mature plants in cultivation demonstrate why wild-collected plants are so difficult to reestablish. Even cultivated plants dislike dividing and repotting to the extent that blooming may be put off for several years after any such disturbance. This wonderful and sought-after species remains uncommon in cultivation, maintaining a premium price when they become available, which is rare.

And what a striking species this is. Densely flowered stems jut straight out from the base of the golf-ball-sized pseudobulbs, which are topped by stiff green, succulent leaves. Color does vary to some extent, but the best are dark wine on an equally dark inflorescence, giving the impression of nearly black foxtails surrounding the plant. Basket culture is advised, as it enables the grower to hang the plant high, where light is bright, and assists in keeping the plant dry during the winter months, when excess moisture can lead to rot and plant loss.

The near-black flowers of Cym. canaliculatum *are presented on a densely packed arching inflorescence. Pictured clone is 'Krull Smith' HCC/AOS.*

CYMBIDIUM LITTLE BLACK SAMBO

Cymbidium madidum is another of the hard-leaved Australian cymbidiums that is much easier to grow and flower. This widespread species comes in a range of colors, but the most popular seems to be var. Leroyi, green with a red dot centrally in the lip. All have strongly cascading inflorescences, up to three feet or longer, with fairly widely spaced one-inch open blooms.

The foliage is not unlike *Cym. canaliculatum* but is significantly larger and more robust, with somewhat thinner leaves. Flower stems emerge from mature growths in late spring and early summer. This is another good basket plant, both for cultural and display reasons.

A variety of hybrids have been made with *Cym. madidum* crossed with more traditional cymbidiums, chiefly to extend the season, and some few are still in cultivation, such as Nonna, Fifi, and Hearts of Gold. But its real claim to fame is in hybrids closer to the species level. *Cym.* Litte Black Sambo (x *canaliculatum*) is an outstanding example. Unfortunately, it appeals to people who have traditional cymbidiums but cannot provide the warmer conditions this hybrid simply must have to thrive. And when it thrives, it is among the most striking of all orchids, with showers of nearly black starry blooms on long, cascading stems. For those in warmer areas, or with a greenhouse, this is a sensational subject.

Cym. *Little Black Sambo 'New Horizon' AM/AOS improves upon the form of* Cym. canalicu atum *and adds attractive bright edging to the flowers.*

CYMBIDIUM PARISH MADNESS

Another *Cymbidium madidum* hybrid that personifies both the best of the species and the unremitting popularity of cascading cymbidiums is *Cym.* Parish Madness (*madidum* x *parishii*). When two parent species of such profound influence in their respective lines of breeding are combined, fascinating results are nearly assured, if only because our knowledge of the two species is increased. *Cym. parishii*, the pendant dwarfish Indian species, is progenitor of the single most currently popular type of *Cymbidium* hybrid among fanatics. Its direct and indirect hybrids, even as seedlings, are sought out and purchased at prices that were unheard-of for cymbidiums even a few short years ago. Many consumers are disappointed when they are left out of the buying frenzy by not arriving on time, let alone early. It is truly an orchid madness unheard of in recent years.

Cym. *parishii* and its hybrids tend to do best in slightly more shade than most commonly grown types. In combination with *Cym. madidum*, which requires strong light, we have a result that is intermediate between the two, growing well under most conditions. Baskets are best, not only displaying the pendant inflorescences well but also freeing up valuable bench space.

CYMBIDIUM GLADYS WHITESELL

Cymbidium Fifi is a *Cym. madidum* hybrid that has been in cultivation for nearly forty years. Only relatively recently, though, has it found new life as an important parent of cascading types. This has resulted from two factors, the option of hybrid fertility induced by polyploidy and demand for cascading types. *Cym.* Gladys Whitesell (Fifi x *parishii*) was the hybrid that pointed the way for *Cym.* Fifi's new popularity. *Cym.* Gladys Whitesell seedlings and meristems, remade at least once since their first introduction in the 1980s, enjoy wide distribution in the United States. Strong growing plants produce arching, pendulous inflorescences with medium-sized blooms ranging from soft lemon yellow through butter cream, most with boldly spotted lips. Shape can be very full though often cupped. Additionally, *Cym.* Gladys Whitesell has the warmth tolerance necessary to enable widespread cultivation in warm summer areas. Because the plants can be rather large, they are not suitable for home culture, though growers with sunrooms or patios that allow abundant summer light and air circulation during the summer months may succeed. Otherwise, this is a plant for greenhouses or areas where frost does not threaten. Grown in baskets or other appropriately sized hanging containers, there are few sights to match a well-flowered plant of this magnificent hybrid.

Cym. *Gladys Whitesell 'New Horizon' AM/AOS.*

PHALAENOPSIS

The species of the genus *Phalaenopsis* are among the most beautiful of all orchids.

There exists a sufficient variety of color, shape, and flowering habit to fascinate even the most discerning orchid collector. From the beginning in the mid-nineteenth century, *Phalaenopsis* have been enigmatic. Their habitats remain largely unknown, with little collection data of any quality available. Originating in warm and humid tropical areas, the plants have little in the way of water-storage organs, making them "ephemeral" in early collectionsl, because they were difficult to import via the very slow transport available at the time and because they were more subject than most to disease.

Perhaps for this reason, hybridizing did not start with the same enthusiasm and vigor that was seen in some other horticulturally interesting genera. But with the introduction of the polyploid white, *Phalaenopsis* Doris, just after World War II, a new standard was achieved in long-lasting and shapely white flowers. The importance of *Phal.* Doris cannot be understated. Not only did it directly contribute shape and substance to its immediate progeny but also was also used to breed into other color lines, improving their quality. Without *Phal.* Doris, such plants as *Phal.* Elaine Taylor (the

Candy-striped "phal hybrids" such as Dtps. Taisuco Melody 'Crownfox' AM/AOS have long been popular and keep getting better as far as form and well-defined markings.

result of crossing an enormous white with a quality pink) simply could not exist; nor could we have the quality seen in all the other "traditional" *Phalaenopsis* types: striped, spotted, and mixtures of the two.

It must be noted that using the intergeneric combination Doritaenopsis (Phalaenopsis x Doritis) is, in many cases, simply a matter of historical convenience for two important reasons. First, the latest monographic treatment of the genus has moved Doritis back into *Phalaenopsis*. Second, in many of the lines where *Doritis* is presumptively in the background, it is the result of a mislabeling from many years ago.

Above: Phal. Elaine Taylor 'Krull Smith' AM/AOS shows improvement for the type with its large overlapping petals that nearly obscure the flower's sepals.

Below: Dtps. Plantation Acres 'Lesa's Freckles' HCC/AOS is a direct descendent from the French spots that began the type twenty years ago and shows refined "pepper spotting".

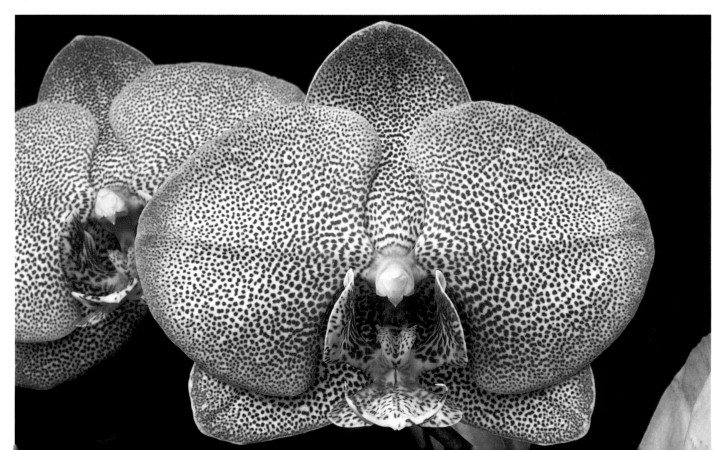

DORITAENOPSIS BROTHER REDLAND & DORTAENOPSIS SOGO BEACH

Dtps. *Sogo Beach 'Adelaide Skoglund'* AM/AOS.

As has been discussed in other genera, the production of a viable new horticultural type is the result of many generations of what amounts to a balancing act of conflicting traits and desired results, which gradually overcome the bad features that inevitably link to the good. Once white *Phalaenopsis* of relatively high-uniform quality were commonplace, thanks to the production of *Phal.* Doris, these polyploid whites began to be used to produce other colors. Two of the earlier attempts, linked by a common species, *Phalaenopsis equestris*, are striped and semi-alba (white with colored lip) forms. *Phal. equestris* is a miniature plant,

Dtps. *Brother Redland 'Evan' AM/AOS.*

often no more than twelve inches across, with a multitude of lightly striped one-inch blooms on upright, branching spikes. This is in stark contrast to the standard *Phalaenopsis* hybrid size of a twenty-four-inch leaf span or more. While hybrids close to the primary level are charming and are making a significant contribution to the potted-plant market today, it is the more complex, multigenerational hybrids that have achieved the highest standards. *Dtps.* Brother Redland is a fine example of its type, showing the richly netted and bright venation that marks quality in this type. It can also be said to show more traditional shape expectations with less petal overlap, the result of the petals being proportionately longer than wide. For the other extreme, see *Phal.* Elaine Taylor, with petals proportionately much wider than long. *Dtps.* Sogo Beach also shows the more ideal petal width and stance, with slightly upswept petals broad enough to nearly touch in the middle of the dorsal sepal.

DORITAENOPSIS SOGO BEACH

When the hybrid between Dtps. Minho Princess and Dtps. Leopard Prince was first seen at the 2000 Miami International Orchid Show, it quickly received four AOS awards. Dtps. Sogo Beach 'Crownfox' HCC/AOS typifies the overall high quality of this cross.

Every so often an orchid hybrid will come along that forces existing standards to be reevaluated, raising the bar for all that come after. In orchid breeding, there are often equal parts skill and luck. Perseverance cannot be discounted. Rarely in the history of orchid breeding can government support be counted a factor. However, in *Doritaenopsis* Sogo Beach, all of the above aspects have come into play. As the world

Phalaenopsis market has grown and changed, it has become increasingly stratified and international. Breeding is done at one nursery, the raising of young seedlings in flask at another, juvenile plants at yet another, with plants brought to flowering and market by a fourth. These efforts can involve several nations. Yet one country has stood out as the source for much of the advances in modern Phalaenopsis breeding over the past fifteen to twenty years: Taiwan.

Taiwanese growers are encouraged in a variety of ways—from direct tax support to government-funded research—to develop new export products and markets. Highly uniform and widely distributed hybrids such as Dtps. Sogo Beach are the result of this industrial approach to orchid breeding. The American orchid industry is beginning to adopt many of the same methods—without government support, it must be added—with increasingly favorable outcomes. The consequences for consumers are manifold, but the most important may be a constantly improving product, again exemplified by Dtps. Sogo Beach. Striped phals of this quality and brilliance were simply unheard-of even a few short years ago. The full shape and outstanding flower carriage on arching stems perfectly display the bright stripes and spots against a sharp white outline on the petals. These represent a quantum leap forward in Phalaenopsis hybridizing.

Dtps. *Sogo Beach 'Holly Frank' AM/AOS.*

Dtps. *Sogo Beach 'Alice Johnson' AM/AOS.*

PHALAENOPSIS BALDAN'S KALEIDOSCOPE & PHALAENOPSIS ORCHID WORLD

For much of the history of *Phalaenopsis* cultivation, uniformity of product was the result of selective inbreeding of known hybrid lines. For example, modern genetic research has demonstrated that most white *Phalaenopsis* are nothing more than highly bred *Phalaenopsis amabilis*, albeit polyploids. Much the same could be said of pinks. Nor did the existing market, consisting primarily of orchid hobbyists, demand much more than incremental improvements. The story was much different in the development of more unusually colored hybrids, where uniformity was essentially nonexistent, owing to the poorly shaped, small-flowered species available as a starting point. Even when a surprise result occurred, of unusual or unheard-of quality, the individual plant remained unique, a novelty for the few. The reason for this was that such high-quality plants generally did not breed, nor could they be tissue-cultured for mass distribution. Occasional crosses of uniform high quality such as *Phal.* Orchid World did occur, which often pointed the way to the parent, presumed to be the source of the quality. This is how *Phal.* Deventeriana 'Treva' has come into widespread use.

Many genera have what has come to be known as their "breakthrough" plants. Such plants achieve great and lasting popularity, often extending far beyond the immediate, foreseen market. Perhaps the best-known example is *Vuylstekeara* Cambria, where an entire class of hybrids has come to be known as "Cambrias." *Phalaenopsis* Baldan's Kaleidoscope is clearly an appealing and desirable cultivar, one that, in past years, with old technology, might have remained "one of a kind." However, its introduction at the dawn of new tissue culture techniques, which allow widespread propagation of *Phalaenopsis*, has enabled it to become nearly an industry standard for brightly colored *Phalaenopsis* potted plants. Where before it was pretty much limited to white or pink, today florists and designers can specify that they want a particular plant. And with its freedom of bloom—often producing multiple, branching inflorescences—and genuine quality, *Phal.* Baldan's Kaleidoscope has become a leader in its horticultural type. It takes its place as a distinct product alongside a range of colors and shapes never before seen in *Phalaenopsis*.

Above: Phal. *Baldan's Kaleidoscope 'Golden Treasure' AM/AOS rightfully set the standard for well-presented, attractively marked Phalaenopsis hybrids. It has been mericloned numerous times and is still one of the most popular phals in the commercial trade.*

Below: Phal. *Orchid World 'Irene Moran' AM/AOS.*

PHALAENOPSIS SOGO FESTIVAL, PHALAENOPSIS BROTHER GOLDEN WAVE & PHALAENOPSIS AMBO BUDDHA

Many modern yellows, such as Phal. Ambo Buddha 'Carib' AM/AOS, *have exotic markings as a bonus.*

One of the most astonishing aspects of the modern *Phalaenopsis* potted-plant market is the quantum leap in uniformity of quality that Taiwan growers have achieved. While tissue culture is becoming an increasingly important part of the overall production of *Phalaenopsis*, it is the Dutch growers who are its main proponents. The Taiwanese remain committed to the production of seed-raised populations. Arguments about which practice is "best"—the advantages and disadvantages of either method—rage on in industry circles. However, when breeders have parents that they know reliably produce high-quality progeny of great uniformity, which they have developed with great effort over a period of years, it is difficult to dissuade them from continuing their proven practices.

And unless their products were of uniform quality, they would not meet the standards set by an increasingly mechanized and

available to the public, in garden centers, and in Big Box suppliers.

Taiwanese breeders started out with the same parental stock as everyone else, but through a combination of perseverance and hard work they have created a legacy of beauty that we enjoy the fruits of every day.

standard-driven market. Thus, it is all the more amazing to note that many of the most highly awarded *Phalaenopsis* of recent years, particularly in the hotbed of *Phalaenopsis* production in South Florida, come straight out of what are potted-plant-oriented populations. Even twenty years ago, yellow *Phalaenopsis* of the quality illustrated here would have been a sensation, truly setting the orchid world on its ear. The clear yellow of *Phal.* Sogo Festival, the dotted yellow of *Phal.* Brother Golden Wave, or the outrageous patterned yellow of *Phal.* Ambo Buddha, would have represented a quantum leap in their respective types. Yet they are representative of plants

---

Above: Phal. Brother Golden Wave 'Crownfox'.

Below: Yellow Phalaenopsis *breeding has improved by light years since a hybrid named* Phal. Golden Emperor 'Sweet' *received an FCC/AOS in 1983. Now we can expect clear, rich color on flowers with excellent substance, such as* Phal. Sogo Festival 'Crownfox Sunrise' AM/AOS.

PHALAENOPSIS BROTHER PEPRIDE & PHALAENOPSIS BROTHER PETERSTAR

Phalaenopsis hybridizing has moved at a consistently faster rate than many other genera because of their more rapid growth rate. This allows breeders to more quickly see the results of their labors and to move along in breeding the next generation. Even so, until recent technological and cultural advances began to be put into widespread use, first-bloom *Phalaenopsis* were generally small and immature, giving only a hint of their adult potential. One result of this was that plants were rushed to the judging room with only a

Phal. *Brother Pepride 'KG's Happy Camper' AM/AOS.*

few flowers, in the hopes of gaining an award before the plant was superceded a short time later. Hobbyists who took the time to grow and culture their plants to a larger size, gaining a proportionately larger and showier inflorescence with more flowers, were often passed by in the march of progress.

However, modern cultural techniques and a demanding market have conspired to enable growers to produce a much more substantial plant in a shorter time. This results in better plants producing their first flowers, giving a more marketable and representative presentation. So what is seen at judging tables now

are plants much closer to their mature floral capability. This is an important gain, especially in hybrids based in species that tend to have lower flower counts, since first bloom plants may not produce enough flowers to be marketable unless well grown. *Phal.* Brother Peterstar is an example of what modern cultural techniques can achieve. On the other hand, the skill of amateur growers may still prevail when their plants, grown an additional year or two, are displayed with multiple branching stems of shapely and unusually colored blooms like *Phal.* Brother Pepride. It is still rather uncommon to see mature, well-grown phals in the judging room, and orchid judges react with pleasure when they see one that is so well presented

Above: Phal. Brother Peterstar 'Crownfox Sunglow' AM/AOS.

Below: The best of the new wave of Phalaenopsis *hybrids bear flowers on a short, branched inflorescence, such as* Phal. *Brother Pepride 'KG's Happy Camper' AM/AOS.*

PHALAENOPSIS H.P. NORTON & DORITAENOPSIS BROTHER TURKEY

Nowhere in *Phalaenopsis* hybridizing have results been slower to be realized than in red shades. Breeders have been frustrated by the lack of a truly "red" species and with the overall poor quality of those species that do exhibit some red coloration. What long passed for red in *Phalaenopsis* was actually more closely related to dark purple or similar colors. Additionally, flowers were generally of relatively small size and borne on short, few-flowered inflorescences that were of interest only to the truly dedicated *Phalaenopsis* fanciers. Two parents were destined to change this sad circumstance, one bred in the United States, one in Taiwan. *Phalaenopsis* Golden Buddha, bred in the 1970s, proved, particularly when selfed and sibling-crossed to intensify desired characters, to be an invaluable parent in the production of larger flowers, on taller stems, that began to approach red as its spotting coalesced. Although *Phal.* Golden Buddha was bred in the United States, and domestic breeders used it to some extent, it was in Taiwan that its true value was utilized.

The other key to the equation of producing red *Phalaenopsis* came about as a result of both breeding and selection of fortuitous mutations resulting from the tissue-culture process. Certain tissue-cultured plants of *Phal.* Golden Peoker showed darker and more coalesced red spotting than the original plant. These were tissue-cultured further, and darker mutations resulted. Breeding on from these enabled the improvement of *Phal.* Golden Peoker and led to *Phal.* Brother Purple and *Phal.* Brother Pirate King. Without such insightful use of chance, we would not have reds of the quality of *Phal.* H.P. Norton or *Dtps.* Brother Turkey. The large blooms of nearly standard shape, borne on inflorescences well above the foliage, are simply beautiful and far removed from what were considered "good" even ten years ago.

The two hybrids shown here, Dtps. Brother Turkey 'Ruben' AM/AOS (above right) and Phal. H.P. Norton 'Ponkan HCC/AOS (right), represent breakthroughs in the breeding of true red Phalaenopsis hybrids.

DORITAENOPSIS BROTHER PUNGOTEAGUE CREEK

What were once small, insipid, and few-flowered, red *Phalaenopsis* have progressed to the high standard we see today. The transition from insignificant to magnificent has been profound. It is not often in the annals of any orchid hybridizing that such a giant leap has been made in such a relatively short time. Often only one or another aspect of improvement is reached. For some time, red *Phalaenopsis* of American bloodlines came ever closer to true red color. However, they were almost exclusively on rather difficult-to-grow plants, and these exhibited short, horizontally held inflorescences with few flowers. Nor were the flowers particularly large. The resultant display was deficient, a "ring" of only a few flowers around the base of the plant, satisfactory only to those who simply had to have red flowers.

Nevertheless, with the advent of the Taiwan lines of breeding, color, size, and flower carriage has improved to such a great extent that the flowers would be considered of good quality no matter the color. When the saturated color is added into a mix that includes a strong, well-held inflorescence, we are left with a truly memorable creation of the hybridizer's art.

The plant pictured would have been nearly unthinkably high in quality as little as ten years ago. Further, this is only a few of the many that are beginning to show up on judging tables, in shows, and even in retail outlets. Due credit must be given to the Taiwanese creators of these truly beautiful hybrid *Phalaenopsis*.

Dtps. *Brother Pungoteague Creek is another successful red* Phalaenopsis *hybrid that retains the traditional "phal shape" and matte texture.*

PHALAENOPSIS BILL GOLDBERG

Phal. *Bill Goldberg 'Orchid World' AM/AOS.*

For many years, there were two choices to *Phalaenopsis* fanciers who wanted spotted flowers. The first were the so-called "French spots" derived from *Phalaenopsis stuartiana* and developed to a high degree by French breeders. These were basically white blooms with varying degrees of fine red spotting and red, often leopard spotted lips. While inflorescences were generally branched, producing a multitude of flowers, size could be lacking as could substance. These were very showy but so inbred that vigor was often lost. The other alternative was the hybrids bred from *Phal. lueddemanniana* crossed onto standard whites, which

produced heavy substanced ivory flowers marked with blotchy spots of varying shades of rose and magenta. Flower count was generally poor, with only a few flowers bunched up toward the end of a longish stem that often needed staking to display the flowers well.

Modern "novelty" spotted *Phalaenopsis* are based in the same breeding lines that gave rise to the rapid increase in the quality of red *Phalaenopsis*. Basically, good red *Phalaenopsis* are produced when heavy red spotting coalesces over a yellow background.

Phal. *Bill Goldberg 'Steve Goldberg' HCC/AOS.*

When the red spots are distinct, they give us our heavily and attractively spotted *Phalaenopsis* of today, which also have far better flower count and flower presentation on stronger stems than was previously attainable. Often, younger plants do not have more than a few flowers but still contain the potential to generate substantial, branching inflorescences when grown an additional year or two.

PHALAENOPSIS BROTHER MAXWELL, PHALAENOPSIS BRIGHT MORNING STAR & PHALAENOPSIS BROTHER JOHN CURTIN

Modern hybrids, like Phal. Bright Morning Star 'Simply Spotted' HCC/AOS, can have spotting that nearly coalesces, making the white base color appear to be the spots.

the art" comprised the direct hybrids of *Phal. lueddemanniana* with large whites.

Shape has improved, of course, as have the intensity of the spots' color and the purity of the background color. *Phal.* Bright Morning Star could pass for an improved *Phal.* Golden Buddha or Golden Peoker, both important background parents. The shape is fuller, and spotting is more red than purple, but the aspect of the flower, borne on a tallish stem above the foliage, is much like that of the progenitors.

No matter how far a line of breeding advances, it is always interesting to see examples of flowers that hark back to the starting point of the line. The spotting of *Phal.* Brother Maxwell is quite reminiscent of how novelty spotted phals looked when the "state of

However, it is in *Phal.* Brother John Curtain that a mechanism of flower color is unmasked. The heavy red spotting has run

together over the entire flower with the exception of a fine edge of

the flower's yellow base color. It is easy to see just how spots and

reds can come from similar, if not identical, lines of breeding.

Above: Phal. *Brother Maxwell 'Crownfox' AM/AOS.*

Below: Phal. *Brother John Curtin 'Crownfox Merlot' AM/AOS.*

PHAL. SUPER STUPID X BROTHER PASSAT, BROTHER KAISER X DORITAENOPSIS LOVE ROSA, & BROTHER TREASURE X BROTHER LAWRENCE

Phal. (*Brother Treasure x Brother Lawrence*).

Fast-growing plants for a fast-growing market undergoing rapid development of improved types; if this sounds like a recipe for intense competition, it is. Competition brings out both the best and worst in people. We have competitiveness to thank for the rapid evolution of the highly improved red and spotted *Phalaenopsis* now coming out of Taiwan. Without the need to excel and stand out from the crowd, the drive necessary to sustain enthusiasm in creation could not exist. The three first-bloom seedlings shown here are examples of the continual rush into the future by Taiwan nurseries, and of the high quality their product has attained. Large blooms with sharp markings highlighted against clean background colors are the goal for each breeder.

Alas, these three seedlings also show what the downside of such competition can be. For example, who, but a disgruntled competitor, would ever name an orchid "Super Stupid"? When all hybrid registrations are preceded by a nursery denominator, such as Brother This, Zuma That, or Ever-spring The Other, consumers may come to recognize a particular "brand"—and this is certainly

the intent—but individual product naming opportunities are lost in the forest of sameness. To ask for a product by name, a consumer has to be able to remember it in a positive light.

Orchids will truly enter the larger horticultural world only when egos are left aside for the more profitable practice of giving attractive product names to the plants.

Above: It is an adventure to buy unbloomed hybrids. They can provide pleasant surprises like the one shown here. Or if not chosen with good information, the surprise can be one of disappointment. The exotic markings of Phal. (Brother Kaiser x Dtps. Love Rosa) are yet another variation on a proven theme.

Left: Phal. (Super Stupid x Brother Passat).

PHALAENOPSIS BROTHER REDLAND SPOTS, PHALAENOPSIS EVER-SPRING KING & PHALAENOPSIS GOLDEN PEOKER

Meristemming of popular and desirable orchid cultivars has become an accepted fact of life for both the industry and for consumers. Product uniformity benefits industry and consumer alike, and uniformity of quality is a matter of faith for both. However, Phalaenopsis, particularly some of the more exotic color types, are not as stable throughout the cloning process as are other orchids. Mutations are not uncommon in Phalaenopsis, especially those affecting floral conformation and color patterning. Some are favorable, resulting in a more pleasing flower; some are not. Some result in plants with superior or new breeding qualities; some do not. The entire premise of the Harlequin line of breeding is based on a succession of mutations resulting from the meristem process. When "improved" meristem mutations of Phalaenopsis Golden Peoker are used in breeding, the successes are great, as in Phal. Brother Redland Spots, which shows

off the intense dark grape purple blotching that gives the group its name. Further mutations take a part in the story of this type. One of the early Phal. Golden Peoker progeny that first gave the Harlequin markings was Phal. Ever-spring King. Some of the best were immediately cloned. Unfortunately, the downside of the

Phal. Ever-spring King 'T.F.' HCC/AOS is representative of first-generation harlequin hybrids. The "spots" were actually raised and had a texture that some people found unattractive.

picture came quickly to light when the first of the cloned plants began to bloom and they often showed substantial differences from the mother plant. Some were better, of course, but many were inferior. Not only did this make sales of the plants difficult, but it also casts doubt on a process that relies as much on consumer faith as anything else. *Phal.* Ever-spring King also demonstrates the deficiencies in shape that can accompany the Harlequin markings.

Above: Phal. *Golden Peoker 'B'.' HCC/AOS.*

Below: Phal. *Brother Redland Spots 'Crownfox' HCC/AOS shows improvement on the texture problems of earlier hybrids.*

PHALAENOPSIS I-HSIN GOLD COAST & DORITAENOPSIS HAPPY KING

More and more breeders began to explore the potentials of this new type. What the genetics were, and how they would work, was still to be discovered. Many breeders concentrated on the "money crosses," those that would result in the highly desired white flowers with dark markings. Others, as might be expected, took other roads. Crossing the boldly spotted *Phalaenopsis* Golden Peoker back to a parent with a yellow background behind its spotting gave flowers like *Phalaenopsis* I-Hsin Gold Coast, with the bold marking over a yellow background. Flower count remained acceptable as did flower presentation with little of the shape anomalies that plague some other hybrids of this type.

A byway in Taiwan breeding that fits here, if only because it fits nowhere else, is the creation of the almost variegated types represented by *Phal.* Happy King. First seen some ten years ago at the New York International Orchid Show as an apparent mutation, debate has been intense as to whether what most closely resembles viral color break is attractive or not. *Dtps.* King Shiang's Rose, normally a very heavily striped flower, subject to streaking, seems to be a source of this type of color patterning. The final test will be, as always, not validation by any judging system but a consumer vote of confidence in terms of plant purchases. Whether or not these will ever amount to any more than a novelty also depends on reliable breeding pathways or meristem techniques that can guarantee a faithful reproduction of this aberrant flower patterning.

Opposite: Dtps. *Happy King 'Pine Ridge' HCC/AOS represents a breeding direction that is controversial. Some* Phalaenopsis *fanciers state that these "spin art" orchids look diseased because of their random markings, which resemble virus color break. Others love them!*

Right: Phal. *I-Hsin Gold Coast.*

MULTIFLORA PHALAENOPSIS: PHALAENOPSIS FAIRY CHARM & PHALAENOPSIS TAISUCO PIXERROT

Multiflora *Phalaenopsis* are not new. One of the earliest registered hybrids was *Phalaenopsis* Cassandra, a cross of *Phal. equestris* and *Phal. stuartiana*. The enduring charm of this particular hybrid is demonstrated by its having been remade several times over the past years, each time creating adherents anew. Unlike other *Phalaenopsis* hybrids made since, *Phal.* Cassandra, and others like it, had a charm and an overall display quality that went far beyond the beauty of the individual flower. Standard whites and pinks in full bloom were majestic, and many of the more highly colored yellows and related shades had their attractive attributes, but when a compactly sized plant gave two or three multiple branched stems of modestly sized blooms, there was simply no comparison.

In the late 1970s and early 1980s, as *Phalaenopsis* breeders began to look for a new way to penetrate the potted-plant market, a few again turned to *Phal. equestris*. This time the intent was not to gain a red lip or stripes on standard size blooms but rather to

miniaturize the presentation and to create a new type of plant. The goal was a plant that would remain a convenient size for the windowsill or under lights while producing a bounty of blooms that would be in proportion to the pot and plant. At the same time, improved strains of *Phal. equestris* were being developed, and the combination of desire and opportunity again led to a hybridizing success that we are still seeing the results of today. Breeders, apparently, do not want to stray far from the species background.

One of the most successful avenues remains the crossing of larger flowered types onto *Phal. equestris* for almost guaranteed success. Both *Phal.* Fairy Charm and *Phal.* Taisuco Pixerrot are outstanding examples of the type.

Above: While multifloral Phalaenopsis *hybrids lack the individual flower size of the standard types, they make up for this shortcoming with floral exuberance.* Phal. Taisuco Pixerrot *uses the* Phal. equestris *hybrid,* Phal. Carmela's Pixie, *to produce a cloud of flowers above the foliage.*

Opposite: Phal. *Fairy Charm 'Denise's Pride' HCC/AOS.*

PHALAENOPSIS ZUMITA BLUSH & DORITAENOPSIS AWESOME JEWEL

One of the problems faced by breeders wishing to breed with the hybrids resulting from direct species use, as in *Phalaenopsis equestris* hybrids, is finding parents that will give seed. Often the results of such hybrids are triploids or other ploidy levels that will not reproduce. One of the happy results of the introduction of polyploid forms of *Phal. equestris* and other species is that their hybrids, which might have otherwise been sterile, will give fertile seed. Pioneering breeders found hybrids such as *Phal.* Carmela's Pixie, *Phal.* Zuma Pixie, and *Phal.* Be Glad that would reliably give seed, thereby enabling them to move away from direct species influence to more complex hybrids. In the case of both *Phal.* Carmela's Pixie and *Phal.* Be Glad, one of the parents was the well-known and loved *Phal.* Cassandra, which carried the additional advantageous trait of giving fine, *Phal. stuartiana*–based spotting to the progeny.

The goal in all such multiflora *Phalaenopsis* breeding is to keep the plant and the flowers in proportion. Balancing various species-derived characteristics is not always easy, especially since how a particular parent will behave in hybridizing cannot be known until the progeny begin to bloom. Again, the opportunity in *Phalaenopsis* development is extraordinarily short generations. When a parent is found to be valuable, it can quickly be incorporated into the breeding program. The development of reliably dwarf, multiflora *Phalaenopsis* has proceeded rapidly as a result. Consumers are thrilled to not only be able to obtain plants of the quality of *Phal.* Zumita Blush and *Dtps.* Awesome Jewel but also to be able to continue to bloom them, reliably, year after year in limited space. The sparkling texture and bright pink tones make an attractive display in the home, where value is prized, lasting so much longer than any comparably priced flower arrangement could ever hope to do.

Left: Soft pink flowers with delicate spotting are set off by a large colorful lip in the hybrid Phal. *Zumita Blush.*

Right: Dtps. *Awesome Jewel has flowers that change color as they age.*

PHALAENOPSIS BROTHER ORANGE RUNABOUT

While American breeders concentrated on "standard" colors and color combinations—white, shades of pink, white with colored lip, finely spotted *Phalaenopsis stuartiana* types, stripes—the Taiwanese put their accumulated breeding prowess behind the creation of new and unusual color combinations. Seedlings of the best multiflora types had traveled to Taiwan from the very earliest point in their development. The Taiwanese breeders, clever and quick to seize any advantage, put the finest from these seedling crosses into their breeding programs. Nor did they limit themselves to the standard, established breeding lines but instead were quick to introduce appropriately sized plants from their existing programs into the multiflora lines.

Phal. Timothy Christopher combined some of the best genes for multifloras (Cassandra x *amabilis*) and—when mated to the brightly colored *Phal.* Sara Gold to make the pictured *Phal.* Brother Orange Runabout—gave a new direction to this quickly diversifying new line of potted-plant subjects. Interestingly, multifloras continue to be more popular in other countries and with American orchid hobbyists rather than with the much more substantial U.S. potted-plant buying public. Mass-market-oriented growers want to be able to grow more of this compact type, but the buying public has been slow to adopt the type, preferring the large and flamboyant standard-sized plants and flowers. The plants also need two to three additional years of growing to reach their full potential.

Phal. *Brother Orange Runabout was registered in 2000 and produces nicely arched inflorescences of perfectly shingled, colorful flowers.*

PHALAENOPSIS TIMOTHY CHRISTOPHER & PHALAENOPSIS ARCTIC THRESHOLD

One of the primary attractive features of orchid flowers as a whole is their distinctive bilateral symmetry, dominated by the highly modified third petal we call a lip, or labellum. It is ironic, therefore, that when an orchid flower is discovered where the petals match the lip, or the lip the petals, we cherish it above all else. The best example is the splash-petal cattleyas derived from *Cattleya intermedia* Aquinii and similarly marked species. Why a regressive mutation should lead to so much fanfare is hard to discern. The easy answer would be that since most orchids aren't that way, a flower that is distinct in having matching petals is prized—even though that is the norm in most commonly grown flowers.

Plants exhibiting this condition are known as peloric.

Phalaenopsis species do not normally exhibit this condition, with the notable exception of *Phalaenopsis equestris*. Even when the species parent does not show the three-lipped, peloric state, its hybrids may. More commonly, clones of *Phal. equestris* hybrids may mutate to show this peloric condition. The charming fleur-de-lis shape never fails to draw admirers, and orchid judges are no exception as in the highly awarded *Phal.* Timothy Christopher 'Zuma Odyssey' AM/AOS.

Petals that match the lip are a fairly common occurrence in a variety of hybrid lines. A less common mutation is when the lip matches the petals. First and most famously seen in dendrobiums, the sheer volume of *Phalaenopsis* in production has led to examples of this trait such as *Phal.* Arctic Threshold, a most unusual result from standard white breeding.

Left: Phal. Timothy Christopher 'Zuma Odyssey' AM/AOS.

Opposite: Some feel that peloric flowers, such as Phal. Arctic Threshold 'White Thunder' JC/AOS, do not truly represent Phalaenopsis because they no longer look like one. For others, they represent breakthrough breeding for novelty types.

PHALAENOPSIS WORLD CLASS
& PHALAENOPSIS ELIZABETH HAYDEN

It is inevitable that, as more and more plants of any type are grown, the incidence of sports, anomalies, and aberrant individuals will rise. Observant breeders and horticulturists, knowledgeable of this axiom, are alert to the opportunities it presents.

The first of the new type of three-petalled *Phalaenopsis* to reach a wide market was *Phalaenopsis* World Class 'Big Foot'. Discovered in a batch of what were bred to be standard pink *Phalaenopsis* hybrids, the large size and bold petal markings of the lip had never before been seen. The discoverer had the means to propagate the plant extensively and has done so, gaining wide distribution and popularity for this oddball. Interestingly, all the other characteristics that make standard phals so widely grown do not seem to have suffered. The tall, arching stems still bear well-shingled blooms of good size and bright color. They just have three petals, rather than two petals and a lip.

Often, new and rare mutations of this sort do not breed on. However, the first hybrids using *Phal.* World Class have begun to bloom, and at least some of the seedlings have shown a similar three-petalled flower. In dendrobiums, similar mutations resulted in the establishment of a new "pansy" type flower. Whether or not this will be the case with *Phal.* World Class remains to be seen, but it continues to be a fascinating sidelight to the larger and better-known lines of breeding.

Phal. *World Class 'Big Foot' JC/AOS (right) was a breakthrough for peloric types and paved the way for hybrids such as* Phal. *Elizabeth Hayden (below).*

PHALAENOPSIS VIOLACEA
(SYN BELLINA)

It is easy to forget, in all the discussion of markets and breeding and horticultural subjects, that *Phalaenopsis* lovers make up the only really successful single genus specialty group, the International Phalaenopsis Alliance. Regional and national meetings of this group are filled with enthusiasm and the latest news about their mutual love for these fine plants. Their newsletter is a model that others might do well to emulate. Collecting and growing *Phalaenopsis* species is an entire subset of the hobby where species are grown for their own intrinsic charm and beauty.

Phalaenopsis violacea, this form now more properly known as *Phal. bellina*, must be one of the most lovely of all species, *Phalaenopsis* or otherwise. Beyond the elegance of the blooms and the simply gorgeous large bright green leaves, this species has something to be prized above all else: a sweet and penetrating perfume. This feature is often passed along to its hybrids, something not to be overlooked. Besides the obvious features, *Phal. bellina* has made a significant contribution to red color in phal hybrids by the continual breeding and extension of the red of its inner lateral sepals over an increasing area of the flower. *Phal.* Luedde-violacea, when backcrossed to *violacea/bellina*, gave one of the most famous red-toned early hybrids, *Phal.* George Vasquez. Although now superceded, many longtime growers have fond memories of the sharp colors presented by this hybrid. Sadly, the short drooping flower stems of *Phal. bellina* are quite dominant in its hybrids with the result that flowers are not presented out of the foliage.

Phal. *violacea (bellina) 'Judy's Delight'* AM/AOS.

PARAPHALAENOPSIS KOLOPAKING & PARAPHALAENOPSIS LABUKENSIS

Perspective is a wonderful thing. Even an untrained amateur has difficulty understanding today some of the decisions reached as entirely reasonable by taxonomists of yesterday. How the plants now grouped into *Paraphalaenopsis* could have ever been considered *Phalaenopsis*, or even closely related, is a mystery. The blooms are showy, granted, but they are borne on a relatively short, stiffly upright inflorescence, whose aspect is closer to that of a *Vanda*. The plants are so different as to defy imagination, with long, terete rattail-like leaves drooping down from a fairly short stem. In fact, they even breed more like a *Vanda* or *Ascocenda*.

Nevertheless, for many years the species in this genus were considered members of *Phalaenopsis* and registered as such. Today this can lead to some confusion, especially among those with less historical insight. The species and hybrids of this genus also respond culturally in a way that is at odds with the appearance of the plants. Generally, terete, narrow leaves are a response to high light as well as to low humidity. *Paraphalaenopsis* grown under such conditions quickly expire. Experienced growers have learned that these very tropical subjects do best in slatted baskets similar to those in which vandas do so well, but hung in a layer under the vandas, where increased shade and humidity suit the plants better. While purveyors of vandas often stock imported plants in this genus, they are not for everyone. Only those who can provide the rather specialized conditions these plants require need apply.

Right: Paraphalaenopsis labukensis *'Crownfox Midnight' AM/AOS.*

Below: Paraphalaenopsis *Kolopaking 'Crownfox' HCC/AOS.*

DEVEREUXARA CROWNFOX SUN SPLASH

Taxonomic changes can cascade down through the registration system, causing confusion and consternation. The logical, reasonable, and fairly recent recognition that, yes, *Paraphalaenopsis* was distinct from *Phalaenopsis* and ought to be treated as such results in problems as we see with this beautiful and unusual hybrid. Is it a *Devereuxara* (*Ascocentrum* x *Phalaenopsis* x *Vanda*) or is it a *Paravandrum* (*Ascocentrum* x *Pps.* x *Vanda*)? To the uninitiated, such questions are arcane and might seem academic. However, the results of the two different combinations would be significantly different, both in floral and cultural characteristics.

Be that as it may, *Paravandrum* Crownfox Sun Splash is a delightful and colorful new hybrid, opening new possibilities for patterning and conformation. Tropical growers will find such hybrids most rewarding as garden plants, while temperate-zone growers must resort to vanda conditions to succeed.

Above: Pvd. *Crownfox Sun Splash 'Pink Glow' HCC/AOS.*

Opposite: Pvd. *Crownfox Sun Splash 'Orange Crush' AM/AOS.*

THE CATASETUM GROUP

The orchid family is an extraordinarily large and diverse group of flowering plants—one, it must be admitted, to which the old adage of "not seeing the forest for the trees" could well be applied.

This is understandable, given the vast array of popularly grown genera, both species and hybrids. However, when a grower begins to become familiar with the more commonly seen varieties, the temptation arises to venture off the beaten path into more exotic and adventurous types. There are groups of genera that, while popular with dedicated orchid enthusiasts, are less often seen in the general trade and are well worth searching out. A group that fits this description very well is the *Catasetum* alliance.

A fimbriate "dust mop" lip set against spotted flower parts make Ctsm. lanciferum *a worthy addition to any orchid collection.*

CATASETUM PILEATUM
& CATASETUM LANCIFERUM

Catasetum is a fairly widely distributed genus of the American tropics, ranging from Mexico to Peru. The plants themselves are among the most handsome of all orchids, with robust cigar-shaped pseudobulbs and broad, thin, soft green leaves that fall during the dormant period. Many are unisexual, that is, bearing separate male and female flowers that are highly distinct, one from the other. These are the "true" catasetums. The best known and most widely grown of these is *Catasetum pileatum*, the former national flower of Venezuela (now *Cattleya mossiae*). While this group is often unisexual, "perfect" or hermaphroditic flowers can be seen as well. The difference between male and female flowers, coupled with their being borne on separate inflorescences and at different times or season, has led to a great deal of confusion in the taxonomy of this group. Add in the facts that the female flowers are often very similar between species and the male flowers different, it is easy to see why early taxonomists had trouble. Today, a core group of dedicated growers are concentrating on cultivating the plants, flowering them, and aiding taxonomists in their proper classification.

Above: The exquisite lunar green flowers of Ctsm. pileatum *have long been valued by collectors. The species has received dozens of awards. Shown here are male flowers.*

Below: Catasetums will occasionally produce hermaphroditic flowers. The flowers are similar to the male flowers shown above, but also show the helmet-shaped lip typical of female flowers. And of course, the flowers are upside down (non-resupinate).

CATASETUM FIMBRIATUM

Because many of this genus are quite showy, it is only natural that they have their own group of specialist growers. These people are willing to go the "extra mile" it can take to grow the plants well. Catasetums exhibit the seasonal growth typical of deciduous orchids, with rapid growth during the warm and moist months in their habitat and a decided rest with the maturation of the pseudobulbs. For this reason, it is important that the plants be grown in a fast-draining but water-retentive medium, to allow the frequent waterings and abundant fertilizer necessary to form their often large growths. Additionally, so many form pendant inflorescences that hanging baskets are indicated, to allow the flower stems to emerge cleanly and easily. The hanging basket culture gives the added advantage of increased air circulation and rapid drying that the plants enjoy. Growers find that when the plants are hung, it allows them to more easily inspect the leaves from underneath, to guard against the number-one enemy of this group: spider mites, which love the broad, thin leaves. Spider mites can quickly build up, disfiguring the beautiful foliage and weakening the plant. These pests can be kept under control by frequent syringing of the undersides of the leaves, another reason to hang the plants. Spider mites are encouraged by low humidity and poor air circulation, so their control is a matter of good culture, as well.

When growths mature in late summer, a dry rest (in the pot, not in the atmosphere) should follow as cooler fall temperatures approach to encourage flowering. Here is where the question, "when should I stop watering?" becomes important. The observant grower applies water according to the plants' needs. When a plant is in active growth, with strong root and shoot activity, frequent watering and adding fertilizer is the rule. As growth and root activity slows, the plants begin to dry more slowly, signaling the grower to slow his watering. When the plant isn't growing actively, water needs are diminished to the point that it may take a week or more before the media dries. The answer then to the question of when to water or not becomes straightforward: water when the plant needs it.

Catasetum fimbriatum is a good example of a more typical, though still highly exotic, member of the genus. The strong flower stem emerges nearly horizontally and then descends, holding the flowers well for viewing from underneath.

As in most species of Catasetum, *the flowers of* Ctsm. fimbriatum *have a trigger mechanism that firmly plants the pollinia on the head or back of the unsuspecting euglossine bee that bumps into it.*

CLOWESIA RUSSELIANA, CLOWESIA REBECCA'S DAUGHTER & CATAMODES PAINTED DESERT

The "true" catasetums have generally unisexual flowers. The "other" catasetums, *Clowesia*, have perfect, or hermaphroditic, blooms. This, of course, is the more usual arrangement in orchids. *Clowesia russeliana* is the most commonly seen member of the genus and is typical with more compact pseudobulbs and a strongly pendant inflorescence of fragrant greenish white blooms. The substance is not as heavy as in many of its allied species. Hybrids in *Clowesia* and with

The soft pink flowers of the recently awarded Cl. Rebecca's Daughter 'JEM' AM/AOS are borne on an arching inflorescence.

closely allied genera such as *Catasetum* and *Mormodes* are relatively uncommon. However, it is within *Clowesia* that one of the most popular hybrids exists, *Cl*. Rebecca Northen (Grace Dunn x *rosea*), created by that master of the unusual, Goodale Moir. This delicate, pink-flowered plant has had a place in connoisseurs' collections for decades and occasionally is used for further breeding as in *Cl*. Rebecca's Daughter (Rebecca Northen x *warscewitzii*).

It is with the closely allied genus *Mormodes* that both catasetums and clowesias make the most interesting hybrids. Another fascinating byway of orchid hybridizing is the search for the "black orchid." Breeders will search out flowers that in some way approach black and attempt to build on the colors already present to try and create "black." These colors are often better described as "wine," "plum," or "burgundy." A truly "black" flower wouldn't be very attractive to most, as is ably demonstrated by some of the paphiopedilums that have achieved this goal. Nevertheless, in some of the *Catamodes* hybrids, breeders have made some progress in this arcane game, though the byproducts, those not anywhere near black, are often the most beautiful. *Ctmds.* Paintec Desert is an outstanding example of this line of breeding.

Above right: Cl. *russeliana is a popular and easy to grow member of the genus. The long inflorescence bears many glassine-green flowers that are fragrant of floor polish.*

Right: The richly colored flowers of Ctmds. *Painted Desert 'Cranberry Delight' AM/AOS resemble a miniature* Cymbidium.

MORMODES DASILVAE

Mormodes, the goblin orchids, are among the most weirdly beautiful of all flowers. The intricate blooms, in Halloween colors with haunting, often medicinal, perfumes, have a dedicated following among orchid collectors. Easily grown in conditions that suit their relatives, the heavy-substanced blooms are borne from bare pseudobulbs in late winter into spring, before new growth commences. In nature, both *Mormodes* and *Catasetum* plants are often found in what would appear to be very marginal habitats, including on old fence posts and telephone poles. Their rapid seasonal growth and deciduous nature helps them to survive these difficult conditions. As with *Catasetum*, the leaves of *Mormodes* are very susceptible to spider mites, which can mar and disfigure the otherwise attractive foliage.

As a genus of more limited consumer appeal, many of the plants in cultivation continue to be wild-collected, since seed propagation, though more desirable, is not often practical for commercial nurseries. Since wild-collected plants are the norm, new species are continually appearing in collections. Some are highly exotic and become sought-after, such as *Mormodes dasilvae*, notable for its subtle bronze coloration and white column.

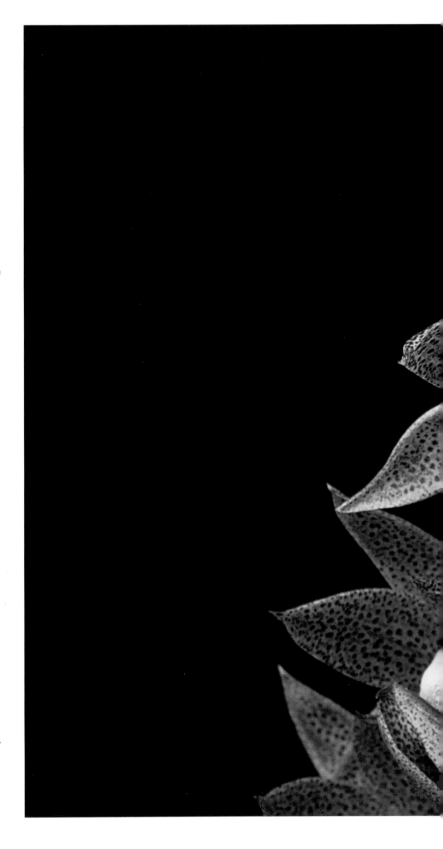

Morm. dasilvae *'Jem' CBR/AOS clearly shows the "twisted" lip characteristic of Mormodes. This trait usually disappears within one generation when a Morm. species is used as a hybrid parent with allied genera.*

CYCNOCHES LODDIGESII
& CYCNOCHES HAAGII

Long known as swan orchids, *Cycnoches* is another of the Catasetum group that is undergoing a renaissance of popularity. Like catasetums, this is a very easy-to-grow group of orchids with a very similar culture. The often quite large, up to eighteen inches or more, pseudobulbs have attractive thin leaves that are deciduous. Flower stems are borne from near the apex of the pseudobulbs and may be erect, arching, or pendulous. As with true catasetums, the flowers are unisexual and strikingly dimorphic, male and female flowers seemingly not belonging to the same species. Additionally, *Cycnoches* blooms are always nonresupinate, or "upside down," with the lip displayed uppermost. This results from the flower stems revolving through an entire 360-degree twist, unlike the 180-degree twist most orchids use to put the lip lowermost. The floral display is often quite long lasting, several weeks or more, and is a source of great comment in any display. *Cycnoches loddigesii* and *Cyc. haagii* have long been in cultivation and are the archetypal swan orchids with their birdlike flowers. *Cyc. haagii*, in particular, is notable for its deep pippin-green coloration, delightfully highlighted by the pure white lip. The male flowers of this group tend to be the more often seen and usually are more prolifically borne on longer inflorescences. Female flowers are generally slightly larger and singly borne. Experienced growers know what cultural conditions lead to the formation of either male or female flowers, and, when able, use differing conditions to induce the desired flowers for breeding or identification.

Left: Cyc. haagii *has apple-green flowers with a contrasting lip of white to pink color, usually with fine spotting.*

Opposite: The graceful flowers of Cyc. loddigesii *have a base color that ranges from greenish to red-brown. An inflorescence can carry ten or more large (four inch) flowers.*

CYCNOCHES BARTHIORUM & CYCNOCHES COOPERI

It is not the species of this group, known the longest, that have led to the recent upsurge in interest. It is the several new and reintroduced species with incredible blooms that have set the orchid world on fire over the past ten years or so. *Cycnoches barthiorum*, from Colombia, was first described some time ago, but was lost to cultivation. The species name honors one of the pioneers of Colombian orchids, Hans Barth, whose family is still in the orchid business in Colombia. The habitat was rediscovered in the mid-1990s, leading to a proliferation of plants available to the trade. One of the most unforgettable sights of my orchid career was on a visit to California in 1999, when I saw some of the first plants to flower on a hobbyist's patio. The pendant inflorescences backlit by the afternoon sun gave the impression of a row of shining copper coins fluttering in the soft breeze.

Depending on the age of the flowers, and the lighting, the color ranges from a bronzy green to a coppery orange. Plants quickly began to appear in the United States, in shows and at monthly judging events. The beauty of this species startled viewers and judges alike, and many high American Orchid Society awards followed. However, as with any quantum leap in the quality of flowers, the sheer newness often led to awards based as much on surprise as relative bloom quality. Nevertheless, if beauty alone is a

Cyc. barthiorum *'Jem III'* AM/AOS.

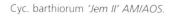
Cyc. barthiorum 'Jem II' AM/AOS.

Cyc. cooperi 'Crownfox' AM/AOS.

criterion, all are worthy. The related and equally showy *Cyc. cooperi* also made its appearance at about the same time. New to cultivation, its species name honors one who first flowered and displayed a plant of this species. As with *Cyc. barthiorum*, a new standard of beauty for the genus had to be recognized by a series of awards. More similar in shape to the classic swan orchid, *Cyc. cooperi* is distinct by its longer and more floriferous inflorescence as well as the unusual chartreuse-to-copper color. Commercial growers can only hope that the exhibitors are beginning to propagate these from seed to enable widespread availability.

CYCNOCHES HERRENHUSANUM

Thanks to increasing activity in the discovery and propagation of the species from Colombia by Colombian nurseries, a spate of heretofore rarely available varieties are now easily found. This is the way it should be, of course, with the range country benefiting from its natural resources. When in-country nurseries propagate their native species for worldwide distribution, a greater portion of the resulting revenue remains in the country. The orchid community as a whole also benefits, as it is a cycle of success that fuels the continuing introduction and availability of a country's finest orchids. *Cycnoches barthiorum* and *Cyc. cooperi* are just two examples. A third notable introduction from this same group may be the showiest of the three, *Cyc. herranhusanum*.

First seen as a single plant, *Cyc. herrenhusanum* created a minor sensation when displayed. Unfortunately, single plants of cycnoches are a problem when it comes to propagation, since often the grower is not able to induce the female flowers that are necessary to seed production. *Cyc. herrenhusanum* also had a reputation of being a bit difficult to grow. Now, with the introduction of additional mature plants from Colombia, as well as seedling populations, this lovely golden-flowered species is becoming more available to growers. Increased availability can often mean that cultural quirks are discovered, leading to the plants' wider success in cultivation. This is a dual benefit: more can enjoy the beauty of the plant as well as lessening demand for fresh material, as more of the existing plants survive.

Orchid students can be grateful for the introduction of these three wonderful species, as any one of them is enough to create excitement. Rarely do three such horticulturally important species, so closely related, come onto the scene in such a short period of time. Nor is so much said so succinctly about the value of responsible artificial propagation as with their relatively rapid distribution to a waiting public.

The beautiful sulphur-yellow flowers of Cyc. herrenhusanum *make this recently discovered species much in demand. Fortunately, seed-grown plants are available.*

GALEANDRA BAUERI, GALEANDRA DEVONIANUM, & CATASANDRA FANFARE

Often confused with Gal. batemanii, Gal. baueri *can be found growing in the tops of Paurotis palms in Central America. Flowers are produced in flushes on the inflorescence providing an extended blooming season. Flowers smell like leather.*

Galeandra, the last of the *Catasetum* relatives to be considered in this section, is an often overlooked, though very showy, genus. Widespread throughout the Americas from Florida south to Brazil, most of the horticulturally known species come from the expanse of Brazil. Tall, cylindrical pseudobulbs have slender, thin leaves characteristic of the group and are also deciduous to some extent. The racemes of blooms are borne terminally, with the sepals and petals forming a circular, backswept backdrop to the round and showy lip. Culture is similar to the others in this group, with a seasonal need for frequent watering and fertilizing.

Not too often seen in modern collections, adherents of the

genus do exist, and occasionally populations of the most desirable species are seen. The discerning grower will not want to pass up such opportunities, as galeandras are easy to grow and give a long-lasting, distinctive, and beautiful display of lip-dominated blooms. Indeed, the cyclical nature of orchid fads dictates the occasional availability of hybrids between *Galeandra* species as well as other related genera. While species such as *Galeandra baueri* and *Gal. devonianum* are the most often seen, and are very worthwhile in their own right, breeders also produce intriguing combinations that draw the speculative interest of curious hobbyists. *Catasandra* Fanfare (*Ctsm. expansum* x *Gal. baueri*) is just such a highly unusual and satisfactory plant. Good for the subtropical conditions where it was bred, it also easily adapts to greenhouse culture due to its easygoing nature.

Above left: Flowers of Gal. devoniana *are larger than others in the genus.*

Left: The interesting intergeneric hybrid, Ctsda. *Fanfare, was created by crossing a* Catasetum *with a* Galeandra.

THE STANHOPEA GROUP

Of all the many byways in the orchid family, none is more rewarding—or more bizarre—than the Stanhopea group.

Nowhere else is there such a variety of color, shape, and fragrance, all of which add up to a floral experience unequaled in the plant kingdom. Despite their massive and showy blooms, however, stanhopeas themselves are not generally common in cultivation. A few species such as *Stanhopea tigrina* and *Stan. wardii* are fairly widely available and regularly seen. And, while many of the genus are wildly colored, there are the more subtly nuanced blooms such as *Stan. reichenbachiana* and *Stan. grandiflora*, said to be representative of the more primitive state of the genus. A sharply pendant inflorescence is characteristic of the group, and flowers droop downward, necessitating viewing from beneath. Petals and sepals often reflex back, exposing the intricate structures of the lip and column, which serve to attract pollinators.

These massive, fragrant, and colorful blooms, clearly representing an enormous energy expenditure on the part of the plant, are ephemeral at best, lasting only a day or two. The weirdly shaped lip and column, with their waxy superstructures, help to ensure that the pollinator, once present, is directed through the pollination process correctly.

Above left: The beautiful, pristine white flowers of Stan. reichenbachiana *resemble falling angels.*

Left: Most stanhopeas, including Stan. wardii, *have very distinct fragrances to attract their euglossine bee pollinators. Most of the fragrances are pleasant, but some smell like cleaning products.*

Right: A bee's-eye view of Stan. grandiflora. *Although the sepals and petals of stanhopeas fade within a day or two, the plasticky "business end" (the lip and column) lasts several days longer.*

STANHOPEA CONNATA

Stanhopea connata is one of the most brilliantly colored of the genus, though it lacks the patterning that marks species like *Stan. tigrina* and *Stan. nigroviolacea*. Its segments are also fuller than most, giving it an appearance that is more generally appealing and traditionally beautiful than many of its close relatives. However, what we see in a flower and what the pollinator sees are two very different things. Pollinators often see in different wavelengths of light and are attracted by colors and markings that are simply not visible to human eyes. Vision is limited by a great many factors and so, for such short-lived flowers as these, their visual appearance is not necessarily the first line of attraction. Scent, on the other hand, is detectable and attractive in very small amounts over an incredible distance. Specific fragrances and floral structures attract very specific pollinators to each different species.

A famous story, first published in a *National Geographic* article about orchids more than thirty years ago, is illustrative of the specificity and power of fragrance as an attractant. Dr. Calaway Dodson, now revered as one of the greatest orchid biologists of all time, has made a study of the fragrances of stanhopeas. While vacationing with his bride in South America, he came across a plant of a species of *Stanhopea* in bud. He brought the plant in bud back to his honeymoon suite, in the hopes of studying the pollinators. The next morning, euglossine bees of a special sort were hovering around the room, but the flowers had not opened. It seems that his wife's perfume had the same active ingredients as one of the plant's fragrant oils.

Opposite: Stan. connata *is one of the most highly colored species of the genus. The sweet fragrance can be overpowering in a closed-in area.*

Below: Two to five flowers are produced on the pendant inflorescence of Stan. connata.

STANHOPEA OCULATA

The downward-growing flower stems of stanhopeas present some challenges for both viewers and growers. Growers must provide the proper environment for the plant to allow the descending inflorescences to emerge easily from the plant, allowing the ponderous flower buds to develop and open. While mounting plants on cork or treefern rafts is an option, it is difficult to keep humidity high enough for success, yet very high humidity can lead to other foliar disfigurements that many would find unacceptable. Most find that wire baskets are the best option, as even slatted teak baskets may not provide enough room between slats for the fat stem to poke out. Interestingly, young *Stanhopea* seedlings grown in regular pots will occasionally be pushed out of the pot by a developing inflorescence. Otherwise, *Stanhopea* culture presents no special problems, and plants prove to be nearly indestructible under most conditions.

Viewers are given several choices for the best presentation of flowers. Some prefer the profile view, while some like the upward-looking view. In profile, the complex lip and column can be easily studied, while the view from below presents a more traditional look to the flower. *Stanhopea oculata* is particularly interesting, presenting the two black "eyes" that give the species its name. Either way, the opportunity to see a *Stanhopea* plant in flower is all too rare and should always be taken.

Left: The species is closely related to, and occasionally confused with, Stan. wardii. Both species are found in Central America and northern South America.

Right: Stan. oculata usually carries four to eight flowers on a chandelierlike inflorescence.

ACINETA SUPERBA

One of the opportunities presented by an increasingly global orchid community is for American Orchid Society judges to visit and judge orchids in their native countries. Judges get the chance to evaluate species that are rarely seen in the United States, grown to the perfection that can only happen in the actual habitat or something very close to it. Species like *Acineta superba*, which is rarely seen in the United States, are often exhibited as large plants with multiple inflorescences of perfectly presented blooms. My experience with such opportunities has been invaluable and much treasured, though it can occasionally "spoil" one for plants back home.

Acineta is closely related to both *Stanhopea* and *Peristeria*, though the lip of the bloom is closer to that of the former genus. Plants are robust, easily cultured under the same conditions that suit stanhopeas. Baskets are a necessity, to accommodate the inflorescences that grow straight down, producing a dozen or more spicily fragrant blooms that remain cupped. Perhaps as plants become more available from range-state nurseries, as certainly will be the case with *Acineta superba*, we will be graced with their presence at our orchid shows and society meetings.

Above: There are close to twenty species in the genus Acineta *with* Acn. superba *being the type. The species is found in Venezuela, Colombia, and Ecuador. Here it is shown growing on a tree near Cali, Colombia.*

Right: Acn. superba *'Vilma Marie' AM/AOS received its award in Caracas in 2002.*

SOTEROSANTHUS SHEPHEARDII

Most of the plants of this group are larger growing, hence demanding of space. The pseudobulbs are often golf-ball-sized or larger, with broad, stiff leaves that can reach more than thirty-six inches. In addition, many often will not flower well or at all on smaller plants of only a few pseudobulbs, so large plants are generally the rule. For these reasons, those with more limited growing areas must shy away from these ephemeral but rewarding species. Where space is not a premium, in warmer summer areas or often under *Cymbidium* garden conditions, growers can afford the space it takes to do well with stanhopeas and their relatives. Even hanging baskets need somewhere spacious to hang!

There are genera and individual species in this group that can be accommodated in smaller collections, on the windowsill or under lights. *Paphinia*, for example, is a great favorite with East Coast growers who favor miniature orchids. The large flowers are out of proportion to the plant and give a showy contrast in a limited space. Another favorite, though not widely known, is *Soterosanthus shepheardii*. Looking much like a dwarf stanhopea, with similar pseudobulbs and leaves, this orchid has six-inch to eight-inch upright inflorescences of beautiful lemon-yellow blooms rising just above the foliage. They are not the easiest plant to grow, but seedling populations from a California nursery have come into the trade and are highly prized. Premature leaf spotting and subsequent leaf drop may be the result of poor water quality, so growers in higher rainfall areas may succeed better with this attractive and desirable species. Very fine-flowering-sized plants can easily be accommodated in three-inch pots, making this ideal for home orchid growers.

Unlike many Stanhopeinae, Strsnt. shepeardii *has an upright inflorescence.*

GONGORA CASSIDEA

Gongoras are another group with bizarrely shaped blooms borne on pendant inflorescences. Two or three broad leaves top the strongly ridged and compact pseudobulbs. The hanging inflorescences often have a dozen or more blooms that hang straight down from the bottom of the plant. Culture is generally easy, under conditions similar to those that suit stanhopeas and similar plants. It seems somehow misleading to picture a species like *Gongora cassidea*, so unrepresentative of the group, first. Nevertheless, this is a truly beautiful flower in its own right and highly worthy of more widespread cultivation. Hailing from Mexico south to Costa Rica, it has fewer flowers than others in the genus, though the flowers are much fuller in shape, as if to compensate. The shape is similar to the closely related *Gga. galeata*, more often seen in collections. Unlike most gongoras, the dorsal sepal is round and helmet-shaped, partially hiding the column.

Gga. gratulabunda is more characteristic of the genus. A profile view shows off the strongly pendant flower, with the reflexed flower parts pulled away to expose the intricate lip and column, structured not unlike the related stanhopeas. Knowledgeable growers claim that the scent of this flower resembles a shrimp boil.

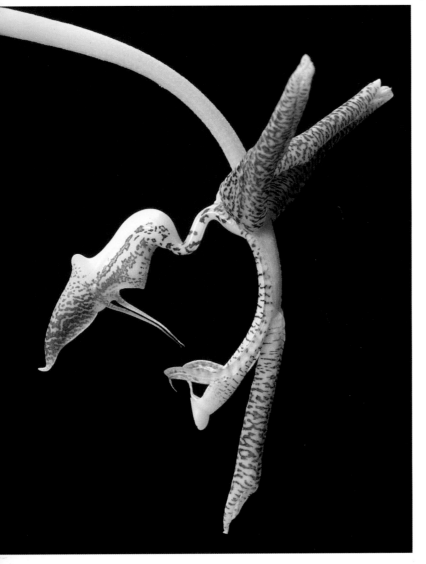

Left: Many gongoras have spotted flowers that are arranged on a long, pendant inflorescence. Gga. gratulabunda *is among them.*

Right: Gga. cassidea *bears little resemblance to other gongoras because of its round, cupped shape.*

GONGORA UNICOLOR

One of my fondest travel memories is of a clothesline hung with dozens of baskets of *Gongora* species. This sight was in the backyard of a Colombian home. The plants were elevated enough to appear as if you were walking down an aisle formed by countless hanging chains of flowers. The array of perfumes, colors, and overall impression was fantastic, as if wandering through the creation of some twisted science-fiction mind. It is difficult to remember, when viewing pictures of individual flowers in genera such as *Gongora*, and species like *Gongora unicolor*, that it is often not the single bloom that creates the beauty, it is the display created by the plant and flowers as a whole. The attractive broad leaves, not unlike those of *Aspidistra*, in a moss-lined basket with garlands of oddly beautiful blooms waving in the breeze beneath is a very compelling picture, to be sure.

There are a variety of reasons why certain genera or species may be less common in horticulture. Some, of course, simply lack sufficient appeal to be worthwhile subjects for the collection. Others are of limited appeal in the sense that fewer people demand fewer plants of any given species.

Below a certain level of demand, orchid businesses find maintenance of stock impractical. Simply because certain plants are rarely seen and difficult to obtain does not mean that they are

Above: Gga. grossa *has a sweet fragrance.*

Right: Gga. unicolor *is found in Mexico, Belize, Guatemala, and Honduras and has long pendant inflorescences.*

not worth the trouble. Any one or combination of several of these unusual and easy-to-grow plants can provide interest and spark to the mix of plants in a collection. The observant grower, prepared with a wide-ranging knowledge, can almost always find one or another of the group offered at an orchid show or tucked into the far corner of an orchid nursery. Worth the search, you may ask? Factor in perfume and floral interest, and you have plants that deserve wider inclusion.

VANDAS

AND VANDACEOUS TYPES

Thailand is home to so many of the wonderful, colorful tropical orchids that are comfortable in the Gulf states and Florida.

Most of the intermediate-sized plants can be grown in greenhouses just about anywhere, while some of the smaller growing types can be accommodated on windowsills or under lights, especially where summers are mild enough to allow them to be grown outdoors during part of the year, to take advantage of better-quality light conditions. The largest plants, including traditional vandas, renantheras, and other related types really need the space and high light that only comes outdoors in subtropical areas like South Florida. Vandas and allied types are monopodial, with no well-defined water storage organs beyond robust root systems, and to thrive, they require good humidity at all times, especially during active growth. The best results are often achieved with basket culture, using little or no medium, which allows the frequent waterings and rapid drying that the plants prefer.

Rhyncostylis gigantea is one of the true success stories of Thai horticulture. The famous Thai orchidist, Professor Rapee Sagarik, searching for improved product to widen the appeal of export orchids, began working with *Rhy. gigantea* in the 1960s. The species is most often seen in the "typical" form of ivory white with rose-purple dotting. Flowers are borne on medium-length stems that arch out from the plant in a most attractive way. The closely arranged blooms form a dense cylindrical display, often referred to as a foxtail. Sagarik bred together the best available forms of the typically colored varieties, as well as the more rare solid-red types. As these grew and were distributed, the species increased in popularity, particularly as a result of their exposure at the World Orchid Conference held in Bangkok during the same era.

Left: Typically, Rhy. gigantea *has white flowers with rose-pink spots.*

Rhy. gigantea, despite its name, is not a large-growing orchid,

staying relatively short and branching from the base to form

clumps at maturity, each fan of which can have several spikes

Above: The solid red form of Rhy. gigantea *has been popular for many years.*

during the late winter blooming season. Not to be overlooked is

the sweet fragrance that is so penetrating on a fully bloomed plant.

Vandas and Vandaceous Types **369**

RHYNCHOSTYLIS GIGANTEA

After a surge of popularity that lasted through the 1970s and 1980s, *Rhy. gigantea* seemed to fade from view. Plants were rarely offered or displayed. Many of the large specimen plants resident to Florida fell victim to Hurricane Andrew or Benlate. In the 1990s, new and improved strains of the species again began to come out

of Thailand to the accolades of a new generation of growers, largely unfamiliar with the plants of an earlier time. Perhaps the first wave of excitement was for the "spotty" strain that resulted from the crossing of a typical finely spotted cultivar with a red. The ivory background was very heavily overlaid with red blotches in a most distinctive pattern. Flower shape and plant vigor was improved as well. In some cases, the spotting nearly coalesced, giving results as in 'Tania' AM/AOS. One of the great breakthroughs in this and other newly introduced strains of the species was a return of the vigor that had been lost in the highly inbred populations that remained in the United States. Plants seemed to grow faster, and the arching inflorescences were longer with more flowers than had been seen in quite some time.

Along with the "spotty" types came improved alba types as well, such as 'Cile' AM/AOS. Again, vigor and floriferousness were vastly improved. More unusual colors also began to be seen. The most unusual was a sort of salmon-colored type, which seemed to lack good growability, unfortunately. The slightly difficult culture often adds just that little bit of a challenge, adding spice to the mix.

Above left: Rhy. gigantea 'Cile' AM/AOS is a fine example of the snow-white alba variety.

Opposite: Line-breeding select strains can produce cultivars with near-solid colored flowers that have what appear to be white markings, as in Rhy. gigantea 'Tania' AM/AOS.

AERIDES LAWRENCIAE

While it does not come from Thailand, but the Philippines, *Aerides lawrenceae* is so closely connected in cultural needs to the related vanda group that it makes great sense to discuss them together. Aerides have growth similar to vandas, though they are often taller—to five feet or more—and usually more profusely branching from the base. In tropical and subtropical areas, large clumps can often be seen, whether in baskets or on trees, where they make a spectacular display when in full bloom. Each stem can bear several arching inflorescences to more than twenty-four inches long, densely flowered with waxy, strongly perfumed ivory blooms to one inch or more. The spurred lip is held up against and obscures the column with a brilliant rose stripe that matches the often rose-flushed sepals and petals.

Aer. lawrenciae and related species, such as *Aer. fieldingii* and *Aer. multiflora*, are very popular in areas where their tropical needs can be met. *Aerides* is occasionally used in vanda hybridizing where it imparts its delicious citrusy fragrance. More often, we see the species, grown as large specimen plants in the landscape, naturalized on trees. Plants of this easy nature and forgiving temperament are invaluable additions to our orchid palette.

Left: Of the twenty or so species in the genus, Aer. lawrenciae *is perhaps the most beautiful. It is from low elevations of the Philippines and requires warm temperatures.*

Right: Most species of Aerides, including Aer. lawrenciae, *have a delicious lemony fragrance.*

ASCOCENTRUM AMPULLACEUM

Asctm. ampullaceum *Aurantiacum is a rare color form of this species. These unusual color forms are eagerly sought by collectors as they are discovered.*

Another Southeast Asian genus of great horticultural appeal and utility is *Ascocentrum*. Traditionally, three primary species have comprised those most frequently grown and used for hybridizing, although recent taxonomic work has modified this to five or six, depending on the authority accepted. Plants of this genus are generally small, upright, monopodial epiphytes to twenty-four inches or more in *Ascocentrum curvifolium*. The other species are usually much smaller, only to eight inches or so, and tend to branch more freely from the base than does *Ascocentrum curvifolium*. *Asctm. ampullaceum* is the smallest-growing of the most frequently grown species, with stiff leaves angled upward on short stems. Inflorescences often will barely emerge from the foliage but are attractively presented nonetheless. *Asctm. ampullaceum* comes from slightly higher elevations than most of the genus, from the foothills of the Indian Himalayas, through the mountains of Laos and Thailand into parts of Yunnan. As a result, it is more tolerant of cooler conditions than many vandaceous types, some growers reporting best success with some cooling to induce flowering.

Flowers of *Asctm. ampullaceum*, up to forty or more closely spaced on the inflorescence, are slightly less than one inch across and are usually in shades of rose to the highly prized cerise types. The variability of shade leads to some of the deepest magenta cultivars being given separate varietal status as Moulmeinense. Seed-raised populations of these richly colored and often-larger flowered types are entering cultivation. An orange-flowered form known as Aurantiacum is also known and is now being raised from seed for wider distribution.

Right: Asctm. ampullaceum *is a compact species that typically has hot-pink flowers. The flowers are borne in dense clusters and have a sparkling texture.*

ASCOCENTRUM AMPULLACEUM

Small plants with brightly colored flowers are always popular, more so in recent years as skyrocketing energy costs often mitigate against the luxury of a greenhouse. Species, especially those with a degree of cool tolerance that approximate larger plants and can be grown in the home, are always in demand. *Ascocentrum ampullaceum* fits all these requirements and so is becoming increasingly in demand. While the standard color form is highly attractive, growers are always searching for something new and different. Moulmeinense and aurantiacum satisfy this urge, as does the lovely pink form, exemplified by the highly awarded 'Crownfox Pink Glow'. With all the deep, rich colors available in this species, it is difficult sometimes to remember that there are those who prefer the softer, pastel colors.

Ascocentrum is an important part of the hybridizer's arsenal as well. Of the major species, *Asctm. ampullaceum* is the least utilized. Two difficulties have been encountered: a failure to obtain seed despite repeated attempts and the rather poor flower arrangement that *Asctm. ampullaceum* imparts to its progeny. What is acceptable and even attractive on a charming species does not always translate well into its hybrids. There have been a few hybrids successfully introduced, perhaps the best being *Ascofinetia* Cherry Blossom (*Neofinetia falcata* x *Asctm. ampullaceum*). This hybrid has been remade several times since its initial introduction and is a very popular potted plant in Japan. While most cultivars are shades of pink, as might be expected, orange clones have appeared, leading to speculation about labeling problems. Nevertheless, *Ascofinetia* Cherry Blossom is available in the United States and is a perennial favorite for many of the same reasons that both of its parents remain near the top of the list for overachieving potted-plant display subjects. Very showy plants can easily be accommodated in three-inch pots and are ideal for those who grow in the windowsill or under lights. Even minimal plants are known to give two flowering stems, adding additional value to what is already a fine plant.

Right: Asctm. ampullaceum 'Crownfox Pink Glow' AM/AOS is another rare color form. The delicate pink flowers are produced on compact plants in the spring.

ASCOCENTRUM GARAYI (SYN. MINIATUM)

Compact, upright plants bear stiff, nearly terete, leaves at right angles to the short stems. The closely ranked leaves form a nearly solid row up each side of the main stem. Leaves are often liberally marked with tiny, purple anthocyanin spots. Basal branching is common, though not as prolific as in *Asctm. ampullaceum*. Just the plant itself has such a handsome aspect that it could be grown for this reason alone. But when the multiple, upright cylindrical spires of small bright-orange blooms appear, the effect is magical. When grown like a small vanda, in a basket or clay pot, an overall beauty occurs that is hard to describe. *Asctm. garayi* is also a significant contributor to the gene pool of modern vandaceous breeding, though unraveling the skein of wrongly labeled hybrids involving *Asctm. miniatum* is nearly impossible. While miniature *Ascocendas* (*Asctm.* x *Vanda*) are one important use of *Asctm. garayi*, like *Asctm. ampullaceum* it has made a very popular and widely distributed hybrid when crossed with the Japanese *Neofinetia falcata*, *Ascofinetia* Twinkle. In varying shades of orange and yellow, *Ascofinetia* Twinkle is popular both in Japan and the United States for its multiple good potted-plant qualities.

What was long known as *Ascocentrum miniatum* now turns out not to be. Eric Christenson, in a fairly recent study, determined that three species are really involved in the complex of what we formerly knew as *Asctm. miniatum*. Briefly, all plants originating in the Philippines are truly *Asctm. aurantiacum*. The "true" *Asctm. miniatum* is a rarely seen species from Java, which, compared to other members of the genus, is fairly drab. What we commonly cultivate as *Asctm. miniatum*, from Indochina, has been given the new specific name of *Ascocentrum garayi*. No matter what it is called, and it will continue in the trade as *Asctm. miniatum* for convenience's sake, it is truly one of the best of all orchid species.

Above left: Asctm. garayi has long been known as Asctm. miniatum. It still can be found offered for sale under this name.

Right: Ascocentrum species require warm temperatures and bright light to flower their best. When grown under these conditions, Asctm garayi will have thick leaves spotted with purple.

ASCOCENTRUM AURANTIACUM

It is not uncommon for growers to attribute some foliar and floral variation to geographic range. In other words, some differences are to be expected as a result of spatial separation. Often, when plants from extreme ends of the range of any given species are viewed, they can and do seem like separate species. However, when seen as part of a continuum, it is easier to see them as all part of a range of variation. This was clearly the circumstance in the case of *Ascocentrum aurantiacum*'s long having been mistaken for *Asctm. miniatum*. The flowers are slightly smaller and the foliage slightly larger, more like the closely related *Asctm. curvifolium*. Nevertheless, good taxonomic methods have determined that it is a valid and separate species.

The confusion persists in the Philippines, however, from whence it is still exported as *Asctm. miniatum*. Rarely used in hybridizing,

Asctm. aurantiacum *flowers in the spring from plants that are less stout than* Asctm. garayi.

the flowers can often appear two-toned, with darker orange near the center of the flower. However, the shortness of the inflorescence, which often barely clears the foliage, may mitigate against frequent use in breeding. It remains a wonderful and desirable species that many may find they have acquired as something else. Thankfully, it is worthwhile no matter the name.

Left: The flowers of Asctm. aurantiacum *are similar to the closely related* Asctm. garayi, *but distinct enough to be considered a valid name. Smaller flowers with a proportionately larger spur are noted for this species.*

ASCOCENTRUM CURVIFOLIUM

The third of the traditionally important *Ascocentrum* species, and arguable the most horticulturally valuable, is *Ascocentrum curvifolium*. Strangely, it is perhaps grown less frequently as a discrete species than its two sister species, *Asctm. garayi/miniatum* and *Asctm. ampullaceum*, but its worth as a parent of literally hundreds of well-known and oft-grown hybrids more than compensates. Not that *Asctm. curvifolium* is not an attractive and worthy species in and of itself. Growth habit, while slightly taller than others in the group and with slightly longer, down-curved leaves (hence, *curvifolium*), is still restrained overall and can be nicely accommodated in no more than an eight-inch basket. Basal branching is common, so moderately sized plants can quickly form a clump, each stem of which can produce two or three (or more) upright inflorescences of up to forty bright orange-to-red, one-inch blooms. Florida gardens are home to big naturalized plants mounted on trees that survive all but the coldest winters. *Asctm. curvifolium* 'Crownfox' CCM/AOS is a good example of the display a specimen-size can present.

Culture presents no special problems for this species, which, like most in the group, prefers to be grown in a slatted basket. Such baskets allow the rather large-diameter roots to range freely in and around the basket, soaking up available moisture before quickly drying. Many growers find the best success with absolutely

The cardinal-red flowers of the typically colored Asctm. curvifolium *generally have a pleasing, full shape and a glistening texture.*

no medium in the baskets, which gives the perfect drainage required by the plants. The wooden baskets and sheer mass of the root structure absorb sufficient water to sustain the plants between the frequent waterings necessary to succeed with this sort of regime. In areas like South Florida, frequent rains and only lightly covered growing areas help growers to maintain the preferred moisture levels. All the grower need do is supplement the rains with weekly fertilization.

This plant of Asctm. curvifolium 'Crownfox' CCM/AOS is over six feet tall.

ASCOCENTRUM CURVIFOLIUM & VAR. LUTEUM

Any species as mportant to horticulture as *Ascocentrum curvifolium* inevitably prompts the search for special cultivars. These extraordinary plants may be noteworthy for intense color ('Red Dragon' AM/AOS is notable for its rich color and very shapely blooms) or for rare coloration (as with var. *luteum*, a rare yellow variant). Not only do such highly select cultivars serve as a source of new colors and color combinations in traditional *Ascocenda* breeding, but clones like 'Crownfox' can be useful for imparting improved vigor. Polyploidy also plays a significant role in the story of *Asctm. curvifolium*, where progeny of sibling crosses of its most famous and influential hybrid *Ascda*. Yip Sum Wah have turned out to be tetraploids.

It is as the progenitor of modern ascocendas that *Asctm. curvifolium*'s true fame will endure. Hawaiian breeders beginning in the early 1960s first created ascocendas, the result of breeding a *Vanda* with an *Ascocentrum*. While *Ascda*. Yip Sum Wah (*V.* Pukele x *Asctm. curvifolium*) was not the first *Ascocenda*, it has proven to be the most important and influential aspect of this large and colorful group. The range of color in today's ascocendas is astounding. Flower size can range, according to the amount of large *Vanda* or small *Ascocentrum* involved, from nearly the size of a standard *Vanda* to more petite *Ascocentrum*-like blooms. The

upright stance of *Ascocentrum* influences ascocendas profoundly, adding strength to flower presentation. When first introduced, ascocendas held the promise of *Vanda*-like flowers on plants of a size that could be easily managed by a greater number of growers. The potential came to pass almost immediately.

Above: Asctm. curvifolium *'Red Dragon' AM/AOS was commended for its extremely full-shaped flowers of exceptional color and substance.*

Opposite: The clear yellow form of Asctm. curvifolium *is sometimes known as variety Luteum.*

ASCOCENDA GUO CHIA LONG & ASCOCENDA CROWNFOX GOLDEN DAWN

Ascda. *Guo Chia Long 'Spotty' AM/AOS has been used as a parent to create generations of colorful, spotted flowers. Photo courtesy R.F. Orchids.*

The center of vandaceous breeding today, as it has been for some years, is Thailand. A variety of reasons favor Thailand's retention of this honor. First, its climate is extremely conducive to naturally rapid growth and flowering of this type of plant. Second, orchids are a very important part of Thailand's export market, given favorable treatment by a supportive government. Also, the Thai simply love vandas and allied hybrids! The real center of *Vanda* and *Ascocenda* excitement in the United States is Florida, where a raft of influential nurseries and their customers grow to perfection and exhibit the very latest that Thai growers have to offer. This is a fine example of the global nature of the orchid business today. Not only does the

enthusiasm of South Florida growers rub off on other U.S. consumers, it leads to the selection of fine cultivars for further breeding, which might otherwise have been unseen. Too, selection for local conditions is an important part of any breeding program, and South Florida growers' selection of plants that do well for them for use in further breeding adds to the mutual benefit.

One of the surprise trends of the past decade has been the emergence of *Ascocenda* Guo Chia Long as a parent. Bred from *Ascda.* Yip Sum Wah and *Vanda* Mem. Madame Pranerm, neither of which are exactly unknown quantities in breeding, *Ascda.* Guo Chia Long and its hybrids have blazed a trail of new colors and color combinations for an eager public.

Yellow and related shades are always highly in demand. When varying degrees of pronounced red spotting is added into the mix, flowers of enormous appeal are the result. As more plants of *Ascda.* Guo Chia Long came into the public eye at judgings and other exhibitions, and more of its hybrids began to bloom, a feedback loop of sorts came into being.

It seems that just about everything that *Ascda.* Guo Chia Long bred was of above-average quality. *Ascda.* Crownfox Golden Dawn is an outstanding example of a more traditional *Ascocenda*

flower with the added attraction of even red spotting that *Ascda.*

Guo Chia Long can give.

Ascda. *Crownfox Golden Dawn 'Miramar' AM/AOS.*

Above: One of the characteristics of this line of breeding is shown in the well-spaced inflorescence of Ascda. Ken Kone 'Crownfox Spots' AM/AOS.

Left: Ascda. Ken Kone 'Crownfox Ruby' AM/AOS.

ASCOCENDA KEN KONE

Ascda. *Ken Kone 'Crownfox Leopard' AM/AOS.*

In the "career" of every great orchid parent seems to come the defining moment, when a hybrid is created that is far and away superior to any that has yet been seen. *Vanda merrillii* is a species from the Philippines little used in hybridizing until quite recently. The lacquer-red coloration of the flowers has led breeders to attempt to infuse this desirable trait into both *Vanda* and *Ascocenda* hybrids.

The flowers resulting from such matings have had merit but are generally consigned to the novelty group. However, when *V. merrillii* was crossed with *Ascda.* Guo Chia Long, *Ascda.* Ken Kone was created. The only concession to some of the poorer qualities of the *Vanda* parent was a somewhat reduced flower count. Otherwise, the shape and size of the blooms was everything that could be desired in a modern *Ascocenda*.

But it was not simply "another" *Ascocenda*. The brilliance of the color combinations, varying degrees of deep-red spotting or blotching over strong-yellow backgrounds, had never before been seen. A spate of well-deserved high awards followed, nearly as quickly as plants could be exhibited to orchid judges in South Florida. These judges, it must be added, are more experienced in evaluating vandaceous breeding than anywhere else in the world. This hybrid represented a quantum leap forward in an already colorful and highly developed line of breeding.

Ascda. Ken Kone is a great hybrid named after a wonderful individual who has selflessly given his time and effort over the years.

ASCOCENDA BANJONG WATERCOLOR & ASCOCENDA VIC FOWLER

Once an orchid is recognized as a useful parent, breeders will often cross it with just about every other parent in their arsenal, if for no other reason than they know they will be able to sell the seedlings. When a parent is truly successful, such a "shotgun" approach yields an entirely new range of flowers of outstanding overall quality. Such seems to be the case with *Ascocenda* Guo Chia Long. The award record of its progeny is one method by which its quality could be measured. This record is long and is growing month by month. Both plants illustrated here are record

enough. However, it is not just the opinion—well informed though it may be—of the judges that matters. For a new hybrid type to be really triumphant, it must capture the public's support. Such support is not the matter of a single generation of progeny but can only be measured against a continuing line of uniformity of quality, as well as influence into further generations. *Ascda.* Yip Sum Wah's legacy is demonstrated in *Ascda.* Guo Chia Long and its progeny. The story of *Ascda.* Guo Chia Long is still being written.

Examination of *Ascda.* Guo Chia Long gives only the briefest entrée into the world of ascocendas. Hybrids from *Ascocentrum curvifolium* and, more recently, *Asctm. garayi/miniatum*, continue to be made, as do hybrids utilizing their further generations. For sheer variety and beauty, in combination with eminently growable and vigorous plants, few groups can match the horticultural value of the *Ascocenda* complex.

Above left: Ascda. Banjong Watercolor 'Adkin's Spottyhead' HCC/AOS.

Right: Depending on the other parent used, Ascda. Guo Chia Long can produce offspring with bold spots, or with fine pepper spots as in Ascda. Vic Fowler 'Orchid Peddler'.

VANDA (EUANTHE) SANDERIANA

Modern hybrid lines can often trace their lineage back to only one or a few seminal, superior species—species that exhibit traits found attractive by established horticultural standards. Without the influence of *Vanda sanderiana*, considered by some taxonomists in the separate monotypic genus *Euanthe*, *Vanda* hybrids would be substantially different. *V. sanderiana* has the large-rounded blooms and strong stems that so many associate with horticultural desirability. The species originates at low elevations in the Philippines, with consistently high temperatures and humidity. The story of its discovery by Western collectors is replete with Victorian angst and adventure, liberally salted with "dreamlike visions" of this magnificent and hitherto unknown species. Cannibals and headhunters abounded in its habitat, according to the explorer who was sent to recover it.

The dangers of obtaining this species from the wild were outweighed only by the difficulty of getting it back to Europe and managing its cultivation. Because *V. sanderiana* comes from an area close to the equator, at low elevations, temperatures must be maintained at a constantly high level, day and night. Humidity must also be maintained, as, like most vandas, water-storage organs are not present. While *V. sanderiana* naturally flowers in the fall,

Above: The alba form of Enth. Sanderiana *has been used to create a number of successful hybrid lines.*

Right: Although properly known as Euanthe sanderiana, *many orchidists still call this species* Vanda sanderiana. *It is among the most beautiful of all orchids.*

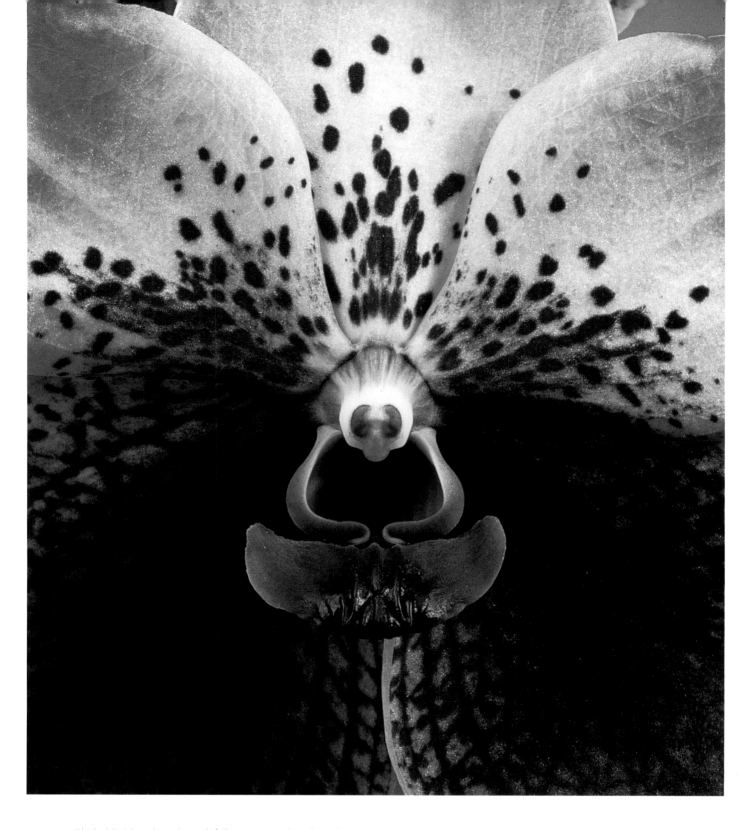

measured in habitat by changing rainfall patterns rather than day length, its hybrids resulting from the fortuitous combination with the higher-elevation *V. coerulea* can often flower throughout the year. *V. coerulea*, the other species vital to what we know today as hybrid vandas, comes from a cooler climate, where it flowers several times during the year. *V. Rothschildiana (sanderiana x coerulea)* is nearly the ideal vanda hybric, in terms of cultural needs and flowering habit, tolerating generally cooler, more attainable, and certainly more comfortable temperatures.

One of the proven avenues to improvement in hybrid lines is the creation of better species stock both by the discovery of newer, better, wild-collected plants and by inbreeding of existing superior cultivars. Over a period of decades, it generally becomes unnecessary to introduce any further "wild" blood, as the inbred stock, so far removed from its ancestry, would only be reduced in value by the addition of inferior genes. However, wild-collected plants can add vigor to inbred species lines, something seen in many rediscovered paphiopedilums, such as *Paph. delenatii*.

Hawaiian breeders were the first to really begin to attempt to improve wild forms of *V. sanderiana*. In the early 1950s, American judges were astonished by the quality of a strain of Hawaiian-bred *V. sanderiana* displayed in New York. That the flowers would even survive the long transportation event was somewhat of a miracle. It is difficult to remember a time when cross-country travel was a big deal, let alone a transpacific flight from the distant Hawaiian Islands. The Kono strain of *V. sanderiana* set a new standard for what, even then, was a well-known and popular species. Later, the Thai took leadership in the breeding of select *V. sanderiana*, helping to take the flowers to the near perfection we see today.

Another breakthrough in *V. sanderiana* has to be mentioned. In the late 1980s, progenies began to appear from a cross of *V. sanderiana* 'Coral Reef' AM/AOS and another, unnamed, cultivar. The quality of these blooms represented a huge leap forward. Indeed, two have gone on to win the rarely awarded and highly coveted First Class Certificate from the American Orchid Society.

Flower color of V. sanderiana *can vary somewhat depending on the temperature and time of year of flowering.*

Such advances in the quality of an important breeding species not only give the immediate result of advancing the quality of the species itself but also affect further generations of hybrids down the line.

Mature plants of V. sanderiana *can produce several heads of large flowers—spectacular!*

Above: Complex hybrids that retain the "sanderiana look," such as V.
Mem. Louise Fuchs 'Crownfox' HCC/AOS, are still being made and are
still popular.

Above right: V. Fuchs Southern Belle 'Crownfox' AM/AOS.

VANDA MEM. LOUISE FUCHS & VANDA FUCHS SOUTHERN BELLE

Vanda sanderiana is extraordinarily dominant. Most modern standard vandas are comprised largely of *V. sanderiana* and *V. coerulea*, with only minor additions of other species that give rise to more unusual colors. The famous primary hybrid *V.* Rothschildiana is happily intermediate between its two species parents. As breeders attempted to overcome perceived floral imperfections in *V. Rothschildiana* and similar hybrids, varying degrees of the *V. sanderiana* "look" resulted.

Continued selection of progeny exhibiting the round, flat form desired in orchids, most often achieved by segment width becoming proportionately greater than length, was often linked to the characteristic *V. sanderiana* coloration.

This is no bad thing. *V. sanderiana* is a strongly marked flower, with its pink base color heavily overlaid with cinnamon brown tessellation on the sepals, matched by similar spotting on the petals. As the proportionate width of the segments grows, greater and greater overlap occurs. Vanda flowers are often known as "platters," at times exceeding six inches. Unfortunately, hybrids heavily influenced by *V. sanderiana* are often also slightly slower to bloom from seed, taking another two years to first bloom, than those with more *V. coerulea* influence, resulting in larger plants, to two feet or more, on first bloom.

FIRST CLASS VANDAS: VANDA ROBERT'S DELIGHT 'CROWNFOX BIG RED' FCC/AOS

Vanda Robert's Delight 'Crownfox Big Red' is one of the orchids that has been awarded the highest accolade as a first-class vanda by the American Orchid Society. No one can deny the power of public acclaim. Without the recognition of the buying public, commercial enterprise would grind to a halt. Consumer demand and breeding trends go hand in hand to produce higher quality products at more affordable prices. Orchids are no different than any other of a hundred other horticultural types, except perhaps in degree. Orchidists are well-known fanatics, whose judgment is too often clouded by a compulsive desire for something bigger, or rounder, or redder, or whatever. Their success in accomplishing such obsessive endeavors cannot simply be on a personal level; validation by a higher authority is essential to the process. n short, when an orchid is awarded by the AOS, it is considered tc have achieved an international level of highest quality.

The hot-pink flowers of V. Robert's Delight 'Crownfox Big Red' FCC/AOS represent the best of modern standard Vanda *breeding.*

VANDA JULIA SORENSON
'ERIC BRYANT MIRRO' FCC/AOS

V. Robert's Delight 'Crownfox Big Red', *V.* Julia Sorenson 'Eric Bryant Mirro', and *V.* Robert's Delight 'Garnet Beauty' have received the highest possible award from the American Orchid Society, perhaps the most coveted award in the world today. All three reached this lofty achievement in the hotbed of vanda knowledge, South Florida. For this reason, it can be safely said that each richly deserved the honors given. Their round, overlapping shape, proportionately broad segments, flat carriage, heavy substance, and strong color all add up to flowers as close to perfection in type as are likely ever to be seen. Of course, each award should raise the bar along with it, so later FCCs will certainly have to attain perceptibly higher standards of quality and perfection.

Rich grape color and a satiny texture garnered a high award for the large-flowered V. Julia Sorenson 'Eric Bryant Mirro' FCC/AOS.

VANDA ROBERT'S DELIGHT 'GARNET BEAUTY' FCC/AOS

Vanda Robert's Delight 'Garnet Beauty' is another vanda that has achieved the highest accolade awarded by the American Orchid Society, the FCC. The FCC, or any other high award for that matter, is not simply the accomplishment of the hybridizer. Many plants, like people, have unrecognized potential. It takes extraordinary attention to detail to bring out the hidden promise in any being. With orchids, a high award is the result of top-notch care given to the plant while growing, to enable it to perform at its best. Well-grown plants produce the best blooms. Indeed, an old orchid adage (from an old orchid grower) states that an average variety well grown will always outperform a superior variety poorly grown. Successful orchid culture is the result of everyday attention to the requirements of the plants. Nothing less will do.

Outsiders often believe that only an experienced commercial grower has a chance at attaining the high levels of culture necessary to high awards. While commercial growers should certainly know what they are doing and have a large array of plants from which to choose, they simply cannot afford to give each plant the individual attention necessary. It has always been my belief that hobbyists should grow the best plants. Why more growers cannot or do not make it to this high level of cultural excellence is a mystery.

V. Robert's Delight 'Garnet Beauty' FCC/AOS received its FCC only two months after receiving an AM/AOS. Sister to the clone 'Crownfox Big Red' FCC/AOS, 'Garnet Beauty' has flowers that are more red but have the same large, flat shape.

BLUE VANDAS: ASCOCENDA ELIZABETH TAYLOR

True blue coloration is not common in orchids. Indeed, the color often seems to be wished for more than actually achieved, like in many of the "blue" cattleyas. However, in the vanda group, we have a species, *V. coerulea*, that is of the desired blue color. Hailing from higher elevations than most other vandas, *V. coerulea* does well under cattleya conditions, tolerating lower humidity than that required by most vandas, down into the sixty percent range, as opposed to the more ideal eighty percent for *V. sanderiana*. The flowers of *V. coerulea* have a soft blue, or nearly white, background, heavily tessellated with a checkerboard of darker blue, sometimes nearly violet color. The plants, which can reach more than five feet, begin flowering at more modest size. Higher doses of *V. coerulea* give us the intense blue-violet colors so sought after. Ascocenda flowers, depending on the proximity of the ascocentrum species in the lineage, can vary from quite small to nearly the size of the vanda parents. As ascocentrums approach vanda flower and plant size, the name vandacenda is sometimes used. *Ascda.* Elizabeth Taylor is a very good example of a vandacenda, using the robust *Ascda.* John DeBiase back onto another standard vanda. Aside from flower carriage and spike habit, very little ascocentrum is evident. For clear blue-violet color and shape, this flower is tough to fault.

Ascda. *Elizabeth Taylor 'Arabella' HCC/AOS has full-formed flowers of intense purple and is an example of the excellence of Ascda. John De Biase as a parent.*

VANDA PAT DELIGHT
& VANDA TOKYO BLUE

Modern blue vandas are the result of many generations of selection and inbreeding. Various desirable traits appear in varying degrees among progeny and the best are used for further hybridizing. Because little species influence beyond that of *Vanda sanderiana* and *V. coerulea* is present, there is both similarity and variety in any given hybrid grex (group of progeny from a specific cross), depending on the particular parents used. For example, for any given hybrid, both pink and blue forms can exist. The use of either form gives differing results in the resultant progeny. Saturation of blue coloration is another example. Whether or not the blue tessellation imparted by *V. coerulea* is attractive is a matter of taste. For this reason, we see both nearly solid blue colors selected for breeding, and strong tessellated patterns.

The continual selection of more and more heavily blue tessellated parents, in what amounts to inbred *V.* Rothschildiana lines, gives flowers like *V.* Pat Delight. Here the tessellation has nearly completely coalesced into a solid blue-violet color, broken only by what are first seen as white spots on the flower. An attractive white edge to the floral segments completes the picture of beauty. On the other hand, when *V. coerulea* itself is a direct parent, as in *V.* Tokyo Blue, tessellation is more pronounced, with a checkerboard effect of darker color over lighter. The superior breeding qualities of highly advanced forms of *V. coerulea* are truly manifested in this flower. Both blooms have the delightful accent of a white column to highlight the vibrant blue color.

Left: V. Tokyo Blue 'Sapphire' AM/AOS.

Right: Like V. Robert's Delight, V. Pat Delight 'Dark Blue' AM/AOS is another hybrid from V. Kasem's Delight and shows variability in color from hot pink through grape purple. How delightful!

VASCOSTYLIS FUCHS PRECIOUS JEWEL, VASCOSTYLIS PRAPAWAN & VASCOSTYLIS KALEIDOSCOPE

Vanda coerulea is not the only source of blue color in the *Vanda* alliance. Over the past ten years or so, *Rhynchostylis coelestis* has made a fantastic comeback in popularity, not only in improved forms of the species but also as a parent of blue hybrids. *Rhy. coelestis* is a species widespread throughout Indochina and is the *Rhyncostylis* species most often used in intergeneric *Vanda* breeding. The plants are relatively short in stature, with closely spaced leaves that result in the plant being wider than tall. It branches freely from the base, and plants quickly form attractive clumps, each stem of which can have multiple upright inflorescences of small blue-tinged blooms. *Rhy. coelestis* was used quite a bit in the middle years of *Vanda* hybridizing, resulting in a spate of hybrids, quickly losing the charm initially found.

Two important drawbacks to *Rhy. coelestis* hybrids have to be considered when using in breeding: first, the flowers may be short-lived, only lasting in perfection for two weeks or so; second, the pedicels (flower stems) are often weak, giving a nodding presentation to the blooms. An advantage of the species is the availability of three color forms: white, pink, and blue. Recent populations of select, seed-raised plants have intensified the colors in all three types.

Above: Using Rhynchostylis coelestis *for breeding, blue* Vanda *hybrids can produce deeply saturated colors such as* Vasco. Prapawan 'Tanzanite' HCC/AOS.

Right: Vasco. Kaleidoscope 'KG's Blue Adagio' HCC/AOS *has much more delicate colors than* Vasco. Prapawan 'Tanzanite' HCC/AOS (above). *Often, the offspring will carry the perfume of the* Rhynchostylis.

Vascostylis is the intergeneric combination of *Rhyncostylis*, *Vanda*, and *Ascocentrum*, most often as an ascocenda crossed with a *Rhyncostylis*. The hybrids in this genus are spectacular, with

spires of dozens of colorful blooms on upright stems. Both *Vasco.* Fuchs Precious Jewel and *Vasco.* Kaleidoscope show the typical pattern of much breeding in this group, crosses of an *Ascocenda* with the species. On the other hand, *Vasco.* Prapawan is both more complex and simpler, with a *Vascostylis* hybrid being crossed back onto the species *V. coerulea*. Deep blue color is the result, though the shape is perhaps more open than preferred. Owing to the compact nature of the *Rhyncostylis* parent, much breeding is focused on the production of smaller-growing, potted-plant types. Perhaps the most popular are *Neostylis* Lou Sneary (*Neofinetia falcata* x *Rhy. coelestis*) and *Darwinara* Charm (*Vasco.* Tham Yuen Hae x *Neo. falcata*). Both give a wonderful display of blue blooms over compact foliage, coupled with the delightful fragrance imparted by the *Neofinetia* parent.

Vandas and Vandaceous Types   409

YELLOW VANDAS: ASCOCENDA CROWNFOX YELLOW SAPPHIRE & ASCOCENDA DHONGCHAI PUSAVAT

The search for yellow in *Vanda* and *Ascocenda* hybrids has been a long, difficult journey. The *Vanda* species with good yellow coloration are uncommon and have a difficult set of traits that have to be removed by generations of breeding. Unfortunately, the further from the species one gets to ameliorate the bad features, the less likely one is to get good yellows or golds. *Vanda dearei*, the species most likely to impart yellow color to hybrids, has several bad features that it tends to pass along with its color. No other *Vanda* species is more intolerant of cold than *V. deari*, and its hybrids may share this tendency, making their culture in cooler areas more difficult. The growth habit and flower count are also problematic. Nor is the flower shape all that could be wished, tending to reflex badly, which, when the often-curled flower parts are added, makes the overall appearance anything but flat. The cultivars with better yellow color may fade to white centrally, which can be considered good or bad depending on taste. Other color anomalies, including broken tessellationlike markings, can also accompany the yellow genes, as in *Ascocenda* Dhongchai Pusavat. One knowledgeable grower strongly warns against gambling on yellow vanda seedlings.

However, recent years have seen marked improvement n yellow and gold ascocendas, thanks to the introduction of *Asctm. miniatum/garayi*, generally through the use of *Asctm.* Viroonchan Gold (*curvifolium* x *miniatum/garayi*). *Asctm.* Viroonchan Gold is one of the parents of *Ascda.* Fuchs Gold, itself the parent of *Ascda.* Crownfox Yellow Sapphire, the other parent a yellow-toned *Ascocenda*, Crownfox Sunshine, bred from more traditional yellow breeding lines. *Ascda.* Crownfox Yellow Sapphire demonstrates that good clear golden-yellow color can be achieved in the group when previously little-used avenues, such as *Asctm. miniatum/garayi*, are used. The shape, color, and especially texture are far superior to flowers of even one previous generation

Above left: Ascda. Crownfox Yellow Sapphire 'Bobby Marcellini' HCC/AOS.

Above: Ascda. Dhongchai Pusovat 'Orchid Acres Sunburst' HCC/AOS has an unusual random red edging that sets it apart from other yellow or spotted types.

Vandas and Vandaceous Types **411**

ASCOCENDA CROWNFOX BUTTERBALL & ASCOCENDA ARUNEE'S HONEY MOON

Ascocenda Fuchs Gold continues to prove itself a parent of worth in the production of very high-quality clear-yellow flowers. *Ascda.* Amelita Ramos is a rather typical *Ascocenda* with a high proportion of *V. sanderiana* in its background. When crossed to *Ascda.* Fuchs Gold, however, beautifully rounded blooms of bright concolor golden-yellow result with little, if any, evidence of the *V. sanderiana* coloration.

In yellow *Vanda* breeding, several parents appear again and again. *V.* Rasri, *V.* Pong Tong, *V.* Thananchai, and *V.* Kultana Gold are among the progenitors of modern yellow vandas. To one degree or another, all carry forward some of the familiar problems with the group, including muddiness of color and occasionally poor texture. *V.* Charles Goodfellow is strongly in this tradition. *Ascda.* Fuchs Gold proves another of its values as a parent by almost completely ameliorating the bad traits in one generation, in the hybrid of *Ascda.* Arunee's Honey Moon. Like *Ascda.* Crownfox Butterball, the lack of any evidence of *V. sanderiana*'s characteristic patterning is remarkable.

Left: Ascda. Crownfox Butterball 'Sunshine' AM/AOS represents the clear yellow Ascocenda so popular with growers of Vandaceous orchids. Depending on parents used, these yellow hybrids can be warm gold or green gold in color

Right: Ascda. Arunee's Honeymoon 'Peddler's Butter Baby' HCC/AOS.

ASCOCENDA CANDACE'S SUNSHINE 'WILLIAM ROGERS' & ASCOCENDA CROWNFOX GOLD DUST 'MARY'

Above: One benefit of using V. denisoniana *as a parent is the delightful fragrance it passes on to its offspring.* Ascda. Crownfox Gold Dust 'Mary' AM/AOS (V. denisoniana x Ascda. Viroonchan Gold) *has a brisk citrus fragrance.*

Opposite: Ascda. *Candace's Sunshine 'William Rogers' HCC/AOS.*

The power of a new direction in hybridizing is amazing. Often, it can lead to unexpected and new colors, even in areas where results would ordinarily be closely predictable. *Ascda.* Yip Sum Wah is considered the single most important and influential parent in ascocendas. A long line of hybrids and tens of thousands of flowered seedlings lead to a proven set of results. However, when

Ascda. Fuchs Gold was bred to *Ascda.* Yip Sum Wah to produce *Ascda.* Candace's Sunshine, a whole new world of clear colors opened wide. We again see the ability of *Ascda.* Fuchs Gold to suppress tessellation from the vanda side of the equation. The beautiful pastel, though strong, orange color is almost indescribable and very pleasing. Future results from this new line of colors will be interesting and worth awaiting.

Another avenue pursued for yellow vandas is with the use of the yellow species, *V. denisoniana.* It is only fairly recently that improved forms of this highly perfumed species have become more widely available. It has its share of faults that must be overcome, including low flower count and a twisting growth habit. The strong yellow color of the best varieties more than compensates for their shortcomings. Its combination with *Asctm.* Viroonchan Gold to make *Ascda.* Crownfox Gold Dust might ordinarily be considered a breeder's cross, one made with the intent of finding one or two cultivars with the characteristics for further breeding. And while the shape of 'Mary' is slightly open, the flower carriage and clarity of color makes for a sufficiently striking display to gain an AM/AOS from the knowledgeable judges in South Florida.

WHITE VANDAS: VANDA ROSE DAVIS

In other groups as large and diverse as the vandas, white flowers are generally fairly common. Indeed, achieving strong color is often more of a problem than arriving at white. Cymbidiums, cattleyas, phalaenopsis, dendrobiums, and other horticulturally important groups all have their white species and hybrids. But vandas do not. The quest for a truly white *Vanda* flower, hybrid, or species, true alba or not, goes on to this day. It is greatly hampered by the lack of any significant white-flowered species. There are, of course, alba varieties of some of the important species, such as *V. sanderiana alba* and the very rare *V. coerulea alba*, as well as white-flowered species of lesser import. None, however, have proven to have what it takes to sire a race of truly white-flowered

Vanda hybrids. Even the alba form of *V. sanderiana* is not entirely white, having green sepals, lip and flushing in the petals.

V. Rose Davis 'Crownfox Snow' is therefore somewhat of an aberration. Bred from *V. Rothschildiana* and the alba form of *V. coerulea*, it is indeed white. It lacks, however, the shape and substance that would make it truly valuable in and of itself. This explains the Judges' Commendation award, given to flowers that exhibit some meritorious feature but lack the overall characteristics necessary for a flower quality award. Ordinarily, this would be considered a breeder's flower, a stepping-stone to further breeding. How history will judge *V.* Rose Davis as a step in the production of white vandas remains to be seen.

V. Rose Davis 'Crownfox Snow' JC/AOS.

PASTEL VANDAS: VASCOSTYLIS VIBOON VELVET & CHRISTIEARA LUANG PRABANG

Monopodial orchids, whether vandas or phalaenopsis, have never been as easy to clone as have sympodial orchids such as cattleyas and cymbidiums. As a result, high quality breeding cultivars are slower to reach wide audiences than in other groups. There are exceptions, and one great example is the white *Ascda.* Tubtim Velvet. Bred from yellow breeding lines, this ascocenda is white with green sepals. Tissue-cultured plants have been fairly widely distributed and it is very popular. Nevertheless, when crossed with the alba form of *Rhy. coelestis*, a very beautiful hybrid resulted in *Vasco.* Viboon Velvet. Again, not truly alba, owing to the presence of color in the lip, it remains an attractive and floriferous addition to the palette of vanda color.

Christieara is the complex hybrid genus resulting from the combination of aerides, ascocentrum, and vanda. Aerides intergeneric hybrids are valued for their floriferous nature and tall inflorescences of many small blooms. When the well-known *Ascda.* Tubtim Velvet is crossed with *Aer. lawrenceae*, *Chtra.* Luang Prabang is created. Very similar in aspect to *Vasco.* Viboon Velvet, the sparkling white blooms are offset by a dark lip and some slight green flushing in the sepals. Both of these *Ascda.* Tubtim Velvet hybrids bode well for the further use of this unusual parent.

Opposite: Chtra. *Luang Prabang 'Charles Bolick' AM/AOS and* Vasco. *Viboon Velvet 'Crownfox' HCC/AOS (below) are two different approaches to producing pastel-colored* Vanda *hybrids.* Chtra. *uses* Aerides, *while* Vasco. *uses* Rhynchostylis.

Below: Vasco. *Viboon Velvet 'Crownfox' HCC/AOS.*

RED VANDAS:
ASCOCENDA FUCHS FLAME
& ASCOCENDA ELANDA BATES

Orchid breeders continually search for what they cannot or do not have. Red, in all its permutations of scarlet, vermilion, ruby, claret, burgundy, and other evocative shades is always highly in demand. The path to red in ascocendas is the utilization of the continually improved species, *Ascocemtrum curvifolium*, which, in its very best forms, imparts clear deep-red color. Two doses of *Asctm.* *curvifolium* create the rich color of *Ascocenda* Fuchs Flame (*Laksi* x *Asctm. curvifolium*). *Ascda.* Laksi is itself a direct descendant of *Asctm. curvifolium.*

Likewise, *Ascda.* Elanda Bates (Vermilion Delight x Meda Arnold) obtains its color from the continual addition of *Asctm.* *curvifolium*, in this case two generations' worth on the Vermilion Delight side of the coin. In their quest for stronger and more unusual colors, breeders can (and often do) lose sight of other important factors such as plant vigor and floriferousness. While *Asctm. curvifolium* gives smaller flowers than might be desired, it has an abundant growth habit coupled with an extraordinarily free-blooming habit that results in display plants second to none. There is nothing quite so striking as one of these cultivars, suitably grown to maturity and flowered to perfection, with spires of brilliant red jewel-like blooms sparkling in the sun.

Above left: Ascda. Elanda Bates 'Crownfox Ruby' HCC/AOS.

Right: Ascda. Fuchs Flame 'Crownfox' AM/AOS.

ASCOCENDA KHUN NOK
& KAGAWARA TEOLINE FAIR

any time of year, and frequently several times. A faint, pleasing fragrance is present in the morning. Its variety boxallii is more brightly colored with purple and crimson markings and is more frequently used in breeding. When crossed with *Ascda.* Madame Panni, a rather typical first-generation *Ascocenda*, the striking and colorful *Ascda.* Khun Nok results. Here is an orchid that, even if never recognized by any judging system, would attain instant popularity for its sheer distinctive beauty. Two-tone flowers have a wonderful yellow background, contrasting with the cinnamon overlay on lower sepals matching the petal and dorsal sepal tips. When the floriferous nature of the species is added in, a sure winner in public appeal is born.

Kagawara is the combination of *Ascocenda* with the brilliant-red species of *Renanthera*. For depth and richness of red color, this one is nearly unmatched. The *Ascda.* Meda Arnold parent tempers the influence of the very tall *Renanthera* parent, resulting in a more compact plant, without sacrificing its wonderful branching habit. Kagawaras generally take lots of space and are very appropriate in areas like South Florida, where they are great patio plants and winter heat is a lesser issue.

Of course, red comes in many shades, from the deep true color to more pastel variations. In combination with other colors, it forms a fabulous accent. *Vanda lamellata* is a very popular species for its distinctive blooms on towering stems that can be borne at almost

Above left: Kagawara *Teoline Fair 'Miramar' HCC/AOS.*

Opposite: Through the influence of its V. Lamellate Boxalii *parent,* Ascda. *Khun Nok has been used to create what would be considered in cattleyas, "splash petal" hybrids. The pictured clone is 'John III' AM/AOS.*

Vandas and Vandaceous Types **423**

(AERIDES LAWRENCEAE X VANDA TANG CHAI) & YUSOFARA CROWNFOX SPECKLED SPIDER

Sometimes the search for unusual shades takes unexpected turns to reach the desired goal. Rose, of course, is a shade of red, and rich rose-colored flowers are striking for their brilliance of color. The sparkling color of 'Susanna' is matched only by the diamond dust texture given by the *Aerides* parent. Nonetheless, it is the candelabra inflorescence that will make this an orchid to remember, standing tall above the foliage with many well-presented blooms.

Demonstrating the length to which breeders will go in their search for unusual and new shades of red is *Yusofara* Crownfox Speckled Spider. This mouthful of a hybrid name denotes a genus comprised of *Arachnis* (the tall, vining "spider orchid"), *Renar:thera*, *Ascocentrum*, and *Vanda*. Lines of fine red spotting come from the famous *Ascda*. Guo Chia Long parent, while the showers of good-sized blooms can be traced to the big sprays of the *Ren. storei* grandparent. This is found only in very tropical areas.

Left: *Most hybrids using* Aerides *such as (*Aer. lawrenciae x V. Tang Chai*)* '*Susanna' AM/AOS have a nice fragrance, while many Vandaceous hybrids do not.*

Above: *Ysfra. Crownfox Speckled Spider 'Crownfox' HCC/AOS.*

Vandas and Vandaceous Types **425**

VANDA TESSELLATA & ASCOCENDA ALICE MOTES

Above: Ascda. *Alice Motes 'X Chromosome' HCC/AOS.*

Left: V. tessellata *is another species of the section that has a rich, distinctive fragrance. One can easily pick out* V. tessellata *hybrids by using their nose! The pictured clone is 'The Orchid Peddler' AM/AOS.*

Modern orchid breeding is not only concerned with the improvement of hybrid types but also the conservation and improvement of desirable species. Well-known species such as *Vanda sanderiana, V. coerulea, Asctm. curvifolium,* and *Rhy. gigantea* are obvious subjects for horticultural improvement. But more "minor" species often get the line-breeding treatment as well. One of the greatest success stories of recent memory is the vast improvement seen in the formerly obscure *Vanda tessellata.* Typically seen with a greenish-yellow background overlaid with muddy brown tessellation, 'improved' forms are nearly solid olive green. Not only is color improved, but shape and size are respectively flatter and larger as well. With so many good features already, such as long flower life, good flower arrangement on strong stems, and lovely perfume, it is easy to see why this new population is creating a stir. Add in the habit of flowering throughout the year, and you have an orchid that creates its own popular demand.

For good or ill, breeders cannot leave well enough alone. Proponents of broadening the species base of *Vanda* hybrids have been hard at work producing a line of highly unusual novelty types that incorporate more than 'just" *V. sanderiana* and *V. coerulea* blood. One attempt is *Ascda.* Mary Motes, a cross of an improved *V. tessellata* with a tetraploid *Ascda.* John DeBiase. Floriferousness is improved as is carriage and separation of blooms.

CORONADOARA MICHAEL'S DELIGHT & CHRISTENSONIA VIETNAMICA

To the victor go the spoils. Whoever wins the race to name a newly discovered species or to flower a newly created hybrid genera may name it. The opening of Vietnam to the West has led to the discovery of many new species as well as the rediscovery of some lost to cultivation for many years. *Paphiopedilum delenatii* is only one example. *Christensonia vietnamica*, a new vandaceous genus and species first described by the reigning expert on *Sarcanthinae*, Eric Christenson, has created a minor sensation among species lovers, with its unusual strongly spurred white lip offset by pippin-green petals and sepal. Plants are compact and a bit vining. Early recipients of plants from Vietnam have been quick to propagate seed-raised populations, so this delightful plant will soon be more widely available.

Strangely enough, the first hybrid genus to bloom using *Christensonia* appeared almost simultaneously with the availability of the species. The hybrid genus has been registered as *Coronadoara*, a combination with *Ascocenda*. Equally amazing is just how little influence the new species seemed to have on the *Ascocenda* look of the flower. Judges were sufficiently impressed to recognize the blooms with a Judges' Commendation, awarded to flowers with qualities worthy of note but not fitting into established judging criteria.

Coronadoara Michael's Delight is, in a way, exemplary of the foment and enthusiasm this group generates in its adherents. New hybrids, new forms of species, and new ways to combine them all are part of the great world of vandas. No matter your growing conditions, there is a hybrid or species for you, often created specifically to extend the range of conditions in which this colorful alliance can successfully be grown.

Crd. *Michael's Delight* 'Crownfox' *JC/AOS.*

Chri. vietnamica *is a recently described species that bears its chartreuse and white flowers on a long, well-spaced inflorescence. Plants are of a compact size.*

OTHER ORCHIDS

In their native Brazil, zygopetalums are among the first to colonize recently disturbed habitats, along roadways, river cuts, and landslips.

The plants grow quickly in the bare soil, taking advantage of abundant light and low competitive pressure. As other plants begin to intrude, lowering light levels and reducing nutrient availability, the initial colonists begin to slowly die out. In ecology, this is known as community succession. However, along road cuts or other areas kept clear by man's actions, zygopetalums, and others with similar habits, continue to flourish. It is ironic that plants that grow in artificial situations, areas where we would expect only "weeds," are popular and valued by both orchid specialists and gardeners where the climate is

Zygo. *Syd Monkhouse 'Everglades' AM/AOS.*

appropriate; and the climate is appropriate in many areas of the United States, especially where cymbidiums thrive. Cool summer areas, where winter frost does not threaten, are very welcoming to this fine group of plants. Best known are the species *Zygopetalum mackayi* and *Zygo. intermedium*, as well as their hybrids. Plants do wonderfully well right alongside cymbidiums, in a

Zygo. *Redvale 'Dabney' AM/AOS.*

similar potting mix, though they will appreciate some shading from the hottest sun. In other areas, plants can be grown in the greenhouse or sunroom. Inflorescences emerge from developing growths in late fall, occasionally again in late winter, growing rapidly to as much as thirty-six inches in *Zygo. mackayi*. Six to eight exotically patterned green blooms are strongly marked with chestnut to mahogany and have a striking blue-veined lip. What attracts many growers to this group is not necessarily the floral beauty but the strong and penetrating perfume that can easily scent a significant area. To smell a *Zygopetalum* is to covet it!

For a genus with a limited amount of horticulturally appealing species, *Zygopetalum* has seen a considerable amount of hybridization. The species involved in almost all intrageneric hybrids are the aforementioned two plus the long-rhizomed *Zygo. maxillare* and *Zygo. crinitum*. The main goals in *Zygopetalum* breeding have been to intensify the coloration, improve the form, and reduce plant

size. Color combinations and patterns remain remarkably constant, with green sepals and petals overlaid with varying degrees of mahogany-to-black barring and white lips veined with blue, some nearly to the point of being solid blue. For this reason, it is always easy to tell a *Zygopetalum*. No other orchid looks like one, and zypetalums look like nothing else. It would seem that a group with relatively limited resources would have a broadly known set of standards of flower quality. Because it can be difficult to bloom zygopetalums from some lines of breeding, some growers have seen only a few. *Zygo.* Redvale is a fine example of a good *Zygopetalum* flower, with flat and proportionately full segments of rich color and a nearly solid-colored lip. While the patterning of *Zygo.* Syd Monkhouse is sharply delineated, the shape is not sufficiently full, particularly in the lip, to measure up to modern standards. None of this, however, diminishes the great appeal of these species and hybrids.

ZYGONISIA ROQUEBRUNE & BOLLEA COELESTIS

The *Zygopetalum* group is comprised of a rather eclectic batch of genera, often collectively called the "soft leaf" types, as many have no or insignificant pseudobulbs and fans of soft green leaves. This group includes genera like *Aganisia*, *Pabstia*, *Bollea*, *Colax*, *Pescatorea*, *Cochleanthes*, and a variety of others. Many of these species are exceptionally lovely in and of themselves, potentially forming the basis of a varied collection. They do have their drawbacks, perhaps the greatest of which is their tendency to bear only single blooms on short stems near the base of the plant. So, while these plants are generally among the most attractive of all orchids, their flowers take some effort to find down in the foliage, which detracts from their popularity. Certain species are strongly colored, like *Pescatorea lehmanii* with its intensely grape-purple blooms, but most are in pastel shades. Many have intriguing perfumes, often medicinal. Some few primary hybrids exist but are limited in distribution and generally appeal only to specialists.

Bollea coelestis 'Elektra' FCC/AOS shows the unusual lip structure of the genus. Colors of this species can range from indigo to raspberry red. Soft fans of green leaves typify plants of many related genera.

Intergeneric hybridizing in this group is still in its infancy, in a period of great experimentation. One of the great facts limiting further experimentation is the tendency of *Zygo. mackayi* to, when used as the female, simply give more *Zygo. mackayi*, regardless of the other parent. Frustrating, to say the least, particularly when some years of growing have been invested. The *Zygopetalum* parent, even when used as the male, is extraordinarily dominant; as a result many intergeneric hybrids show little influence of the other side of the cross. Also, when good hybrids are made, they can often be very difficult to grow as well as shy to flower. Nevertheless, dedicated breeders persist, stretching our knowledge of genetic affinities by the production of new combinations of genera. *Zygonisia* Roquebrune is bred from the famous hybrid *Zygo.* Artur Elle and the beautiful-blue species *Aganisia cyanea*—one of the most attractove members of this group but also one of the most difficult to grow. This stunning flower incorporates the finer features of both parents while being considerably more compact than the *Zygopetalum* parent, as well as more warmth-tolerant. Of course, the dominance of *Zygopetalum* can be overcome by simply not using it. Where the broad-ranging hybridizing taking place in this group today will lead remains to be seen. The goal of horticultural success is nowhere more elusive than here, where ease of flowering will have to be improved along with vigor and cleanliness of foliage.

Although the colors of the Zygopetalum *parent are mostly dominant, the Amazonian species* Agn. cyanea *imparts a distinct bluish cast to* Zns. Roquebrune *'JEM' HCC/AOS.*

YELLOW LYCASTES: LYCASTE CORRIMAL, LYCASTE AROMATICA & LYCASTE MACROBULBON

Lyc. *Corrimal 'Orestes' AM/AOS produces large flowers on plants that are adaptable to a broad range of temperatures.*

Lycaste skinneri, the national flower of Guatemala, presents to most the "mind's eye" image of this genus. Small wonder, when the imposing beauty of the species, with its broad pastel pink sepals framing the darker pink petals and lip, is so well known. An entire race of exceptionally fine hybrids, heavily dominated by *Lyc. skinneri* influences, have been created over the years and form an important part of spring exhibitions. Unfortunately, with their large broad leaves to over thirty inches and dislike of temperature extremes, many find them difficult to grow, if not house, owing to their overbearing size. However, there is a broad range of *Lycaste* species, perhaps less well known, that are much easier to grow, more floriferous, and take up significantly less space. Indeed, the group of deciduous species originating at mid-elevations of Mexico and Central America are among the easiest and most rewarding of all orchid species.

Lycaste aromatica is a perennial favorite that finds suitable homes both under *Cattleya* conditions and outdoors where cymbidiums thrive. As with many of this type, it drops its leaves in late fall and so prefers a dry rest. As days begin to lengthen again, new growths emerge from the base of the older bulbs, surrounded by many individual flower stems, each capped with an upward-facing sulphur-yellow bloom. Each new growth may have twelve to fifteen or more flowers around it, giving quite a display, especially when the delicious cinnamon perfume is considered. *Lyc. macrobulbon*, a Colombian species, is similar in color to *Lyc. aromatica* but is dramatically fuller in shape. *Lyc. macrobulbon* is more robust in size but also tends to flower after the leaves have fallen and given an equally imposing show, with many of the brightly colored blooms emerging from the base of developing growth. Little hybridizing has been done with this group of lycastes, but one promising result utilized *Lyc. aromatica* with the widespread, large-flowered *Lyc. macrophylla* to produce *Lyc. Corrimal*. *Lyc. macrophylla* occurs throughout Central America into northern parts of South America and is named for its very large leaves. However, when crossed with the much smaller-growing Mexican *Lycaste*, a plant happily intermediate in size resulted, with the prolific flowering habit so beloved in this type of *Lycaste*. Additionally, *Lyc. Corrimal*, like most of the related species, is very easy to grow under a variety of circumstances. Hopefully, this sort of *Lycaste* hybrid will become more widely available, since they represent a worthwhile and versatile flowering plant.

The sulphur-yellow flowers of the Colombian species, Lyc. macrobulbon, *are produced from the base of the previous year's pseudobulbs in late winter.*

The compact-growing Lyc. aromatica *has flowers that smell like cinnamon. Like all deciduous lycastes, allow plants to dry when leaves drop in late fall.*

BIFRENARIA HARRISONIAE

Bifrenaria harrisoniae is a truly beautiful orchid that deserves to be better known. Described in 1825 as *Dendrobium harrisoniae* in honor of Mrs. Arnold Harrison, an avid orchid collector and relative of its discoverer, William Harrison, Reichenbach transferred the species to the genus *Bifrenaria* in 1854. There are about two dozen species in the genus, which ranges throughout South America but has the heaviest concentration in Brazil, also the home of the illustrated species. *Bif. harrisoniae* is an attractive plant

Pink forms of Bif. harrisoniae *are sometimes horticulturally known as "Rosea." This species has a distinctly pleasant fragrance.*

even when out of flower, with a single leathery leaf topping the quadrangular pseudobulbs. The inflorescences arise in the spring from the base of the pseudobulb and produce one or more two-inch to three-inch flowers. The waxy flowers have a hairy lip and beautiful gold veining on the side lobes. A seductive perfumelike fragrance is an added bonus. Under certain conditions, there may

be a second flowering a month or so later. Conflicting reports as to habitat refer to the species growing as a lithophyte in full sun or as an epiphyte on low shrubs. Most experience indicates moderate light and intermediate temperatures. However, growers in areas where cymbidiums grow outdoors report success under these conditions, though some find the species a bit more difficult to flower.

Bifrenaria is related to *Lycaste*, and some intergeneric hybrids have been made. Unfortunately, as this combination could be so lovely, the plants are essentially never flowered. One hybrid, *Lycasteria Darius*, notorious as a nonflowering mule, finally did flower in the hands of one of the Pacific Northwest's most fastidious growers (through luck or skill will never be known). While the blooms were pretty, neither the pictures taken at the time nor the memories of those present credit the wait as worthwhile. Other lycasterias that have occasionally been offered have proven to be either equally

More typically, flowers of Bif. harrisoniae *are white to cream with a contrasting lip. Bifrenarias benefit from drier conditions in winter.*

reluctant to flower or have been mislabeled. Whether because of distance of genetic relationship or other, less easily determined reasons, little further hybridization has been done. *Bif. harrisoniae* remains like a lovely orchid spinster, occasionally courted but never successfully wed. This in no way diminishes the appeal or beauty of this fine, underappreciated orchid.

MAXILLARIA TENUIFOLIA & MAXILLARIA RINGENS

Maxillaria, also closely related to *Lycaste*, is a large, varied, and underappreciated genus. Indeed, one famous orchid researcher told me that he switched from the study of paphiopedilums to maxillarias because "they are so obscure that no one will ever bother me and I can study more freely." Ironically, not six months later, the specialist group known as the Maxillaria Tribe was formed. Even cursory knowledge of the genus is enough to understand why they are so enigmatic and little known. While some higher-elevation members of this New World genus have larger blooms approaching *Lyc. skinneri* proportions, many more have small, drably colored blooms sparsely borne around the base of the plant. So insignificant are some of the species that they have been used for packing material around other, more valued, plants as they are shipped from the forest collection sites. Plant size ranges from extraordinarily small, sometimes under two inches in *Max. ubatubana*, to many yards long in some of the vining types. Two growth habits seem to dominate the horticulturally important species: close-set pseudobulbs and those with some distance between bulbs, but not so much as to be overwhelming. The flowering habit in *Maxillaria* is as in the related *Lycaste* and *Bifrenaria*: multiple inflorescences bearing single blooms emerge from the base of the most recent growth. This flowering habit can lead to magnificent flowered specimen plants in the showier types.

The most widely grown and best-known member of the genus is *Max. tenuifolia*, the "coconut pie orchid." While the individual pseudobulbs are only an inch or so high and the leaves are not too long, up to eight inches or so, the distance between bulbs on climbing rhizomes can quickly overwhelm any pot in which a grower might attempt to contain this plant. Most growers prefer baskets or mounts, which allow the plant to produce a large and attractive ball of foliage. The oxblood-red blooms, about an inch across, are borne individually on short stems, two or three per new lead. The prolific and free-branching character of the plant provides a wonderful show. But it is not just the flower's beauty that draws admiration. The fragrance is what has given this orchid its popular name, being strongly and convincingly of coconut pie. Delicious! Some clones seem to be more difficult to flower than others, so if no evidence of past flowering is present in the form of old flower stems, the consumer may want to search out another plant.

Attractive foliage makes Max. ringens *a valuable display plant.*

Although similar to the showy, higher-elevation types, *Max. ringens* is found at lower elevations of Central America, from Mexico to Panama and possibly into South America. The pretty yellow and white flowers are produced three to four per pseudobulb in the fall and held singly on upright stems. A well-grown plant makes a beautiful presentation of upright leathery leaves surrounded by a base of cheery flowers.

CYRTOPODIUM ANDERSONII & CYRTOPODIUM PUNCTATUM

While there are two distinct groups in this genus, one approximating *Catasetum* in size and the other quite large, the most frequently seen in contemporary collections are the big boys. Indeed, the sheer size of the plants can render them nearly impossible to accommodate except in the very largest greenhouses or outdoors. This widespread genus occurs from South Florida to Brazil, most of the most commonly seen species hailing from Brazil. Both of the species pictured here can only be described as big plants, with spindle-shaped pseudobulbs reaching four feet or more. The palmlike leaves are arranged up the pseudobulb in a very attractive manner and are winter-deciduous, leaving spiny leaf sheaths behind encasing the stems. *Cyrtopodium punctatum*, native to South Florida and throughout tropical America, is one of the showiest of all orchids that occur naturally in the continental United States. Deep in the Florida Everglades, where humans seldom intrude, wild plants may still very occasionally be seen high in the trees, where they can form enormous clumps. The common name for this species is the "cow horn" orchid, in recognition of its appearance when

The large club-shaped pseudobulbs of Cyrt. andersonii *can reach thirty inches and produce an inflorescence twice as tall. Because of its large size, the species makes a good garden subject in frost-free areas.*

deciduous. *Cyrt. andersonii* is found from the West Indies into Brazil, and its appearance out of flower is not dissimilar to *Cyrt. punctatum*.

Both species inhabit areas with seasonal rainfall, where they grow and mature rapidly, fed by abundant moisture to immense final proportions. The flowering stems erupt from emerging growths in the spring, quickly outstripping the growth rate of the new leads, and ultimately reaching six feet or more with copious branching. *Cyrt. punctatum*'s spotted yellow blooms, about one inch across, are subtended by showy bracts that add to the overall presentation. The individual blooms, while impressive enough, are part of a mass display—towering flower stem, colorful subtending bracts, and many bright flowers—that impresses when seen in the full sun. *Cyrt. andersonii* has shapely pure-yellow blooms with an arresting and sweet fragrance, borne on an equally imposing inflorescence.

The very best plants of these two species are seen in areas like South Florida, where the high light, ample moisture, and warm temperatures allow orchid enthusiasts to grow these as patio or garden subjects in large pots or in the landscape. Experienced growers recommend that, unlike many other potted orchids, somewhat overlarge pots be selected, not only to allow for several years' undisturbed growth but also to help keep these large and top-heavy plants upright. When well grown, there are few sights to compare with one or both of these in full bloom. Those who have conditions appropriate to their use in the landscape will also find that nature does a fine job of watering these plants with the frequent summer rain so common to the American South.

Cyrt. punctatum, *the "Cow Horn" orchid, was once common in the Florida Everglades. A dry, cool rest in winter, when the plant loses its leaves, will produce the best flowering.*

CHYSIS BRACTESCENS

Few New World orchids make as handsome a display as *Chy. bractescens*, whether in or out of flower. The growth habit is unusual, seeming to be a combination of several plants in one.

The beautiful Chy. bractescens *is found from Mexico south to northern South America. Because of the pendant nature of the deciduous pseudobulbs, grow Chysis in a basket or mounted on a tree fern or cork slab.*

The pseudobulbs are prominent and club-shaped with leaves not unlike a *Catasetum*, which is also eventually deciduous like *Chy. bractescens*. But the pseudobulbs are pendulous like many dendrobiums, such as *Den. pierardii*. Because of the drooping pseudobulbs, most growers find that these plants do best in a hanging basket or mounted on a raft. Not only does this exhibit the plant at its best, it allows the rapid drainage that is preferred. Flower stems are produced along with the new growths in late winter, with large, fleshy blooms of purest white offset by a hairy yellow lip. Inflorescences have six to twelve blooms, and there may be more than one per growth.

Chysis plants, while large, adapt themselves to a variety of cultural regimes owing to their seasonal growth. Like most plants from seasonally warm and moist areas—*Chy. bractescens* can be found from Mexico south into Peru and Venezuela—growth is rapid once begun, requiring abundant watering and copious fertilizer. When the new pseudobulbs begin to reach maturity, signaled by a terminal leaf, water should be lessened and eventually withheld to allow the rest that helps trigger flowering. This translates into a plant that will do well in areas even with the cold winters that prevent year-round outdoor culture, if the plants are summered out in the garden with good light and air circulation.

Resting plants may then be brought indoors to a sunny window or sunroom for their winter rest. As growth commences in spring, water needs increase gradually, and often the flowers, long-lived though they are, come and go before the plant really needs to go back outdoors.

COELOGYNE MOOREANA
& COELOGYNE CRISTATA

Coelogyne is a very widespread genus, occurring throughout Southeast Asia, China, India, and the foothills of the Himalayas. While some have been widespread in cultivation for decades, for some reason they are not a genus that engenders the same excitement as paphiopedilums or vandas. Why this should be so is difficult to understand. Species come from a wide variety of growing conditions, from cooler and higher elevations to intermediate-type areas to truly tropical. Growers everywhere can find plants that suit their growing area. Nor are the flowers "just"

Coel. mooreana 'Brockhurst' HCC/AOS comes from Vietnam at about 4,000 feet elevation and requires intermediate to cool conditions.

white, though white is a very common color. Coelogyne pandurata is deep apple-green with a nearly black lip, while Coel. speciosa is an unusual salmon color and Coel. massangeana is tan with a deep-brown lip. Flowering habits vary, as well, from the long arching inflorescence of Coel. pandurata to the sharply pendant Coel. dayana and massangeana to the ramrod-straight upright flower stems of Coel. mooreana and ochracea.

Personally, I have a soft spot for white flowers. So, a plant of *Coel. ochracea*, purest crystalline white with an ocher-marked lip and a heavenly scent, was one of my first orchids. If only it had grown for me. For this is the drawback to coelogynes for many: they can be very hard to maintain in a collection. The secret seems to be managing potting so as to minimize both frequency and disturbance. Coelogynes just hate to be repotted and will often take a year or more to recover from the inevitable. Growers must observe rooting behavior carefully to ensure that potting and any attendant disturbance comes only when the plants are ready to make fresh roots.

My love of white flowers leads me to judge *Coel. mooreana* 'Brockhurst' as one of the most beautiful of all orchids, period. The sparkling white blooms have a yellow throat, are shapely, and emerge just far enough from the developing growth to clear the attractive deep-green foliage. Simply lovely. *Coel. mooreana* is one of the species that will stand a little more warmth but, like so many, comes from an area where moderate temperatures are found, varying little from day to night, season to season. Too hot or too cold are equally bad for this fantastic species. White coelogynes perhaps are best

represented by the higher-elevation *Coel. cristata*, a standard of horticulture since Victorian times. Many English found *Coel. cristata* perfectly suited to their conservatories or sunrooms, which are much cooler in winter than those in the American South would be accustomed to in their homes. Here, the hanging baskets would explode with pendant stems of pure white blooms in late winter, often covering the ample plants and scenting the area with their sweet fragrance

Coel. cristata *'Woodland' CCM/AOS shows the beauty of a specimen plant. A Certificate of Cultural Merit recognizes the skills of the grower.*

INDEX